# Activist and Socially Critical School and Community Renewal

*Social Justice in Exploitative Times*

# TRANSGRESSIONS: CULTURAL STUDIES AND EDUCATION

*Series Editors*
   **Shirley Steinberg**, *McGill University, Canada*
   **Joe Kincheloe**, *McGill University, Canada*

*Editorial Board*
   **Heinz-Hermann Kruger**, *Halle University, Germany*
   **Norman Denzin**, *University of Illinois, Champaign-Urbana, USA*
   **Roger Slee**, *McGill University, Canada*
   **Rhonda Hammer**, *University of California Los Angeles, USA*
   **Christine Quail**, *SUNY, Oneonta*

*Scope*
Cultural studies provides an analytical toolbox for both making sense of educational practice and extending the insights of educational professionals into their labors. In this context *Transgressions: Cultural Studies and Education* provides a collection of books in the domain that specify this assertion. Crafted for an audience of teachers, teacher educators, scholars and students of cultural studies and others interested in cultural studies and pedagogy, the series documents both the possibilities of and the controversies surrounding the intersection of cultural studies and education. The editors and the authors of this series do not assume that the interaction of cultural studies and education devalues other types of knowledge and analytical forms. Rather the intersection of these knowledge disciplines offers a rejuvenating, optimistic, and positive perspective on education and educational institutions. Some might describe its contribution as democratic, emancipatory, and transformative. The editors and authors maintain that cultural studies helps free educators from sterile, monolithic analyses that have for too long undermined efforts to think of educational practices by providing other words, new languages, and fresh metaphors. Operating in an interdisciplinary cosmos, Transgressions: Cultural Studies and Education is dedicated to exploring the ways cultural studies enhances the study and practice of education. With this in mind the series focuses in a non-exclusive way on popular culture as well as other dimensions of cultural studies including social theory, social justice and positionality, cultural dimensions of technological innovation, new media and media literacy, new forms of oppression emerging in an electronic hyperreality, and postcolonial global concerns. With these concerns in mind cultural studies scholars often argue that the realm of popular culture is the most powerful educational force in contemporary culture. Indeed, in the twenty-first century this pedagogical dynamic is sweeping through the entire world. Educators, they believe, must understand these emerging realities in order to gain an important voice in the pedagogical conversation.

   Without an understanding of cultural pedagogy's (education that takes place outside of formal schooling) role in the shaping of individual identity--youth identity in particular--the role educators play in the lives of their students will continue to fade. Why do so many of our students feel that life is incomprehensible and devoid of meaning? What does it mean, teachers wonder, when young people are unable to describe their moods, their affective affiliation to the society around them. Meanings provided young people by mainstream institutions often do little to help them deal with their affective complexity, their difficulty negotiating the rift between meaning and affect. School knowledge and educational expectations seem as anachronistic as a ditto machine, not that learning ways of rational thought and making sense of the world are unimportant.

   But school knowledge and educational expectations often have little to offer students about making sense of the way they feel, the way their affective lives are shaped. In no way do we argue that analysis of the production of youth in an electronic mediated world demands some "touchy-feely" educational superficiality. What is needed in this context is a rigorous analysis of the interrelationship between pedagogy, popular culture, meaning making, and youth subjectivity. In an era marked by youth depression, violence, and suicide such insights become extremely important, even life saving. Pessimism about the future is the common sense of many contemporary youth with its concomitant feeling that no one can make a difference.

   If affective production can be shaped to reflect these perspectives, then it can be reshaped to lay the groundwork for optimism, passionate commitment, and transformative educational and political activity. In these ways cultural studies adds a dimension to the work of education unfilled by any other sub-discipline. This is what Transgressions: Cultural Studies and Education seeks to produce—literature on these issues that makes a difference. It seeks to publish studies that help those who work with young people, those individuals involved in the disciplines that study children and youth, and young people themselves improve their lives in these bizarre times.

# Activist and Socially Critical School and Community Renewal

*Social Justice in Exploitative Times*

John Smyth
*University of Ballarat*

Lawrence Angus
*University of Ballarat*

Barry Down
*Murdoch University*

Peter McInerney
*University of Ballarat*

SENSE PUBLISHERS
ROTTERDAM / TAIPEI

A C.I.P. record for this book is available from the Library of Congress.

ISBN 978-90-8790-652-8 (paperback)
ISBN 978-90-8790-653-5 (hardback)
ISBN 978-90-8790-654-2 (e-book)

Published by: Sense Publishers,
P.O. Box 21858, 3001 AW
Rotterdam, The Netherlands
http://www.sensepublishers.com

Printed on acid-free paper

All Rights Reserved © 2009 Sense Publishers

No part of this work may be reproduced, stored in a retrieval system, or transmitted in any form or by any means, electronic, mechanical, photocopying, microfilming, recording or otherwise, without written permission from the Publisher, with the exception of any material supplied specifically for the purpose of being entered and executed on a computer system, for exclusive use by the purchaser of the work.

# FOR JOE

As this book goes to press, we have been rocked by the sudden and tragic loss of our dear friend, teacher and mentor Joe Kincheloe. As series editor, Joe has been a powerful influence not only on the ideas contained in this book but in our ongoing struggle to create a more socially just world. We can think of no better way to celebrate Joe's life than by engaging with him about education, justice and activism. This was his passion, commitment and life.

We last met Joe, Shirley and their daughter Bronwyn in July 2007 in Ballarat, Victoria. Joe and Shirley spent time talking with local educators and community activists about the importance of developing an 'evolving criticality' around questions of social and educational disadvantage. We shared ideas about a range of complex issues confronting young people, teachers and the wider community.

We talked about the fallout from neoliberal policies of marketization, standardization, high stakes testing and other 'backlash pedagogies'. In these situations, Joe was at his brilliant best. Articulate, courageous, provocative and passionate. There can be no doubt about where Joe stood on the big issues confronting society and education. In the tradition of great public intellectuals, Joe had a deep understanding of democracy and the collective good. Drawing on these insights, he was able to create a vision of what a truly democratic and just society might look like and how we might go about the task.

Above all, Joe was a person who lived the principles and values of humility, lovingness, courage, tolerance and respect advocated by his mentor Paulo Freire. Like Freire, Joe's legacy is rich, generous and timeless. He will continue to inspire the next generation of critical scholars and teachers who will be a testimony to his ideas. Fittingly, we leave the last word to Freire when he says "One of the tasks of the progressive educator ... is to unveil opportunities for hope, no matter what the obstacles may be. After all, without hope there is little we can do" (Freire, 1999, p. 9). Joe has made a truly remarkable contribution to this broader critical democratic project.

*John Smyth*
*Lawrence Angus*
*Barry Down*
*Peter McInerney*

# TABLE OF CONTENTS

Acknowledgments ix

**Chapter 1.  What this book is about** 1

  Why activism, what is it, and why now? 2

  In what sense then, is this book activist? 5

  How have we gone about our intellectual craft? 7

  Something about the Australian context 11

  Snapshot portraits of the communities 12

      Wirra Wagga 12

      Bountiful Bay 13

  Organization of the book 13

**Chapter 2.  Putting teachers and communities into policy reclamation: countering educational 'discourses of deceit'** 17

  Introduction 17

  Neoliberalism and educational reform – a discourse of deceit and false promises? 19

  The illusion of choice 20

  New standards, old inequalities? 21

  Teaching to educate or teaching to the test? 22

  Local empowerment? 24

  Reclaiming educational policy and practice: towards community-oriented and socially engaged schooling 26

  Building a community of learners 27

      The Wirra Wagga story 28

  Developing a critical pedagogy of place 32

      Stories from Bountiful Bay 33

  Educating for a better world 37

  Community-oriented schooling: high hopes? false promises? 39

  Concluding remarks 42

TABLE OF CONTENTS

**Chapter 3.  Relational solidarity: harbinger of a paradigmatic shift in school and community renewal**    **45**

Introduction    45

The possibility of a relationally-led backlash    49

A relational politics for school and community activism    51

How then, does 'a different kind of politics' play out practically?    52

The architecture of a 'community voiced' approach to neighborhood and community renewal    57

     1. Relational Immediacy    59

     2. Investment in Indigenous Leadership    60

     3. Interdependency    61

     4. Painting a Bigger Picture    62

Renovating relationships as well as buildings    62

Building people through de-institutionalizing relationships    65

Affirming working class identity    66

From client to authentic partnership    69

Concluding remarks    73

**Chapter 4.  Taking a stand against school effectiveness: pursing a pedagogy of hope**    **75**

Introduction    75

The confused origins of 'school effectiveness'    76

The 'scientific' appeal of school effectiveness    82

School effectiveness, authentic school reform, and ideology    84

Social context and social agents in educational change    90

Imagining alternative, really effective, ways of 'doing' education    96

Concluding remarks    101

**Chapter 5.  Engaging meaningful work**    **103**

Introduction    103

Confronting the 'big lie' that training creates jobs    105

Deconstructing job hierarchies 110
Reclaiming symbolic spaces for meaningful work 116
Developing an understanding of Good versus Bad work 119
Integrating the vocational and academic curriculum 121
Fostering critical citizenship, democracy and social justice 123
Conclusion 125

**Chapter 6.   New Storylines on school/community renewal** **127**

Introduction 127
Reclaiming educational policy: pursuing a pedagogy of hope 128
   1. Looking beyond 'school level effects': context matters 130
   2. Building 'a different kind of politics' 131
   3. Becoming 'radical listeners' 131
   4. Fostering people-centered 'capacity building' 131
   5. Investing in indigenous leadership 132
   6. Developing a democratic participative/professional culture 132
Reinventing pedagogy: towards a critical pedagogy of school/community engagement 132
   7. Reasserting the primacy of teaching and learning in schools 133
   8. Promoting socially critical approaches to schooling 134
   9. Deconstructing stereotypes and pathologizing practices 134
   10. Linking the local and the global 135
   11. Valuing craftsmanship and good work 135
   12. Creating a new 'social imagination' for doing school 135
   13. Engaging place-based learning 135
Reinvigorating research: advancing an activist and socially critical research agenda around school/community renewal 136
   14. Puncturing categories of social identity and exclusion 137
   15. Generating grounded and dialectical knowledge 138
   16. Coming to critical engagement 138

TABLE OF CONTENTS

    17. Locating ethnographic and narrative data into context     138

    18. Thinking critically and theoretically     139

What can be done?     139

    1. Redistribution     140

    2. Recognition     140

    3. Political representation     140

**References**     **141**

**Author Index**     **155**

**Subject Index**     **159**

# ACKNOWLEDGEMENTS

Books always come into existence with interesting, complex and intriguing histories, and this one is certainly no exception.

This is the fourth book in a series I have led as the chief investigator, with a varying team of co-authors who have worked with me for over a decade, in which we have explored various aspects of a particular theme. The work started with the intrigue we had around what was happening inside the lives of the increasing number of young people in western countries who we making the active choice that schooling was not for them, even when these decisions seemed to be against their long-term economic interests. Our focus was on the process of 'dropping out' of school, or as we came to frame it less pejoratively, the act of early school leaving.

The first research we undertook into this topic, funded by the Australian Research Council (ARC) through a Linkage Grant, culminated in a report appropriately titled, *Listen to Me, I'm Leaving* (Smyth, Hattam, Cannon, Edwards, Wilson, & Wurst, 2000). This was transformed into a book called *'Dropping Out', Drifting Off, Being Excluded: Becoming Somebody Without School* (Smyth & Hattam, et al., 2004).

Our second foray, this time with support from an ARC Discovery Grant, was into more optimistic territory with a group of schools that were attempting innovative strategies with young people against the prevailing policy grain. This precipitated into the book with the double entendre of *Teachers in the Middle: Reclaiming the Wasteland of the Adolescent Years of Schooling* (Smyth & McInerney, 2007).

The third phase of this work which extended into new territory for us of communities and community politics, was made possible through two further ARC grants, a Linkage Grant (Smyth & Down, 2005) and a Discovery Grant (Smyth & Angus, 2006a), and led to our recent book entitled *Critically Engaged Learning: Connecting to Young Lives* (Smyth, Angus, Down & McInerney, 2008), and to the present volume.

The storied and narrative accounts in this book derive from the latter two grants— *Individual, institutional and community 'capacity building' in a cluster of disadvantaged schools and their community* (2006–2008), and *School and Community Linkages for Enhanced School Retention in Regional/Rural Western Australia* (2005–2007). We extend our grateful appreciation to the ARC for their continued financial support of this research, and acknowledge the assistance and involvement of the Western Australian Department of Education and Training and the Victorian Department of Education and Early Childhood Development. We are especially grateful to the educational administrators, teachers, students, community activists and residents who spoke with such passion and conviction about the importance of critically engaged learning and schooling for a more just society. We also thank our respective institutions, Murdoch University and the University of Ballarat for providing us with the conducive and supportive conditions so crucial to

## ACKNOWLEDGEMENTS

high level rigorous scholarship. Naturally, we take full responsibility for the ideas expressed which are not necessarily those of any of the organizations involved.

I want to express particular appreciation to my fellow authors who have labored hard over long distances separated from one another, Barry Down and Lawrence Angus and I especially thank Peter McInerney who is not only a co-author but also has been a vital research associate in all of this work.

Thank you to Jan McInerney for her assistance with copy editing, and to Solveiga Smyth as research assistant and fieldworker in both of these projects who has cheerfully, capably and most efficiently held all aspects of the research together from the beginning. We simply could not have done it without her!

To Joe Kincheloe, series editor, Michel Lokhorst and Peter de Liefde at Sense Publishers, who lived up to their publishing motto of *For Wisdom and Awareness*, we thank you for having the wisdom and confidence to take us on.

Finally, we express our collective gratitude to our families for their forbearance towards us during the long periods of familial disengagement while we were putting this work together.

This has been quite some intellectual journey, and we make no claims to have fully plumbed the depths of the issues yet, but we think we have made a courageous start.

John Smyth
Mt. Helen, Victoria
July 2008

CHAPTER 1

# WHAT THIS BOOK IS ABOUT

This is a book about social and educational activism.
　While we will go on to explain in a moment what we mean by activism, this is a book that is fundamentally committed to some very specific social ends. The idea that education is supposed to be the great equalizer, the escalator for social and economic mobility, is in deep and possibly terminal trouble. In most affluent western countries at the moment, school completion rates, or high school graduation rates as they are referred to in the U.S., are falling dramatically in respect of public schools. At the time of writing, in the island state of Tasmania, Australia, for example, which is symptomatic of many similar places that have suffered badly in recent times from globalization, de-industrialization, and international economic restructuring, public schools are struggling to get 40-50 percent of the students who commence year 10 through to completing year 12 (Worley, 2008). If we take the collective situation in the U.S., somewhere around 1 million students each year are not graduating from high school, and the situation is most dire in areas of exacerbated 'location disadvantage' (Nader, 2008) such as large cities with protracted urban poverty, declining rural and remote communities, and communities in which the 'politics of place' (Gulson, 2008) seem to conspire intergenerationally to blight the 'capacity to aspire' (Appadurai, 2004) to a meaningful education. The completion of an adequate level of schooling (Belfield & Levin, 2007) is the most compelling social and economic indicator of the capacity of a society to equitably share in the distribution of its resources, as well as ensuring the capacity of individuals to contribute more widely to collective social well-being.
　When the politics of place looms as large as it does in terms of who benefits and who loses educationally, then the starting point in terms of re-imagining how the problem is framed as well as how things might done differently, has to commence with and be located in schools, communities, and with young people themselves. This is not to say, that all of the action has to be completely handed over, but it does mean a quantum shift of mindset from where we at the moment.
　We are bone weary of the ad nauseam victim-blaming analyses and the patronizing, pathologizing and paternalistic amelioratives that continue to masquerade as solutions to this issue, served up by politicians and policy makers who are not only demonstrably lacking in courage and imagination, but who are too distant and remote form the issues to have any hope of understanding them, let alone resolving them.
　We have had enough too of the incessant political spin and impoverished policies that continue exacerbate and deepen the damage that comes with the

CHAPTER 1

exclusion of so many young people from participation in shaping their educational futures in the most affluent countries. In this book we are making a clarion call not only for an equitable share of public resources to go towards producing viable learning opportunities for the most vulnerable groups, but we are also arguing strongly that the groups for whom schools appear to be the most inhospitable, need to be the ones most actively included as part of more inclusive solutions (Smyth, 2008).

## WHY ACTIVISM, WHAT IS IT, AND WHY NOW?

Good question! The title of our book, its conceptualization, its substance, the fieldwork research on which it is based, and the process of jointly writing it considerably preceded our knowledge of Gary L. Anderson and Kathryn Herr's (2007) monumental three volume *Encyclopedia of Activism and Social Justice*. As we write this overview introductory chapter we have the distinct feeling that our book is extremely timely. Our feeling is that Gary and Kathryn's contribution presents a fabulous opportunity for us to connect our work with their volume, even if only in passing, and to show that not only is activism very much alive and even thriving in difficult times, but that it can have many faces in quite different places.

In their introduction, Anderson and Herr talk of their schizophrenic and quite bizarre existence as U.S. academics in earlier times as they worked as compliant technicians and as well as activists, speaking back and undermining the status quo:

> By day, we produced positivist knowledge to feed the information society; by night, we engaged in political activism to change it. (p. xlix)

Knowing Gary and Kathryn as valued, long-time and forthright socially critical colleagues, we take this self-effacing confession somewhat with a grain of salt, but their wider point about the tension is quite true. There will be little argument from us about how we are increasingly required to live our lives as academics in ways that involve both complying with regimes imposed upon us, while also having a much wider responsibility to speak out as public intellectuals about the damaging effects such policies have—and by this we don't mean just complaining about political interference with our work, but speaking out at a much deeper level, actively exposing and working against powerful injustices.

Place, history, context and timing are always much more than mere background, despite what we might be told by those who deem to know better than us regarding what is important about academic and scholarly work—notably, by those who tout the benefits of so-called 'scientific' or 'evidence-based' approaches. From where we sit, context is everything! The fact that four of us, and we are by no means exclusive or alone in Australia, have been able to sustain a healthy, productive and activist approach to research and scholarship within universities for over 30 years in one case, and over twenty in each of the others, is testimony the fact that the situation alluded to by Anderson and Herr in the U.S. is by no means the norm in other parts of the English speaking world, and possibly elsewhere as well. We do indeed believe in the idiosyncratic and place-based nature of how things work—perhaps this is somewhat indicative of our stance as sociologists and scholars who bring a critical perspective to our research and scholarship.

None of this is to suggest that we have not felt the disciplining effects of the blowtorch of neo-liberal policies as they have been applied to us in our work nor the sharp edge of the institutional disciplining that Anderson and Herr refer to, but we regard ourselves as having been blessed with the opportunity of having found spaces within our culture and our work as academics in which to operate productively and to not have to be apologetic about that. Anderson and Herr (2007) in speaking of the U.S. remind us of the more general point made by C. Wright Mills (1959[1970]) about the confluence of history and biography, when they talk about the timeliness of activism:

> Increasingly, scholars see themselves as 'public intellectuals' who no longer apologize for advocating for the powerless in society. The brazen advance of neoliberalism, the resurgence of nativist and racist policies, and the arrogance and aggression of a post-9/11 American empire has given scholars a greater sense of urgency. The once-tight boundaries between academia and activism have been breached, to the consternation of some and the approval of others. (p. xlix)

We could not agree more with Anderson and Herr about the propitious timing in this upswing of scholars who are finding the courage to confront and contest the ugly and disfiguring work being done by marketization, individualism and consumerism. The urgency accompanying this has significantly raised the stakes for ways of enabling those who have been excluded, silenced, marginalized, and deeply scarred by these grotesque tendencies, to find the voice with which to speak back and for us to help them do this. We are grateful to Brian Martin, one of the associate editors of the *Encyclopedia of Activism and Social Justice* for providing some conceptual clarity on what he regards as distinctive about being an activist, when he said:

> Activism is action that goes beyond conventional politics, typically being more energetic, passionate, innovative, and committed. In systems of representative government, conventional politics includes election campaigning, voting, passing laws, and lobbying politicians. Action outside of these arenas includes neighborhood organizing, protest marches, and sit-ins. The boundary between activism and conventional politics is fuzzy and depends on the circumstances. (Anderson & Herr, 2007, p. xlx)

In this book we want to markedly increase the stakes in this process of crossing boundaries, in ways that further enrich, deepen and extend the notion of activism as it relates to schools and communities put at a disadvantage. Our starting point is the commitment and passion we have to puncture some of the enduring myths and mischievously constructed false and misleading claims that are allowed to increasingly go unchallenged.

In this opening chapter we want to provide something about the nature of what C.Wright Mills (1959[1970], p. 215) appropriately titled our 'intellectual craftsmanship'. We are particularly enamored by Mills' notion of displaying our intellectual craft because as socially critical scholars we feel this to be an honest and appropriate way of revealing how it is that we do things intellectually. Most importantly, doing this reveals something about ourselves and how it is that we have come to do what it is we do. The more detached and conventionally used terms of research 'method' or research 'methodology' are far too diminished and impoverished for our liking because they are highly suggestive of a degree of neutrality and distancing that is realistically and practically impossible in doing good social science. Mills put it in these words (the more inclusive language is ours):

> Scholarship is a choice of how we live as well as a choice of career; whether [she] knows it or not, the intellectual work[wo]man forms [her] own self as [she] works towards the perfection of [her] craft; to realize [her] own potentialities, and opportunities that come [her] way, [she] constructs a character which has at its core the qualities of the good work[wo]man. (p. 216)

We believe that what defines 'good' socially critical intellectual work are approaches that profoundly challenge taken-for-granted constructions of the way things are, and how they came to be like that.

To give an opening example into how we do our craft, we want to suggest that the term 'disadvantage' as it is attached as a descriptor to individuals, schools and communities, is highly problematic. Cass & Brennan (2002) name our concern and the nature of the misrepresentation and distortion, in this way:

> ... individuals and communities are not naturally disadvantaged, their disadvantage is economically, politically and socially constructed by the operations of financial markets, labor markets and housing markets and by government economic and public policies. (p. 257)

What Cass & Brennan (2002) are referring to, is the way in which disadvantage and misadventure in the area of social policy get constructed as if they were individual deficits or problems that reside in individuals in terms of causation, rather than being seen as structural or institutional issues. When categories like disadvantage are portrayed in this kind of partial and misleading way, the effect is a kind entrapment way of thinking. C. Wright Mills (1959[1970]) argues that when people become induced or habituated into thinking and feeling 'that their private lives are a series of traps', then they have diminished agency and 'the more trapped they feel' (p. 9). What he is saying is that we seldom define the troubles we endure in terms of 'historical change and institutional contradictions' (p. 10). That being the case we desperately need to interrupt this is a way of thinking so as to reveal the patterns and interconnections that are deliberately packaged and obfuscated so as to keep things shrouded and concealed. It is not that we need more information, nor on their own, better skills of analysis, but rather as Mills argues, we need a 'quality of mind that will help [us] use information and to develop reason in order to achieve lucid summations of what is going on in the world ... ' (p. 11). What we need is a way of interrupting this introverted way of thinking, with what Mills famously labeled 'a sociological imagination'.

What is most significant about Mills' thesis for our purposes in this book is the crucial analytical and practical distinction he makes between 'personal troubles' or private matters, and 'public issues' that transcend local circumstances and that have to do with social structures. The difficulty, Mills argues, is that 'an issue often involves a crisis in institutional arrangements' (p. 15), which is to say that it can be difficult to define and even more difficult to solve. In contrast, personal troubles are attributable to individuals as 'biographical entities', and to that extent, the articulation of what is going on and 'the resolution of troubles properly lie within the individual' (p. 15). Where the difficulty arises is in the mis-labeling of a public issue as a personal trouble. Mills gives the example of when a single person in a city is unemployed, then this is a personal trouble 'and for its relief we properly look to the character of the man, his skills and his immediate opportunities' (p. 15). But, when unemployment occurs on a widespread, protracted and exacerbated scale, then both the construction of the problem and the possibility of its solution lie beyond 'the personal situation and character of a scatter of individuals' — rather, it may be that 'the very structure of opportunities has collapsed' (p. 15).

The slide from the former to the latter is incredibly easy to do in a policy sense, and when it occurs, it leaves behind devastating consequences. The requirement to look in more complex ways at the workings of social and institutional structures, or the ways things are organized and for whose benefit, is let entirely off the hook. Fine (1989) refers to this as 'seeking private solutions to public problems' (p. 169), and likens this to the public sphere in effect packing up and walking away from its designated constitutional responsibility (Weis & Fine, 2001, p. 499). The more substantive point lying behind this, is that:

> The life of an individual cannot be adequately understood without references to the institutions within which his biography is enacted ... To understand the biography of an individual, we must understand the significance and meaning of the roles he has played and does play; to understand these roles we must understand the institutions of which they are a part. (C. Wright Mills, 1959[1970], pp. 178–179)

## IN WHAT SENSE THEN, IS THIS BOOK ACTIVIST?

Our over-arching aim in this book is to tackle two intractable, interlocking, conceptual and practical issues in a radically different way. The literatures and research on *school reform* and *community renewal* have existed historically apart and have rarely if ever come together and spoken to one another except in awkward and ultimately unhelpful ways. The consequence has been that schools and communities that have been most severely damaged as a consequence of globalizing tendencies, and that have had 'solutions' imposed upon them that demonstrably don't work, are about to experience the even worst excesses of the worldwide move to elitist so-called 'scientific research' (also known as evidence-

CHAPTER 1

based research). The stage is indeed being set for a situation in which complex schools and communities of disadvantage are going to have their situations dramatically and markedly exacerbated by an even more inappropriately imposed 'totalizing epistemology' (St. Pierre, 2004, p. 135; see also Gordon, Smyth & Diehl, 2008).

What makes this book different, therefore, is the way in which it contests this existing state of affairs by seeking to bring issues of school reform and community renewal in disadvantaged settings into conversation with one another.

The problem with conventional approaches to school and community renewal is not only their hortatory nature but the self-assured infallibility of the way they define what is the problem, and the research approaches that will produce 'solutions' that will work—if only we get the mix of variables right, and then apply the treatment together with the right degree of acquiescent compliance from those whose lives need to be turned around. Symptomatic of this is what Muijs, Harris, Chapman, Stoll & Russ (2004) say the research points to in terms of omnibus lists of things that need to occur in order to change schools in challenging circumstances, namely:

> A focus on teaching and learning, leadership, creating an information-rich environment, creating a positive school culture, building a learning community, continuous professional development, involving parents, external support and resources. (p. 149)

Free-floating lists like this avoid completely the circumstances of power and privilege that have made things the way they are, and that operate to keep them that way.

This book starts from the premise that no amount of external leverage on its own can change educational disadvantage, and that three inter-related conditions of people-centered 'capacity building' (Eade, 1997) are necessary. The first condition is a respect for the knowledge, language, class location, culture and experiences of communities of disadvantage; the second, an understanding that 'awareness, learning, self-esteem and the capacity for political action are mutually reinforcing' (Eade, 1997, p. 11); and the third, a realization that people from contexts of disadvantage have the right and, more importantly, the capacity to challenge authoritative 'solutions' to their problems (including the application of resources) that may not be in their interests, and to supplant such imposed solutions with better alternatives. What this book does is try to simultaneously get inside theoretically and practically two largely unconnected literatures, but to do that in the context of what happens when disadvantaged communities and their schools embark on community renewal and local school reform approaches designed to rejuvenate schools and communities.

Trying to get at deeper 'insider' understandings of the inter-related conditions necessary for turning around something as complex as disadvantaged schools and their communities, is a significant departure from current interventionist and performance-driven policy approaches to improving social and educational disadvantage. In this respect, this book opens up space for a 'new policy agenda' of how to bring a sociological imagination to the illumination of social and educational disadvantage. In O'Connor's (2001) words, when pursued in this way, 'a genuinely different kind of poverty knowledge' (p. 7) is possible.

## HOW HAVE WE GONE ABOUT OUR INTELLECTUAL CRAFT?

While we are not prepared to go quite a far as John Law in his book *After Method: Mess in Social Science Research* (Law, 2004) and his confessional piece 'making a mess with method' (Law, 2003), we are certainly in agreement with Law's sentiment that in social science research at the moment we are 'caught in an obsession with clarity, with specificity, and with the definite' (p. 3). While we would not want to convey the impression of ourselves as methodological luddites, because we do pursue our research in reasonably robust ways, we do find ourselves like Law 'at odds with method as it is usually understood'(Law, 2003, p. 3) and for the kind of reasons Law so cogently advances that seem to have more to do with hygienic superficialities than with in-depth substance:

> [Research methodology], it seems to me, is mostly about guarantees. Sometimes I think of it as a form of hygiene. Do your methods properly. Eat your epistemological greens. Wash your hands after mixing with the real world. Then you will lead the good research life. Your data will be clean. Your findings warrantable. The product you will produce will be pure. Guaranteed to have a long shelf-life.

We take some heart from Law's point that there is a certain seductiveness to what is on offer by the research methods industry, but there is also a very severe downside, because of what it is they refuse:

> ... they assume [a] hygienic form, [that doesn't] really work, at least for me. In practice, research needs to be messy and heterogeneous. It needs to be messy and heterogeneous, because that is the way it, research, actually is. And also, and more importantly, it needs to be messy because that is the way the largest part of the world is. Messy, unknowable in a regular and routinised way. Unknowable, therefore, in ways that are definite or coherent ... Clarity doesn't help. Disciplined lack of clarity, that may be what we need. (p. 3)

The kind of research form we used, if that is the correct term, is more in tune with Lawrence-Lightfoot's (2003) notion of the 'essential conversation'. While Lawrence-Lightfoot was not advancing an articulate research approach, what she was referring to was what can be learnt in teacher-parent conferences across the school-home boundary. We believe that the complex tensions and contested terrain of the 'borderlands'(p. xi) between bodies of theories about how schools and communities work, and new possibilities for school and community renewal, involved all of the same emotions, vulnerabilities, risks, complexities, anxieties, and uncertainties encountered by Lawrence-Lightfoot in her teacher-parent conferences. In our case, we confronted, negotiated and re-negotiated the full range of these perplexities in our research, as we engaged with the informants with whom we had conversations.

There are two further reasons we are attracted to Lawrence-Lightfoot's (2003) notion of the 'essential conversation'. First, it seems to convey something about the urgency of the need to puncture the mythology that can often reside in bodies of theoretical ideas that are seriously out of kilter with the real world because of the way they have become hermetically sealed by the action of interest groups. In other words, ideas can become dominant when they are insulated from critique and analysis. Second, the tenor of the notion of an 'essential conversation' conveys something about what is necessary for university researchers to do, if they are to make sense of the practical (and messy) world of students, teachers, schools, and communities as they work in grassroots ways to contest and re-work policies imposed upon them.

At both of these levels, we hope to demonstrate in the remainder of this book, something, not only of an 'essential conversation', but of a conversation that we had to have!

Let us begin the conversation by saying that we are seeking in this book to carve out some new and distinctive territory in two ways.

Firstly, to pose some substantively different questions that pre-dispose themselves to qualitatively different answers to a number of compelling and increasingly urgent issues that are largely being ignored, or else obfuscated, by current social and educational policy and research, namely:
- how disadvantaged schools and their communities 'read' the issue of disadvantage and its impact on their educational outcomes and futures;
- how disadvantaged schools and their communities situate, understand and confront the wider 'causes' of educational under-achievement;
- how disadvantaged 'insiders' develop alternatives to the 'official' deficit views of educational disadvantage;
- how educational debate can be refocused away from so-called 'students at risk' towards more optimistic scenarios of how to enhance learning in disadvantaged schools and communities; and;
- how everyday curriculum and pedagogical practices, processes, and application of resources, can be actively directed in ways that confront persistent educational inequalities, and lead to improved learning.

Secondly, and in terms of the intellectual craftsmanship we bring, we hope to begin to reinvigorate and rehabilitate notions of critical ethnography that have fallen somewhat on hard times as a consequence of the neo-conservative restoration.

Ethnography has come a long way since the days of Malinowski and Boas – particularly within its 'home' discipline of anthropology but also within education where ethnography seems to have become a preferred methodology within critical sociology and what has generally become known as policy sociology (Bowe & Ball with Gold, 1992). Critical versions of educational ethnography, that is, versions informed by theories of class (neo-marxist), feminism and post structuralism, have been particularly significant. However, the critical dialectic between data and theory, the key feature of versions of critical ethnography, would seem, according to some commentators to be losing its edge. Stephen Ball (2006a), for example, one of the early prime-movers in advocating theoretically-informed ethnographic work and one of the founders of 'policy sociology', has recently been critical of the state of theory in much education research. Speaking on behalf of Youdell (2006) and Gillborn (2006), as much as of his own views, Ball (2006a) writes:

> Theory when it is talked about is either spoken in hushed tones before speakers move on present their 'findings', or it is some kind of add-on or aside that does little or no real work within the research reported, or is an unreflexive mantra which tells us everything we need to know about the social world and makes research redundant. (p. 1)

> This is a problem and a danger ... [W]e argue that social theory, rather than being an indulgence or irrelevance to research, plays a key role in forming and reforming key research questions, invigorating the interpretation of research, and ensuring reflexivity in relation to research practice and the social production of research. (Ball, 2006a, p. 1)

The point being made here is that understanding and exploring complex and protracted social questions requires sophisticated investigative approaches which take theory seriously but which do not simply apply a pre-conceived theoretical template.

What we seek to reveal through our own socially critical account 'against the flow' (Abbs, 2003) in this book, is how neo-liberal policy attempts to domesticate schools and communities through school effectiveness reform mentalities by making such reforms appear sensible and unchallengeable. We also strike out indignantly asserting our right to construct our research in schools and their communities in ways other than the officially endorsed narrow and impoverished evidence-based ways. Through the assertive voices of the participants in our research we seek to show how a socially critical approach enables an unmasking of schools as 'classed spaces' (Ball, 2006b, p. 7) that deserve, as Willis (2000) argues, a research approach that emphasizes 'imagination' rather then 'method'—in order to push the theory and practices of inequality a little further. Along with Knights & McCabe (2000), we believe that identity—in our case a learning identity in disadvantaged communities—cannot be produced 'as if the self were independent of the broader social relations and institutions about which entirely different stories are told' (p. 426). Rather, our critical ethnographic approach is one that aims to exemplify the situation of how 'power is rarely so exhaustively and totalizing as to preclude space for resistance and almost never so coherent as to render resistance unnecessary or ineffective' (pp. 426–427). In other words, we hope to illustrate how 'resistance can occur at any point in a series of power –knowledge relations' (p. 427).

In particular the book does this in three main ways, by:

# CHAPTER 1

(i) *foregrounding the central role of theory as a precursor to data collection* with theory not only acting as a medium and an outcome of the ethnographic writing itself, but with theory shaping the pattern and texture of ethnographic data as they are interrogated, with theory at the same time being open to the possibility of being re-fashioned in light of the data.

(ii) *having a central concern with the cultural politics* of what it is that is being investigated so that the social actors in the research are able to acquire ethnographically informed knowledge around what is happening to their lives, and in the process acquiring the agency with which to act back on the forces shaping their lives.

(iii) *bringing a critical focus to bear on the research as well as the writing* in ways that highlight inequalities of power so as to produce 'socially relevant ethnographic accounts' (Mills & Gibb with Willis, 2004, p. 215) that enable 'sensuous practices of 'meaning making'' (Willis & Trondman, 2000, p. 9).

In this regard, the research we undertook used an ensemble of practical and theoretically critical ethnographic strategies, including:
- embedded interviews
- purposeful conversations
- dialectical theory-building
- voiced research from the data
- data representation through portraiture
- speaking data into existence
- advocacy oriented approach
- editing ourselves as researchers into the research
- listening for silences

In the end, we believe that it is the 'renovating of educational identities' (Gulson, 2005) that we are attempting through the relationship we seek to forge between theory and data, that give us the license to ask new and urgent questions, like:
- How do so-called 'disadvantage' schools and their communities understand and talk about the circumstances of their lives?
- How do these schools and communities respond to well meaning efforts by outsiders to 'change', 'reform' or 'improve' their lives?
- What happens when outsiders attempt to interrupt inter-generational histories of low educational participation, engagement and success?
- What do communities such as these bring to processes of neighborhood, community and school renewal?
- How do people inside these schools and communities think about themselves in relation to the wider community and their prospects for the future?

This book is part of a much wider multi-locale ethnography of schools and communities that have been put at a disadvantage (see: Smyth & Angus, 2006; Smyth, Angus, Down & McInerney, 2008; Angus, 2008; Smyth, Down & McInerney, forthcoming). Rather than reiterate much of the detail of what we have already presented elsewhere, we will instead provide a synoptic view and refer the reader to the more detailed sources of how we undertook our research and the specifics of the particular contexts in which we did it.

Rather than providing the kind of extensive detailed portraits or portrayals of the kind we have used elsewhere (Smyth, Angus, Down & McInerney, 2008), what we intending doing instead is to present ethnographic 'slices of life'. In this we draw on Green (2002), who said:

> The term 'slice' emphasizes that, while the depictions of their lives are only partial, they are not random or lacking coherence (p. vii)

As Green (2002) points out, what these slices look like, has much to do with what it is we are looking at, who has done the cutting, which bits get to be included, and for what reasons. To put this another way, what we have tried to do is present some 'snapshots', taken at a particular time and in particular places, to help us present a point or carry a larger argument or thesis. Our intent, as it was in the kind of 'slices of life' approach of Green (2002), is in multiple ways to 'describe', 'document', 'ponder' and 'critique' as well as 'construct and deconstruct meanings' (p. vii). At some places in our text we do more of this ethnographic insertion than at other times. Sometimes we have chosen to concentrate instead on advancing and reconstructing the complex arguments that need to be won more widely, if the viewpoints and groups currently excluded are to be given an airing.

Some brief contextual portraits of the two communities that we draw from and present in some sections of the book may be helpful to the reader. However, before we do that, and in order to situate the book more generally as well as ourselves as the writers, we need to say something about Australia and the place both from within as well as about which we are writing.

## SOMETHING ABOUT THE AUSTRALIAN CONTEXT

Almost two thirds of Australian children attend public (government) schools that provide secular and supposedly free education from Reception to Year 12. Typically, schools are organized into primary (elementary) and secondary (high school) divisions although middle schools are now coming into vogue. There is a movement towards community schools in some quarters but this is very much in its infancy. In most states and territories schooling is compulsory until 16 years of age although governments are now legislating to raise this to 17 years of age. Constitutional responsibility for the provision of public education in Australia resides with state and territory governments. However, because the Commonwealth government has sole authority over taxation collection it wields the fiscal authority and in recent years has begun to exercise a much stronger influence over educational policy. In order to qualify for federal funds, state education systems now have to comply with national goals of schooling and accountability measures, such as national literacy testing programs in years 3, 5, 7 and 9. Although schools across Australia vary somewhat in terms of local curriculum priorities and areas of specialization they tend to have a common curriculum framework incorporating essential learnings in the arts, design and technology, English, health and physical education, mathematics, science and society and environment, and vocational education. At the senior school level this learning culminates in a certificate of education.

During the ascendancy of neo-liberal governments there has been a retreat of governments from the funding of public education and human services and a consequent shift of responsibilities to parents and school communities. Because of shortfalls in Commonwealth and State government funding, school councils on behalf of parents have to raise funds through fees, levies and corporate sponsorship—a process that reinforces the disparity between the well-endowed schools in middle-class suburbs and those situated in poorer communities like the ones we draw from in this book, where the capacity for parents to supplement school budgets is markedly reduced. Coincident with this funding reversal has been a movement by state authorities to devolve educational responsibilities to school councils and to promote the concept of the self-managing school.

## SNAPSHOT PORTRAITS OF THE COMMUNITIES

### *Wirra Wagga*

The community of Wirra Wagga (a pseudonym) exits on the outskirts of a provincial Australian city of some 100,000 people. The community was established as a public housing estate in the 1950s and since then has had something of a 'reputation' in the eyes of outsiders. Since 2001 Wirra Wagga has been a priority area for a state government neighborhood renewal that has had as its objective greater involvement and ownership of residents in bringing about a range of community improvements in terms of built environment as well as human capacities. The population of this community has remained remarkably homogenous in terms of its predominantly Anglo-Celtic ancestry, in spite of the multicultural mix of migration to Australia in recent years. This is an area that has experienced protracted inter-generational disadvantage, with only 7% of public housing tenants citing 'a wage' as the primary source of income. Perhaps because of this and other related reasons, this is a community that has suffered from the stigmatizing and stereotyping discourses around family dysfunction, welfare dependency, criminal behavior, lifestyles and educational aspirations and attainment. These disparaging portrayals rest somewhat uneasily with what we quickly discovered to be a proud community, that was resilient, caring, and that had an extensive reservoir of largely unacknowledged and untapped human assets, talents and resources. There was a strong ethos of volunteering that fed into extensive local leadership and networking, and this contributed to a passion to build and extend capacity among residents in a variety of ways. As part of the community renewal process there was a strong disposition on the part of government officials to listen carefully to residents, and the residents in co-operation with government had prepared an action plan in areas of housing, community well-being, community safety, employment and education, and aspects of the environment. While there were undeniable and daunting challenges to be confronted in terms of the many complexities in the lives of residents of Wirra Wagga, there was also a remarkably up-beat view that this was a 'great place to live', and for reasons that were still largely invisible to and not well understood by outsiders.

*Bountiful Bay*

Some 3000 miles distant from Wirra Wagga educators and residents in the Bountiful Bay (also a pseudonym) Education District are also struggling with issues of student engagement and early school leaving. At first glance this might seem somewhat surprising. Bountiful Bay is a resource-rich region with a strong economic base and a unique maritime heritage. Tourism, agriculture, fishing, mining, petro-chemical production, steel fabrication and a host of manufacturing and service industries all contribute to the development of a prosperous and expanding urban region. It is apparent, even from a cursory glance at the proliferation of high rise apartments, that the wealth generated by the state's mineral boom had penetrated the region. However, pockets of affluence on the seafront mask the extent of poverty in the hinterland. These beautiful coastal locales may be playgrounds for holiday-makers and week-end trippers but they are also home for working class families who have largely missed out on the 'new money'. Compared with state averages, Bountiful Bay townships have low levels of weekly earnings, low levels of adult workforce participation, low levels of parental education, reduced levels of life expectancy, a greater percentage of single parent families, high levels of welfare dependency and a youth unemployment rate of 12%. These statistics point to a considerable degree of educational disadvantage in the four senior high schools serving the Bountiful Bay district, and that we refer to later in parts of this book.

## ORGANIZATION OF THE BOOK

The book falls into four parts, each of which builds on and extends the others.

**Chapter 2** sets up the argument that the most damaging aspect of education in recent times, especially for communities and schools pushed to the margins of society through no fault of their own, has been the progressive narrowing of the goals and options that have been the center-piece of neo-liberal reform approaches. The loss of moral, philosophical and political compass that accompanies this turn, has collapsed schools down to annexes of the economy and allowed the forces of privatization free reign through technologies of effectiveness, performativity and accountability. The effect has been to ride rough-shod over issues of social justice, equity and the common good. What we argue in this chapter, is that neo-liberalism constitutes a discourse of deceit that masquerades as a set of false promises—illusions of choice, old inequities re-packaged as new 'standards', teaching to educate that is subverted by teaching to the test, and local empowerment that is replaced by a thin consumerist version of parental involvement in schools. In a

CHAPTER 1

very real sense what we take up in this chapter is the point behind the provocative title of Frank Coffield's (2008) book: 'Just suppose teaching and learning became the first priority ...'

The activist position we take in this chapter is around our unwillingness to give up on the institution of public schooling, especially for those unable to buy their way into private education. We are simply not prepared to allow public education to become yet another cost-center of business and commerce. The kind of re-casting of educational policy and practice necessary to counter the debilitating and corroding effects of the current assault on public schools, can in our view only come from the inspirational efforts of community-minded and socially-engaged schools.

How this might happen and what the features of such a grassroots reclamation might look like, are provided in this chapter through a series of ethnographic slices from two communities and their schools—Wirra Wagga and Bountiful Bay. Through extracts of stories from both of these communities, we are able to give some hopeful glimpses of what a more optimistic critical pedagogy of place might look like. Examples like these provide the central source of inspiration around which an alternative must coalesce, for schools and communities that have been the most damaged by the neo-liberal discourse of deceit.

**Chapter 3** carries this trajectory into the new, urgent and largely uncharted territory of 'relational power'. The central claim, invoking Boyte with Gust (2003), is that profound transformational change of the kind we are alluding to can only happen as part of a much broader 'different kind of politics'. The basis of the backlash against the unremitting agenda of economic instrumentality is our assertion that conventional political approaches no longer work. Not only is there widespread indifference and cynicism with mainstream politics, but it has become deeply implicated in the forms of individualism that make this impossible as a viable platform. The kind of revitalization needed has to be embedded in community activism around the collective will, desire and imagination of active citizens. In this regard, we explore what is meant by citizen politics, and the architecture of a 'community voiced' approach through the eyes and experiences of some of the key players in Wirra Wagga.

In this chapter we map some of the experiences in a Community Renewal process in Wirra Wagga against the key ideas of the Saul Alinsky tradition of community organizing (we explain this in more detail in the chapter itself). This part of the chapter reveals something about how relational power can be spoken into existence through a focus on community strengths rather than continuing to focus in remediating deficits, though de-institutionalizing relationships, through an affirmation of working class identity, and by supplanting a client and service mentality with notions of authentic partnership. But the renovation required is of an order of magnitude that goes beyond even the rejuvenation of relational power on the part of communities. What lies at the core is the need to profoundly question how schools are being constructed metaphorically-speaking, for whom, and how they work for the most excluded. These are questions that are highly contestable given the prevailing educational policy orthodoxy, as the following chapter reveals.

In **Chapter 4** we turn to the regime that has had the most damaging effect of all on schools and communities put at a disadvantage—the ideology of the 'school effectiveness' movement. While it might seem like an innocuous enough concept at a superficial level, the way in which the school effectiveness ensemble of narrow utilitarian practices has been allowed to do its work, is that it excludes, expunges or puts under erasure wider notions of social class, community context, and student and family background. Options, opportunities, and avenues for action are constrained, distorted and rendered down to matters that are certain, predictable, measurable and controllable by schools themselves. The result is that what gets to be included in the school effectiveness approach is what is deemed to 'make a difference' in terms of immediacy, measurability and controllability—to the exclusion of the wider social and economic agenda that are relegated to the status of background 'noise'.

This chapter gets up close and inside the school effectiveness approach and provides an exhaustive critique of how it has become the single dominant educational policy discourse, and what it means to present problems of educational disadvantage as if they are issues that can be resolved instrumentally. The chapter concludes with a contrast between the technical/managerial view of school organization implicit in school effectiveness, and the participative/professional orientation that represents a more socially activist way of pursuing what we refer to, invoking Freire, as an approach embedded in a *pedagogy of hope* rather than of despair.

**Chapter 5** returns us full circle to the fundamental question of the purpose of education, particularly for schools and communities of disadvantage. Against the background trajectory of the rest of the book, this chapter questions the way in which message systems get to be constructed for young people who are most precariously placed in terms of the brutalizing effects of globalization and economic restructuring. We pursue these wider issues by having a final look at schools in Bountiful Bay as they struggled to find some spaces within which to both contest the 'big lie' that training creates jobs, while looking to the features of a more ethically honest and engaging alternative.

Often portrayed as being less academically talented, trouble-makers, unmotivated, or simply educationally unchallenged or uninspired because of family background, young people in communities like Bountiful Bay are positioned in ways that appear to present them with no other avenues other than options that prepare them for a 'vocational' orientation—which is code for, low paid, low skill, insecure, casualized fodder for the capitalist industrial complex. Some schools, teachers and communities have the courage to question, from within the vocational orientation itself, what might be possible by shifting the focus away from the unremitting deficit portrayals of young people from disadvantaged contexts, and concentrating instead on forms of learning that foster collective, critical, democratic and socially just approaches that reveal their true learning potential and capacities. As we show, such approaches can be rare, they require very special teachers, and they need to occur in schools that have created a more expansive vision, within programs that profoundly understand the importance of 'being in community'. We can think of no more appropriate comment with which to conclude this chapter, than the Bountiful Bay student with whom we start chapter 5, who said:

> At the start they thought we were the stupid class until they saw what we can produce, now they don't think we are so stupid.

The conclusion, **Chapter 6**, reassembles the activist and socially critical theme of the book around a heuristic of intersecting central 'storylines', comprising—policy, pedagogy and research. Through a constellation of eighteen elements we present an architecture of what an activist but discomforting imagination might look like when taken in concert with a counter-hegemonic model of social justice like that advocated by Fraser (1997) around the discursively linked notions of *redistribution*, *recognition*, and *political representation*. We agree with Fraser & Naples (2004) that a socially just world is predicated on interpreting the world in order to change it.

CHAPTER 2

# PUTTING TEACHERS AND COMMUNITIES INTO POLICY RECLAMATION: COUNTERING EDUCATIONAL 'DISCOURSES OF DECEIT'

## INTRODUCTION

February 13th 2008 will go down as a landmark in Australia's history. On this day, before a packed parliamentary gallery in the nation's capital, Canberra, the incoming Labor Party Prime Minister, Kevin Rudd, apologized to indigenous people for the grievous harm inflicted on them by successive Commonwealth government policies. Since European occupation in 1788 indigenous Australians have been dispossessed of their lands, separated from their families and communities, decimated through frontier violence and diseases, subjected to gross violations of their culture and heritage and pushed to the margins of society. Today the living standards of many Aboriginal people are more akin to third world conditions as evidenced in the huge gap between indigenous and non-indigenous Australians in life expectancy, educational achievement and employment opportunities. In uttering the word 'sorry' to Aboriginal people, Kevin Rudd did what his predecessor, John Howard, had been unwilling to do for more than a decade of conservative rule, despite the disturbing findings of a national inquiry into the separation of Aboriginal and Torres Strait Islander children from their families (Commonwealth of Australia, 1997). Acknowledging the need to right the wrongs of the past, Rudd proclaimed:

> We apologize for the laws and policies of successive parliaments and governments that have inflicted profound grief, suffering and loss on these our fellow Australians. We apologize especially for the removal of Aboriginal and Torres Strait Islander children from their families, their community and their country. For the pain, suffering and hurt of the stolen generations, their descendants and their families left behind, we say sorry. To the mothers and the fathers, the brothers and the sisters, for the breaking up of families and communities, we say sorry. And for the indignity and degradation thus inflicted on a proud people and a proud culture, we say sorry. (Hansard, 2008, p. 1)

Although many Australians view this apology as merely a symbolic gesture and argue for more practical measures to ameliorate injustices and inequalities, its significance should not be underestimated. A key feature of Rudd's address was his confession that the lawmakers of the land, not the administrators, missionaries and settlers, must ultimately be held accountable for the injustices experienced by indigenous peoples.

> The uncomfortable truth for us all is that the parliaments of the nation, individually and collectively, enacted statutes and delegated authority under those statutes that made the forced removal of children on racial grounds fully lawful ... We, the parliaments of the nation, are ultimately responsible, not those who gave effect to our laws. And the problem lay with the laws themselves. (Hansard, 2008, p. 3)

We have dwelt on the apology to highlight the gross injustices facing indigenous people and to reveal the complicity of governments in sanctioning racist policies and practices. The Prime Minister's words serve as a salutary reminder that, although public policies may leave spaces for more benevolent and humane courses of action, they nonetheless set parameters within which individuals, groups and institutions are predisposed to conduct themselves. Discussing contemporary education policy, Ball (2006c) observes:

> Policies do not normally tell you what to do, they create circumstances in which the range of options available in deciding what to do are narrowed or changed or particular goals are set. (p. 21)

The uncomfortable truth is that many education policies enacted by neoliberal governments in Australia, New Zealand, the United Kingdom, the United States and elsewhere, have narrowed the options and changed educational goals to the point where they are damaging not only the wellbeing of young people (especially those in economically disadvantaged communities), but are having a detrimental effect on the overall economic and social health of these societies. Increasingly, the roles of schools are being redefined in response to economic imperatives, rather than a commitment to social justice, equity and the common good. According to Fielding (2006, p. 349), lack of a 'philosophic compass' to guide education policy has led to a deepening crisis in the United Kingdom as notions of effectiveness, performativity, accountability and managerialism have taken hold. We contend that these trends are apparent in many Western countries, including Australia. Countering the 'discourse of deceit' (p. 356) embedded in these reforms demands a reorientation of educational philosophy and practices so that schools become far more creative, humane and personally fulfilling places for young people and their teachers. In Fielding's words, they must become person-centered learning communities.

In this chapter we want to engage in some policy reclamation by exploring democratic, community-oriented and socially critical alternatives to market-driven and functionalist approaches to schooling. We acknowledge that contesting dominant ideologies is difficult in a policy environment that muffles the voices of teachers and students, rides roughshod over local communities, and refuses to engage with (let alone tackle) the 'savage inequalities' described by Kozol (1992) in his searing expose of the extremes of wealth and poverty in America's school system. Nonetheless, from our studies in Australia and accounts from the United

States and elsewhere, we believe that there are 'pockets of hope' (de los Reyes & Gozemba, 2002) within schools and communities where committed teachers and social activists show what can be achieved by embracing Freire's conception of transformative education. At the heart of this approach is the democratization of pedagogical power, the fostering of socially just relationships and a capacity to be critical (Freire, 1998). This chapter will contribute to the overall theme of activist and socially critical school and community renewal through:
- a critique of contemporary educational policies and their manifest failure to address educational disadvantage
- an account of educational policies and practices that foreground the role of teachers and communities in developing curricula which is (a) inclusive of the needs and aspirations of young people (b) promotes critically engaged forms of learning, and (c) contributes to civic engagement and community capacity building
- a critical analysis of the potential of community-oriented schooling to redress educational inequalities.

## NEOLIBERALISM AND EDUCATION REFORM–A DISCOURSE OF DECEIT AND FALSE PROMISES?

For the past decade or so, much of the educational discourse in Western countries has been dominated (if not captured) by the New Right—an alliance of neoconservative and neoliberal forces wedded to a market model of education, parental choice and the restoration of 'traditional family' and 'national values' (Apple, 1996). With the retreat of the welfare state and adoption of user-pay principles a good deal of the responsibility for education, health and social wellbeing, has been sheeted back to individuals and their families. Now, more than ever, the goals of education are being set within a narrow frame that subverts the social and aesthetic domains of learning to technical and utilitarian purposes. In an effort to lift national economic goals and global competitiveness, governments have sought to make curricula more responsive to the workplace through an emphasis on basic skills and competencies, entrepreneurialism and vocational education. A business ethos manifests itself in education through the promotion and adoption of corporate managerialist practices such as target setting, audits, mission statements, performance appraisals, and the marketization of schools. Perhaps these new ways of operating are best encapsulated in the idea of a school as a high performance organization incorporating a measure of local autonomy within strict accountability guidelines laid down by central governments.

At first sight some of the neoliberal reforms may appear to be quite benign or even enlightened. After all, shouldn't parents be able to exercise freedom of choice in selecting a school for their children? Isn't it reasonable to expect that all children should attain functional levels of literacy and numeracy achievement? Shouldn't schools, teachers and education administrators be held accountable to the community for their educational outcomes? Surely local, state and federal governments have a responsibility to ensure that public funds are used efficiently

CHAPTER 2

and wisely, that no children are left behind in the education stakes and that education serves the national interest. The trouble with such rhetoric is that much of it rests on a false set of claims and promises that constitute what Fielding (2006) labels a 'discourse of deceit'. These are strong words and they require some unpacking.

## THE ILLUSION OF CHOICE

In the first place, the language of the market with its call for competition, accountability and choice is fundamentally an illusion. In a market democracy real choice is the prerogative of the well-to-do—those with the social, cultural and economic capital who can gain access to a private education or better-resourced public schools. Families without the power of the purse have no recourse but to enroll their children in neighborhood schools often badly blighted by years of neglect. However, those who dare question the fairness or logic of school choice are likely to be accused of being undemocratic, a situation which creates what Macedo calls 'a pedagogy of entrapment' (de los Reyes & Gozemba, 2002, p. x). Barely concealed behind the rhetoric of the New Right agenda is a blatant disregard for the 'markers of disadvantage' (Broadhurst, et al., 2005) adhering to children's lives. Those students most often missing from schools (or underachieving) tend to come from low income families, live in poor housing conditions, are cared for by single parents, depend on welfare benefits, exhibit emotional and behavioral problems, and often have a history of poor physical and mental health. There is a racial and ethnic dimension to this scenario with a large proportion of indigenous children in Australia experiencing high levels of disadvantage.

Typically, the suffering and diminished opportunities engendered by these circumstances are attributed to a combination of cultural, family and individual deficiencies rather than oppressive economic and social conditions. However, there is no denying the intimate relationship between academic success and social power in Australia. Teese (2000) reminds us that:

> There is more than a mere parallel between the poverty of many unemployed workers and the failure of many students in schools. Often these groups are drawn from the same population. Scholastic failure leads to casual, poorly paid work. Economic failure leads to frustrations, loss of self respect, loss of commitment, loss of means—all fatal to the confident sense of purpose, the inner integrity and personal wellbeing on what childhood learning most readily builds. (p. 1)

Structural inequalities of global significance are a key element in this cycle of poverty. Bardsley (2007) argues that students from economically disadvantaged backgrounds—the 'rust belt kids' (Thomson, 2002)—are most vulnerable to globalization since they are less likely to achieve academically, are more likely to leave before completing formal school requirements, and in all likelihood will go on to poorly paid jobs or experience underemployment or unemployment. Bardsley goes on to suggest that without a proper injection of funding for public schools obtaining a quality education in Australia is likely to shift from right to a privilege in a neoliberal society.

What we now have is a stratified education system marked by high concentrations of wealth and privilege in some districts, and abject poverty, welfare dependency and educational disadvantage in others. Because schools are funded by state and federal governments rather than local authorities, the extent of disadvantage is less marked in Australia than the United States; nonetheless the residualization of public education is a major issue for schools serving low socioeconomic communities. Teachers in a high school that was part of our study claimed that public schooling was now being viewed in some quarters as a safety net for those parents who could not afford to send their children to private schools. In the wake of a pronounced 'drift to private schools', government schools in the region had a tendency to focus on vocational education. However, this brought its own set of problems as a school leader explained:

> One of the biggest problems we've got is that we only obtain about 67 per cent of primary school students and it's the top 30 plus per cent that go to other schools [including] other government schools and a few private schools. On the reverse of that, the school has developed a very strong vocational program. It's a very strong VET school, and in some ways that works as a disadvantage because the parents see this as not providing for university entrance. We have 180 year 12s; but there are only 22 students undertaking courses that will prepare them for university. We have to try and turn that around. (Principal)

What this meant in practice was a strong drive to promote the school and to find a niche in the educational market through the provision of specialist programs to attract students with particular gifts and talents in sport and the arts.

## NEW STANDARDS, OLD INEQUALITIES?

The second myth we want to expose concerns the claim that neoliberal reforms have raised educational standards and led to greater equality of opportunity for minority groups. There is little evidence that the push for a standardized curriculum and high stakes testing embodied in the No Child Left Behind (NCLB) legislation has resulted in any improvement in educational attainment for children from minority groups. These, and similar reforms in Australia and the United Kingdom, have failed to deliver on the promise of lifting achievement levels, participation rates and student engagement for a large proportion of young people (Hursh, 2007; Lipman, 2004; Anyon, 2005; McDermott, 2007; Darling-Hammond, 2007). School retention rates have in fact declined in many parts of the United States and Australia (Smyth & McInerney, 2007).

In a study of the impact of accountability policies in four US states, McDermott (2007) argues that far from ensuring greater equity outcomes, the move to standards-based reform has effectively disempowered local communities and singled them out for the failure of their children to reach national standards. From a comprehensive analysis of National Assessment of Educational Progress (NAEP) scores, Hursh (2007) concludes that exams used to assess schools have increased the number of school dropouts, resulted in less rigorous curriculum and actually widened the achievement gap between student cohorts. In a similar vein, Lipman's (2004) research in Chicago's public schools reveals how testing policies have led to students of color and students living in poverty being subjected to more regimented and uninspiring forms of instruction than their peers from middle class and professional families. What Haberman (1991) has described as a 'pedagogy of poverty' is very much a reality for students in these schools.

On the question of standards, Collin and Apple (2007) suggest that it is rather ironical that many of the reforms proposed by business interests in the neoliberal state, including high stakes testing and reductions in government spending on public education, are likely to create a situation in which there is less emphasis on the kinds of literacies needed to enhance critical thinking skills that are supposedly so highly valued in the new economy.

For Darling-Hammond (2007) it is a case of 'new standards old inequalities' as she laments the disparities in resource allocation amongst American schools, the lack of investment in teacher education, and the shortcomings of curriculum and assessment reform. She observes that a small fraction of the $3000 billion spent on the Iraq War could have established a world class teaching force in all US communities. It is difficult to escape the conclusion that neoliberal policies have ultimately shifted the blame for student failure away from unfair, discriminatory policies and practices to the inadequacies of individual students, their families and their communities.

## TEACHING TO EDUCATE OR TEACHING TO THE TEST?

A third misconception that we want to dispel is the idea that these reforms with their emphasis on standardized curriculum, measurable outcomes, and school and teacher accountability have led to an improvement in teacher quality, professional standards and classroom instruction. On the contrary, there are signs that teachers are losing their creative energies and capacity for curriculum innovation as they seek to cover the objectives and requirements of externally prescribed curricula. Commenting on the impact of reforms in the United States, Ohanian and Kovacs (2007) go so far as to suggest that 'NCLB is sucking the very life blood from our professions, demanding that teachers become readers of scripts rather than professionals engaged in the critical work of educating children in their care' (p. 270). They go on to state:

> It is time to respect the informed judgments of classroom teachers and to stop paying outside testing companies to produce measurements that have been shown to be poor indicators of student success. (p. 272)

According to Valli and Buese (2007), high stakes policy directives have intensified teachers' work and promoted an environment in which teachers are asked to relate to their students differently and 'enact pedagogies that are often at odds with their own vision of best practice' (p. 520). Although teachers in Australia still retain a fair degree of freedom in the choice of curriculum content and teaching methods, standardized testing regimes have undermined school-based curriculum and moves towards more integrated studies. In these circumstances, 'teaching to the test' can become an overriding imperative, as we were to observe in one of the research sites:

> Accountability processes impact on teaching and learning. Our year 9s will be taking the standardized tests in literacy and numeracy next week so the innovative group of teachers I have referred to will be gearing up their students for the test. So you won't see any innovative practices in their classroom this week. Ironic, isn't it? They're happy to talk and meet with you but it might be better to visit their classrooms in your next visit. (Principal)

When teachers have to put on hold engaging and socially relevant forms of learning for the sake of testing functional literacy skills we have indeed reached a sorry state of affairs. Increasingly it appears that teachers are being reduced to mere 'functionaries' (Kincheloe, 2003), whose task it is to implement externally produced curriculum. Ronald, a deputy principal, summed up the impact of this kind of top–down decision making in the following words:

> We have so many people driving policy now outside of the school that it interferes with the structures that we have set up. It's not stopping teachers from doing what they have always done but it's wearing them out. It's the tiring effect of accountability. (Ronald, 26 July 2005)

Ronald has chosen his words carefully. He notes that the public policy environment has not brought a halt to local school initiatives, but it has led to a frustrating and unproductive situation where teachers have to be seen to be toeing the line when it comes to meeting accountability measures imposed by state and federal governments. In another school we were given the following explanation of the link between accountability processes, student learning and professional development:

> We link performance management to school planning, targets and strategies. The targets for success are basically the discussion points for staff performance management. Staff talk of performance management and school planning in the same sentence. It's not just a compliance tool that people sign off in term four. Targets are discussed throughout the year. The big emphasis is getting the process right ... making connections to planning, targets and performance management. Every part has been done in consultation with staff. The staff and management own this. Most welcome the opportunity to set targets because it gives them some structure and a layer of accountability. (David, 26 July 2005)

What is most interesting here is the way in which David justifies target setting in terms of serving the interests of teachers and the school. However, classroom teachers in the same school were not so enamored with the jargon and rationale behind this corporate managerialist approach. Frank, a senior school science teacher expressed his concerns as follows:

> We are into target setting in our school but it's very difficult to decide on appropriate targets at the beginning of the year. If you set a target that 65 per cent of students are going to get a 'C' or better does it mean that you are going to work any harder than if you set the target at 50 per cent? Measurement is one area that confuses me as it does a lot of other people, including parents. Kids have many ways of demonstrating knowledge of outcomes that are much better than just doing a test. (Frank, 26 July 2005)

Frank and his colleagues have a well-honed view of what is needed to engage students in disadvantaged schools but his knowledge and wisdom have been ignored by policy makers. Commenting on the situation in the United States, de los Reyes and Gozemba (2002) argue:

> Too often the voices of students and teachers, the very people who understand best what works in educational settings, are ignored in favor of listening to corporate and political leaders, who have not set foot in a classroom in years. (p. 30)

Not only are teachers out-positioned in the policy making process but according to Gale and Densmore (2003) they are often at the sharp end of policies where they tend to be treated as objects of policy interventions, most notably through the thinly disguised surveillance mechanisms of standardized testing regimes. Teachers are charged with immense responsibilities but their 'capital … has a low exchange rate in contexts of policy text production' (Gale & Densmore, 2003, p. 42). The same is true of parents and students.

## LOCAL EMPOWERMENT?

Much is made in policy statements of the educational value of school–community engagement and indeed in some quarters there is a strong push for full service schooling as well as a renewed emphasis on local school management, parent participation and community-based forms of learning. Local empowerment has become a catchword but the policy imperative to reinstate the local amidst the global is often underpinned by deficit views of low socioeconomic neighborhoods (Thomson, 2006). Typically, these neighborhoods are perceived as lacking in assets, social networks and funds of knowledge to build sustainable and cohesive communities. Correspondingly, students in these schools are often categorized as emotionally vulnerable or 'at-risk' learners with low self-esteem and fragile identities—images of the 'diminished self' (Ecclestone, 2007, p. 455), which are commonly translated into institutional beliefs and practices through the normalization of 'at-risk' policies.

The net effect of these pathologizing discourses is to reinforce a view that parents and students in poor communities are in need of external support and have little to contribute to educational policy and practice. Much of this thinking is

sustained by prejudice and mythology. To a large extent, the difficulties confronting low income families are often ascribed to deficiencies in parenting skills and/or to material and cultural differences, rather than inequitable social structures. In a study of literacy practices in the United States class, Compton-Lilly (2004, pp. 33–50) challenges prevailing myths about parents in poverty-stricken neighborhoods, for instance the common assumptions by educators and policy-makers that:
– parents are content to rely on welfare
– poor households are vacant of print
– parents have no interest in their own learning
– parents do not care about school
– parents can't read
– parents lack resources to help kids with reading.

Compton-Lilly argues that explanations that blame people in these circumstances are not only simplistic in the extreme, but they also fail to acknowledge the multiple funds of knowledge which exist in many poor homes and neighborhoods. Reporting on the findings of a study of school–community links in disadvantaged schools in Australia, Hayes and Chodkiewicz (2005) reached a similar conclusion:

> There was a very limited recognition [amongst principals and teachers] of how the school could resource and contribute to the community, nor how the community could contribute to school progress and student learning. (p. 16)

Studies of this kind add weight to Corson's (1998) assertion that there is frequently a discord in terms of what is valued in schools and families when it comes to working class and middle class communities.

> Much of the cultural capital valued in school is only partly available to children who come from class, gender, or cultural backgrounds that differ from the school recognized norms. (p. 11)

We will revisit this notion in this chapter, but we want to stress that current policy leaves little space for parents and members of the community to determine the goals of education and to engage directly with the pedagogical issues affecting their children. This is especially so for working class parents.

In summary, coercive policies developed at arm's length from teachers and local communities have failed in their goal of improving educational standards and equality of opportunity for young people. Research shows that allowing the market to dictate the fate of students has widened the achievement gap amongst the haves and have-nots, undermined teacher agency and morale, and seriously eroded the social and democratic purposes of schooling. The imposition of standardized curricula, high stakes testing regimes and other authoritarian and generic solutions will not succeed in improving the life chances of disadvantaged youth. Nor will such measures allow schools to address in any pedagogically enabling manner the major social, ecological and economic issues confronting humanity today.

CHAPTER 2

## RECLAIMING EDUCATIONAL POLICY AND PRACTICE: TOWARDS COMMUNITY-ORIENTED AND SOCIALLY ENGAGED SCHOOLING

In this section we explore elements of a counter-discourse to the corrosive effects of the 'conservative assault' and 'new authoritarianism' (Giroux, 2005) infecting our school systems. Our account is informed by insider perspectives of democratic, community-oriented and socially critical forms of schooling that offer a sense of hope and possibility for those young people whose lives and aspirations have been dealt a cruel blow by contemporary education policies. We acknowledge that 'teaching to transgress' (bell hooks, 1994) is a dangerous pastime that demands a great deal of personal and professional courage, especially in the current political environment. Not surprisingly, radical efforts to transform schooling are often relegated to 'pockets of hope' (de los Reyes & Gozemba, 2002), rather than widespread movements for change. As such, they are usually characterized by isolation, fragmentation and vulnerability within larger institutions and (more broadly) the political economy.

Our research in Australia suggests that such efforts are often confined to a handful of teachers within a school or to a school leader who is willing to contest inequitable practices and work with local communities to bring about progressive changes. We have also observed at close hand a group of education administrators working cooperatively with a neighborhood renewal team to establish a community-based alternative to mainstream schooling for disaffected youth. Having noted the somewhat disparate nature of these efforts, we recognize the longstanding commitment to progressive school and community renewal in such United States organizations as the Highlander Research and Education Center, the Coalition of Essential Schools, the Coalition for Community Schooling and their counterparts in Australia, the United Kingdom and elsewhere. These centers do provide a sense of hope and inspiration for those committed to the creation of more just communities.

Much has been written about what is required to reclaim educational policy and practice to advance more egalitarian goals of schooling. In *Rethinking schools*, Christensen and Karp (2003) argue that unless schools and classrooms are animated by a broad vision of equity, democracy and social justice, they will never be able to realize the widely proclaimed goal of raising educational achievement for all children. Fielding (2006) offers an antidote to the school effectiveness movement through the ideal of a 'person-centered learning community', while for bell hooks (1994) these emancipatory intents are best captured in the notion of education as 'the practice of freedom'. Goodman's (1992) vision of transformative education is based on the idea of schooling for critical democracy that seeks to maintain a balance between the values of individual freedom and communal rights and responsibilities. Drawing on the philosophy of Paulo Freire, Shor (1992, pp. 33–35) presents a case for a critical pedagogy that incorporates (amongst other principles) a commitment to dialogic learning, democratic practices, critical reflection, student activism and multiculturalism. Broadly speaking, each of these writers articulates a democratic and socially just alternative to market-driven and

utilitarian approaches to education but we will confine our discussion to three areas, all of which connect quite strongly to the overarching theme of activism and a socially critical approach to school–community renewal:
- building a community of learners
- developing a critical pedagogy of place
- educating for a better world.

## BUILDING A COMMUNITY OF LEARNERS

The idea of community is generally accepted as a 'redemptive solution' (Noddings, 1996, p. 246) to the isolation and individualism associated with traditional schooling—so much so that the desirability of creating such entities as a 'community of learners', 'professional communities', 'schools as communities' and 'community partnerships' are almost taken-for-granted. However, as Noddings reminds us, community also has a dark side in 'its tendency towards parochialism, conformity, exclusion, distrust (or hatred) of outsiders and coercion' (p. 258). By setting up fixed boundaries and single identities, we run the risk of inferring 'insiders and outsiders', 'inclusion and exclusion', 'us and them', 'centers and margins', and other exclusionary notions which often lend legitimacy to racism, ethnocentrism and dangerous forms of nationalism. Notwithstanding these limitations, we believe a strong case can be made for nurturing a sense of belongingness, a commitment to the common good and collective solidarity when it comes to school–community relationships. In what follows we explore some of the contemporary understandings of community building and discuss an Australian instance of school–community renewal.

Although a good deal of rhetoric supports the merits of school–community engagement, we agree with Hayes and Chodkiewicz (2005) that 'the interface between school and community is a boundary that contains and excludes, whilst affording limited views of the other side' (p. 12). This is most apparent in disadvantaged communities where residents often harbor bitter memories of their own schooling experiences, and a degree of mutual suspicion may well exist between educators and parents. For the most part, parent engagement tends to be confined to voluntary support in learning programs, fundraising activities, parent–teacher interviews and consultation (rather than direct participation) in school planning processes. Ownership of the substantive business of schools—the curriculum— remains firmly in the hands of educators and policy makers.

As we have already observed, a marketized approach tends to frame school–community relations in terms of contractual arrangements with students positioned as clients, principals as business managers, and teachers as producers. Although this view of school as a business organization is gaining currency in Australia, it does exist alongside democratic alternatives that attach greater weight to local decision making and community building programs—ideals embodied in the work of the Disadvantaged Schools Program (DSP) and the National Schools Network (NSN). During the 1970s and 1980s, the growth of community schools in Australia fostered closer links with local communities through shared resources, community outreach programs, integrated health, welfare, education and family services, and community education courses. Arguably, these initiatives—traces of which still exist in some schools—helped to break down the traditional divide between schools and communities by promoting greater parent participation in the life of schools and encouraging the concept of the school as a learning community for all.

To view a school from this perspective is to affirm that education, participation and inclusivity, are important ideals for the whole community, that the spaces in which teaching and learning occur are not just confined to classrooms, and that the community has pedagogical resources that can actively support the work of schools. A number of these ideals are contained in the community school model that is being developed in conjunction with the Wirra Wagga neighborhood renewal program.

## *The Wirra Wagga story*

Sibley (1995, p. ix) contends that 'the human landscape can be read as a landscape of exclusion'. Such is the case in Wirra Wagga where the 2500 people who call the neighborhood 'home' have to contend with negative and disparaging portrayals of their lifestyles from outsiders. Undoubtedly, a shared experience of poverty and social exclusion has helped to forge a strong sense of neighborhood identity, but it is also reinforced with positive elements of working class solidarity, care for others, and a tradition of voluntarism within the community. As described in Chapter One, the suburb is a priority site for a government-funded neighborhood renewal project that seeks to strengthen social institutions and improve the wellbeing and economic opportunities for residents.

Commencing in 2001, neighborhood renewal has involved an extensive phase of local consultation, asset mapping, leadership formation and the preparation of a residents action plan to guide community development. Job creation, accredited training programs and an expansion of adult education facilities are key components of renewal. Governance operates through a neighborhood advisory board comprising residents and agency representatives, but much of the community building occurs through a network of committees which address priorities such as health and wellbeing, community safety, housing, community works and environment, and learning, employment and economic development. Administrative support is provided through the state government department of human services neighborhood renewal team and a community house serves as a meeting place, communications center and educational resource for local residents. The district education office has been a major player in developing a community-based model of education in consultation with local schools, parents and community personnel.

'Education is at the heart of neighborhood renewal in Wirra Wagga. We are not going to move on unless we do something with education. Even though good things are happening, they are not going to go far because there are not many who can read and write.' These remarks from a local parent give some indication of the importance attached to schooling in improving the life chances of people. They also point to the extent of educational disadvantage in a community where few children have experience of preschooling; literacy and numeracy standards are well below national averages; attrition rates are high; and the majority of students fail to complete formal high school requirements. Olive Kennedy, the local member of parliament and a strong advocate of neighborhood renewal, summed up the concerns and aspirations of parents arising from a community meeting on the future of schooling in the neighborhood:

> One of the things that came out was a concern about the high rate of absenteeism of the Wirra Wagga kids when they go to the secondary school at the end of year 6. Often they go back to the primary school and hang around there. They have no security at secondary school and they want to go back to the safety of their primary school. The kindergartens here are badly run down—especially one of them which is run by a church group. Attendance is poor and we know we need better preschool services. We hope to improve education facilities at Wirra Wagga with the amalgamation of the two existing primary schools. Both principals have a commitment to it but a lot of the ideas came from the community. The community needs to own them or they won't work. (Olive Kennedy, 19 March 2007)

From Olive's perspective, the question of ownership is crucial to the success of schooling in Wirra Wagga. Unless parents have a major say in the organization of education provision in their community, there is little prospect that things will change. Equally, the mainstream curriculum and modes of instruction need to be critically reviewed, a point emphasized by Barry Jones, a school improvement officer in the district education team:

> Pedagogy is probably the most important thing that we have to address with the new community school. Our data says the kids aren't learning. We've got an education system based on middle class values, and until you understand the language of poverty you can't build a relationship with kids. We could build the best building but not change teaching ... the teacher makes the difference. If we can get a curriculum framework to work at Wirra Wagga it could become the lighthouse for schooling in the district. The new school will comprise three learning communities: preschool to year 2; years 3–5; and, years 6–8. Each will have a specific pedagogical emphasis. The foundation years will focus more on direct instruction, integrated studies and literacy. As students move into the 3–5 learning community they will be engaged in more collaborative and project based learning. In the 6–8 community, students will be supported to become more independent learners with an emphasis on ICT and a thinking curriculum. We are also looking at the childcare center aspect of renewal. (Barry Jones; 1 March 2006 and 5 June 2006)

Beane and Lipka (2006) argue that schools have to find ways to reach out to families and communities by creating small learning communities, developing high quality relationships and providing strong transition support for students. Major steps towards the realization of these ideals at Wirra Wagga took place in 2007 with the demolition of a run-down primary school and the construction of a community school incorporating kindergarten to year 8 learning communities, adult education facilities, a gymnasium, library and shared community facilities, and a more integrated approach to the delivery of health and community services. With support and cooperation from the Wirra Wagga Community House, government departments and local businesses, the secondary school has developed a community-based program aimed at reconnecting disaffected students and early school leavers to education. Known as Connect, the new arrangements attach particular emphasis to individual pathways, personalized learning, community mentoring, and the use of interactive technologies, small group instruction, hands-on-learning and community-based studies. According to the principal, the school plans to draw on community funds of knowledge to enhance learning for students:

> There are resources in the community that can support the education agenda. We have people with skills in the arts, computers and so on who can work productively with students. Some of the residents have been skilled up with various certificates as part of the renewal process, and are already teaching craft and computing courses. The school received 70 obsolete computers from the university and a local woman runs a club where young people can build their own computers. A group of men are constructing 'coracles' (Saxon boats) and their skills and experiences can be used to advantage in the school. Under the one roof you will have three to four staff with helpers but you may also have four to five people from the community assisting as well. We will modify the school times so these people have the state of the art things that the kids have access to. When they work with the students they also learn things from the kids. The kids are going to get more out of home grown role models than anything I can do for them because they can speak the same language as them. With the learning communities we are getting away from the teacher as the focal point. The teacher will be the facilitator and people will be able to work as part of a team. It won't be a teacher directed thing always. (Peter , 8 June 2006 ; 20 March 2007)

It is too early to say that the new community school is succeeding in its aims to break down the traditional barriers to learning, improve school participation and enhance job prospects. Certainly there are signs of improved attendance and student engagement, but generational change of the kind envisaged at Wirra Wagga requires a paradigm shift in approaches to school organization, curriculum and pedagogy. Creating employment opportunities is a huge task that cannot be realized solely through schooling. Although new training positions have been created through a community jobs program, many are restricted to part-time employment of limited duration. Much will depend on long-term funding commitments on the part of governments to maintain educational programs and the social and economic infrastructure to sustain neighborhood renewal. Undoubtedly, the new arrangements have heightened community expectations about the possibilities of education making a difference for young people and adults alike, sentiments echoed by Jenny, the parent chair of the school council:

I am really excited about the new adult community center. We are going to be pushing to get more people into it and we'll have a child care facility. A quarter of people accessing community and disability services in the city are from the Wirra Wagga area, so there's a big need for education. My son who is 19 has just gone back to the School of Mines but he can't read and write. And my son-in-law is illiterate and he's going back to school. You just need that bit of support. There are a lot of good learning facilities out there now for kids that dropped out at year 7. There's also welfare and social support agencies such as United Care and the Salvation Army, and it would be good to have them incorporated into our new facilities. We have Vinnie's (St Vincent de Paul charity organization) coming up here soon to open a supermarket. When the new school center comes on stream I'm hoping that we won't just be a Wirra Wagga school but we will have something to offer the entire city. (Jenny, 9 June 2006)

For parents like Jenny the community-oriented model of schooling in Wirra Wagga offers a source of hope and possibility. She acknowledges the value of an integrated approach to community services and expresses confidence in the capacity of new arrangements to improve educational outcomes for the students with special needs. It remains to be seen if the goals of lifelong learning envisioned in the action plan can be achieved, but some major steps have been taken towards the development of a learning community that accords a high level of respect for the knowledge, language, culture and experiences of local residents. Community ownership is at the center of the Wirra Wagga story. Here the education of young people is regarded as everybody's business—something that cannot be achieved without the cooperation and active involvement of parents, teachers, students and community groups.

What we have described above is an instance of a community-engaged school that exhibits a concern for the social conditions of the life of students and their families. In contrast to the high performance, managerialist model, the school is part of the community and education is for the whole community. Rather than relying on externally prescribed solutions, the community (with the support of external agencies) works cooperatively to address issues of student engagement, participation and achievement. In schools of this kind:
- a large measure of trust and goodwill characterize school–community relationships
- there is a focus on community strengths rather than deficiencies
- community funds of knowledge enrich the curriculum
- a culture of inclusion is the norm in school decision making processes
- there is a strong sense that the school belongs to the community
- the school is a community resource and major contributor to community capacity building.

Creating the conditions to nurture a community of learners is a vital element in transforming schooling for young people, but the question of what students learn in

CHAPTER 2

the context of their local and global community is also a crucial issue. In the next section we turn our attention to community-based learning and the possibilities of reclaiming the curriculum discourse that has become so emaciated by contemporary education reforms.

## DEVELOPING A CRITICAL PEDAGOGY OF PLACE

Schools and their neighborhoods are significant sites in the identity formation of young people. Here students 'are brought into contact with different social/cultural practices, texts and narratives' (Thomson, 2006, p. 92) that shape their view of themselves and their worlds. Traditionally, teachers have utilized local resources, spaces and funds of knowledge to develop curriculum that enriches the academic, vocational and aesthetic domains of learning. However, in recent years moves towards generic learning outcomes and standardized testing regimes have diminished opportunities for teachers and students to engage in learning which has both a strong sense of connection to place and an emphasis on critical pedagogy (Gruenewald, 2003a). All too often students are confronted with mandated programs that pay scant attention to local contexts and tend to eschew the facts and skills over critical reasoning. In particular, curricula often endorse the acquisition of knowledge and understandings deemed relevant to the national economy and business interests, rather than the values, history, culture and economics of local communities. As a consequence, a good deal of what students do in schools has little connection to their immediate lives, communities and cultures.

In advocating for place-based learning we acknowledge that communities are integral to curricula and that community members are 'valid bearers of knowledge' about the world (Gale & Densmore, 2003, p. 113). Community-based studies allow students to connect what they are learning at school to their own lives, communities and regions (Smith, 2002, p. 587). Learning beyond the walls of the classroom creates opportunities for young people to develop positive relationships with community members and organizations. Ideally, educational goals connect personal achievement to public purpose as students are involved in learning which promotes community development, civic responsibility and a commitment to the welfare of others (Melaville, Berg & Blank, 2006). These are important ideals but we agree with Gruenewald (2003a) that place-based learning needs to incorporate a critical dimension that encourages educators and young people 'to reflect on the relationship between the kind of education they pursue and the kind of places we inhabit and leave behind for future generations' (p. 3). Rather than endorsing the status quo, a critical pedagogy of place seeks to raise young people's awareness of inequitable structures and oppressive relationships within communities. Just as importantly, it invites young people to contemplate social action in support of the most oppressed and to work for a more just society.

What does this look like in practice? What are some of the problematic aspects of place-based learning? We will explore these questions with reference to a cluster of high schools in the Bountiful Bay education district of Australia.

## Stories from Bountiful Bay

As outlined in Chapter One, Bountiful Bay is a resource-rich region with a strong economic base and a unique maritime heritage. However, not everyone has benefited from the state's mineral boom. Compared with state averages the district has low levels of household income, low levels of adult workforce participation, a greater percentage of single parent families and high levels of welfare dependency and unemployment.

The district is served by four high schools with enrolments ranging from 700 to 1000 students. To varying degrees, all are grappling with issues of student engagement, school retention and educational disadvantage. A high proportion of students receives government assistance and schools operate breakfast programs and homework centers for the neediest students. All schools offer a comprehensive education from years 8 to 12 but increasingly much of the curriculum focus is on work-related studies and enterprise education. Only one in five senior school students undertakes courses leading to university entrance. 'Private schools cream off the smart kids,' explained a teacher. All schools have developed a strong sense of community through the formation of subschools, middle schools, pastoral care programs and collaborative teaching arrangements.

One of the distinguishing features of the Bountiful Bay schools was the high level of school–community engagement and the vibrancy of place-based learning. Whilst community-oriented studies operated under the umbrella of subject disciplines, they commonly involved cross-curricula themes and varying degrees of service learning. In what follows we look at what teachers had to say about the value of environmental, cultural and community studies in supporting the needs and aspirations of students who typically don't fit the system.

### Story 1. The plant nursery

As a qualified environmental scientist, Clyde quickly discovered that his unique knowledge and talents were to be put to good use when he embarked on a teaching career. 'I got a phone call from a Bountiful Bay principal who asked if I was interested in running a horticulture course for students at risk. The principal at the time said, "This is your baby; you've got a free rein to develop a course. We need to keep these kids at school so do what you want with them."'. Clyde says he met the kids, shook their hands and asked them what they wanted to do in horticulture. 'Grow marijuana,' said one boy. Clyde explained that, within reason, he would support them in whatever they wanted to do. His message from the start was: 'You get what you want out of this program.' The course has now been running for five years and involves a range of enterprises as Clyde relates. 'We take orders from industry and grow the plants and every year we supply these industries with plants. We have done plant displays, supplied the plants and put on the displays. We ran a 'rent a plant' project for classes in the school. Kids get rewards in the form of vouchers, T-shirts and so on, but no payment. We have done a rehabilitation study and decided what plants can be planted. We have jobs in the horticulture section at school and students have to apply for positions like horticulture manager and ground manager.' According to Clyde, students virtually run the whole place and he just watches what they do. 'They come self-motivated and they take responsibility for it all,' he says. 'Students know that to get funds for equipment that they have to get produce plants to an industry standard. They have a purpose to what they do over there and get some realism into their learning. We also operate Flourish Café twice a week in conjunction with the hospitality program. We grow our own produce and take the orders for the cafe' (Clyde, 27 July, 2005).

The horticultural course was one of a number of projects that combined entrepreneurial activities with an ethic of care for the local environment. Students were also engaged in recycling projects, tree planting schemes, stream restoration, wildlife conservation, and activities that encouraged hands-on learning, personal responsibility, community service and awareness of the importance of ecological sustainability. Many of these ideas were brought together in a courtyard project.

*Story 2. The courtyard*
The courtyard was Brendan's idea. As head of a subschool he saw that there was nothing for the so-called 'at risk' kids in year 10, many of whom he viewed as potential early school leavers. 'I realized that we had to give these disengaged kids—mostly boys—some life skills,' he says. 'So I put together a courtyard restoration program in which they could do literacy and numeracy as part of a vocational studies project.' The students costed all the materials and put together a five page report on the project. They interviewed the principal to seek funding for the project. 'She signed off okay,' said Brendan, 'and then the kids ordered the materials and we went ahead with the construction.' Brendan says the project got them out of the classroom and gave them a purpose in their learning. Brendan didn't have a background in maths so he did the numeracy part of the course in a more practical way.' I started with 18 kids and I still have 17 now, so that speaks for itself,' he says. Students are studying a first aid course and we are now going to do a certificate one in construction. I'm trying to create an environment for them so they come to school and have fun' (Brendan, 27 July 2005).

*Story 3. The maritime boardwalk*
Part of the appeal of community-based projects is that they provide students with a direct access to local funds of knowledge, traditions and resources that enable them to gain a better appreciation of their local heritage. A good deal of Bountiful Bay's identity is shaped by a maritime history with tales of shipwrecks, thriving ports and seafaring ventures, but the community also has a somewhat neglected legacy of indigenous culture and traditions. Lisa, a middle school enthusiast, saw the curriculum possibilities of this unique heritage, and with the support of local organizations arranged for her students to build an interpretive trail along the seafront. This is what she had to say about the project. 'The aim was to create a series of plaques commemorating people, organizations and events in the city's history. Artists were commissioned to work with a group of my year 10 students to design and construct the murals and markers with information about pioneer

families, maritime and forest industries and environmental themes. Students were given an overview of the community's rich history and were organized into groups, with each group being responsible for researching a particular aspect of local history, such as shipping and shipwrecks, settlement and trade, and the timber industry. Research was followed up by a visit to the local museum where students could engage in displays. It is here that they gained the inspiration for their drawing on paintings, photographs, models and objects that were on display. Original sketches were taken back to class where they were refined and further research was carried out. Students prepared a power point presentation displaying their designs with a summary of their meaning and significance. A presentation was made to all involved at the local council. The students were very focused and proud of their achievements' (Lisa, 5 August 2006).

The boardwalk project reveals the potential of schools and students to contribute to community development and civic pride—something which comes to the fore in the next story from Bountiful Bay.

*Story 4. Civic engagement: The Lone Pine Project*
Jason, a teacher with a passion for horticulture and Australian history, managed to combine both interests in a tree planting project of particular significance to Australia's wartime heritage. Here is what he had to say about the project. 'Last year we started a Lone Pine Tree project with a group of year 9 students—predominantly boys. The original idea was to put up a shade house and to teach students how to grow Lone Pine trees from seed supplied by the War Memorial Gardens in Canberra. The seeds were originally brought back from Gallipoli by returning World War One soldiers [so called because of the solitary tree standing amidst the carnage of battle. Lone Pine is the site of the official Australian war memorial on the Gallipoli Peninsula, Turkey.] Students will be assigned to branches of the Returned Services League (war veterans association) and they will look after the plants and hand them over on Anzac Day [a public holiday in Australia originally set aside to commemorate those who lost their lives in the Great War of 1914–1918.] From little things, big things grow. The project has expanded well beyond our original plan and has brought many benefits to the school and community. We now have an accredited nursery in our school and students have opportunities to develop skills which may lead to employment in the field. They have gained community recognition for their work in assisting the Department of Conservation and Land Management and other organizations in the raising of endangered flora for reintroduction into the wild' (Jason, 3 August 2005).

The stories reveal how a group of creative and enterprising teachers in Bountiful Bay schools were willing to step outside the boundaries of traditional subject disciplines to provide relevant and challenging learning for the most disengaged students. In some instances they were given a license to experiment largely because the mainstream curriculum had failed these young people, but the majority found spaces within the official curriculum to negotiate significant aspects of learning with students, as well as utilizing community resources and incorporating new technologies and popular culture into the curriculum. By fostering respectful relationships, a strong sense of belongingness and a success-oriented approach to learning, these teachers encouraged kids to hang in with their schooling when all else seemed lost.

Beyond supporting individual students, these programs contributed to community development. Goodman and Kuzmic (1997) contend that teaching for democracy in schools means 'working towards a connectionist pedagogy' (p. 81) that develops 'compassion, altruism, cooperation, civic responsibility and a commitment to the welfare of our planet' (p. 81). Often expressed in the concept of voluntarism, the idea of 'giving to the community' was an integral part of learning in these schools. We heard how senior students conducted coaching clinics and mentoring programs for younger students and were involved in organizing sporting, cultural and craft programs for the benefit of the wider community. Many resident teachers also assumed civic responsibilities and were strong advocates for their communities and local schools.

There is always a risk that a strong focus on place-based learning may lead to an uncritical acceptance of community traditions, practices and attitudes. Interrupting students' insular and prejudicial views of other people and cultures was seen as an especially challenging task for teachers in the Bountiful Bay schools, as illustrated in the following comment:

> A teacher who is doing a unit on Asia has run into the attitude that we get all the time: 'We hate Asians.' Kids say, 'They're all "povo" (poor) or "SALVO" (welfare recipient). 'Why do they have rice every meal?' they ask. It's not the kids' fault that they're like that. You have to challenge understandings and stereotypes. (Teacher)

Although the teacher had attempted to broaden her students' experiences through exchange programs, excursions and cultural activities, she acknowledged the difficulties of tackling racist and homophobic attitudes within the community. All schools in the district had anti-harassment policies to address bullying and other forms of abuse, but the real challenge was to develop more inclusive curricula that promoted cultural understandings and acceptance of difference, rather relying solely on punitive measures. What we are alluding to here is the importance of developing a socially critical approach to place-based learning which involves students in a political process of understanding and shaping what happens in communities. When teachers and students employ a critical lens in learning they are prompted to ask such questions as: Whose culture and heritage is reflected in the museums, galleries and public buildings? Which groups are missing or undervalued? What might we do to redress the imbalance? However, Gruenewald (2003a, p. 7) cautions educators against highly politicized pedagogies that focus almost exclusively on what is wrong with society. Especially amongst young children, this is likely to engender feelings of anxiety, fear and hopelessness, rather than a sense of agency and possibility. Citing Sobel (1996, p. 10), Gruenewald states:

What's important is that children have an opportunity to bond with the natural world, to learn how to love it, before being asked to heal its wounds. (p. 7)

Community-oriented learning must therefore combine a deep respect for the social institutions, histories, cultures and environments that constitute students' lifeworlds with a critical reading of what might be done to improve communities. In this context, the question of what needs to be conserved and protected is just as crucial as the question of what needs to be transformed. Equally important, models of community learning need to position students as active initiators, rather than passive recipients of teacher-imposed projects, however well-intentioned they may be. According to Holdsworth (2005), a great deal of what passes for community engagement fits within a community service model in which student participation is restricted to fundraising, helping to maintain community facilities, assisting in organizing local sports days, cleaning up the environment, and/or providing support for community groups. Holdsworth contrasts this with a model based on student action teams developed in the state of Victoria in 1998 in which young people play active roles in identifying, investigating and proposing solutions to community issues and concerns. To cite two examples, a team researched traffic conditions around a local school and organized a seminar on road safety, whilst another group of students developed and made recommendations to the local shire to improve community safety in dangerous streets.

Critically engaged, community-based learning, as we have described above, does not resonate well with conservative reformers who seem more preoccupied with standards, rubrics and measurement, whilst the deeper problems of society go unattended (Eisner, 2005, p. 187). It also represents a major challenge to teachers whose work is often construed in narrow, instrumental ways that threaten to subvert their autonomy and transformative roles in society.

## EDUCATING FOR A BETTER WORLD

Rejecting the efficacy of market-driven school reform and high stakes testing, Hursh (2007) argues for the reassertion of deliberative democracy and deeper sense of commitment on the part of educators to community engagement and social justice. Rather than producing workers for a global economy, teachers, according to Hursh, have a prime responsibility to 'engage students in continually working to question how we best develop a world that supports human welfare and planetary health' (p. 515). We suggest that it is more urgent than ever that students take a profoundly critical look at the direction the world is headed, given the gravity of the environmental, social, political and moral issues confronting humanity today. To cite examples of particular relevance to young Australians:
- Gripped by the most severe drought in recorded history, many Australians are coming to the realization that global warming is a fact of life, and that, after years of government indifference and community ignorance, fundamental

decisions need to be made about the use of renewable energy resources to ensure our very survival.
- Australia is experiencing a period of economic prosperity fuelled largely by the export of mineral resources to China; yet the wealth and social opportunities generated by this boom are very unevenly distributed.
- In spite of the perception of Australia as an advanced Western society, high rates of poverty, homelessness, unemployment, welfare dependency and ill-health prevail in many low socioeconomic communities.
- An Oxfam Report in April 2007 revealed a gap in life expectancy of indigenous and non-indigenous Australians of 17 years. It noted that 'much of the disease is preventable, being the result of poverty, overcrowding, poor sanitation, low levels of education, poor nutrition and poor access to accurate diagnosis and treatment'. (Mackay (2007, p. 18)

Pursuing a critical pedagogy is not an easy path for teachers but there are resources for nurturing the critical capacities of students (Dobozy, 2007) and promoting social activism (Schultz & Oyler, 2006). Some of these have been revealed in the stories of school–community engagement in Wirra Wagga and Bountiful Bay, and teachers can also draw inspiration from the writings of critical educators. Goodman (1992) argues that teachers can make a start by creating 'islands of democracy' in their own classrooms and by designing learning experiences that promote democratic sensibilities among young people. In *Rethinking globalization*, Bigelow and Peterson (2002) claim that teachers can assist students to gain an understanding of social justice getting them to connect their everyday habits to global concerns, such as climate change, water scarcity, poverty and trade. However, beyond explaining injustices, they also suggest that teachers can encourage students to think about what action they can take to make a difference within their own communities. An example of one such project in the United States is described by Compton-Lilly (2004) who drew on the knowledge of her students and their families to investigate concerns about lead poisoning in the district. The study involved students in a scientific analysis of the levels of lead in the environment, research into the medical problems associated with lead concentrations, and a presentation of the findings to parents and local government officials. Another example of a student-led campaign for social justice described by de los Reyes and Gozemba (2002, p. 27) involved a group of students from Massachusetts who testified before the legislature to get a safe school bill passed that would provide counseling and support for gay and lesbian students in the state's public schools.

Promoting students as agents of social change is fundamental to the challenge of building democratic communities and a better world. It is also crucial to the task of re-engaging young people in education. All too often students are positioned as passive consumers rather than active creators of knowledge in their own right. Moreover, what passes as official knowledge in schools tends to validate the values, histories and norms of white middle class males (Berry, 1998). Traditionally, students in disadvantaged communities like Wirra Wagga and Bountiful Bay have struggled to see the relevance of schooling, partly because much of what was taught had little connection to their own lives, cultures and experiences. However, a new sense of possibility has arisen with the movement towards community-oriented schooling.

## COMMUNITY-ORIENTED SCHOOLING: HIGH HOPES? FALSE PROMISES?

The idea of community schooling has been around for some time, but over the past decade the movement has gathered momentum in Western countries, most notably in areas of socioeconomic disadvantage (Dyson & Raffo, 2007). Now there is a growing expectation that schools, in conjunction with private and public providers, will offer a range of services to families, ranging from preschool education and child care to health, welfare and counseling. At first sight the concept of community-oriented schools makes a great deal of sense. As we have shown in the case of Wirra Wagga, a coordinated approach to the provision of human services acknowledges the multidimensional nature of neighborhood disadvantage and the necessity of a whole of community response. Schools in this situation can become vital resources for the community—places where people can gather for cultural, sporting and recreational activities, participate in adult education programs and access information and communication technologies. Ideally, the community has a strong sense of ownership of the school and a major say in developing curriculum priorities.

The most fervent advocates of community-oriented schooling claim that schools have a potential for community development by virtue of their capacity to enhance social capital—'the processes between people which establish networks, norms and social trust and facilitate co-ordination and co-operation for mutual benefit' (Cox, 1995, p. 15). But are these realistic expectations? To what extent can community schools reduce the extent of educational disadvantage without significant social and economic reforms in society at large? In exploring these questions we will briefly consider the experiences of school and community reform in the United Kingdom, the United States and Australia.

Discussing the progress of full service extended schools in England, Dyson and Raffo (2007) suggest that there is little empirical evidence to suggest that they are having a dramatic impact on education, health and other social outcomes. They contend that rationales are generally under theorized and tend to rest on shaky assumptions about the reproduction of inequalities and capacities of schools to lift achievements of students in disadvantaged neighborhoods. With reference to Feinstein, et al.,'s (2004) notions of 'distal' and 'proximal' factors, Dyson and Raffo claim that many of the efforts to ameliorate disadvantage are focused on classroom and institutional processes which impact most directly on children's learning. However, what is largely missing are the more distal or peripheral factors, 'those which might be thought to underpin and explain the proximal factors' (p. 305). So while community-oriented schools are expected to drive up educational standards in the quest for a highly skilled workforce and improved economic growth, it is very unclear how they can do so without major government investments in housing, public transport and community development. Moreover, since community-oriented schools in the United Kingdom sit within a marketized model there is every chance that educational disadvantage will become even more concentrated as middle class parents exercise their choice in sending children to better endowed public or private schools. In short, school reforms that are unaccompanied by major structural and social reforms are unlikely to alter the patterns of disadvantage in communities.

Similar criticisms have been voiced about the limitations of community-oriented schooling in the Unites States. Writing about recent education reforms in Chicago, Lipman (2004) claims that monetarist policies linked with neoliberal reforms emphasizing deregulation, privatization and cutbacks to public services have led to deep social fractures within the city and great disparities in the resources allocated to schools. With the passing of the a law recentralizing control of public schools in the hands of the mayor and a hand-picked board of trustees, many of the democratic and community-based approaches to schooling set in place in the 1988 Chicago School Reform Act have been seriously eroded. Lipman argues that although committed, culturally-relevant, critical educators can make a difference in schools, 'any serious effort to transform public schools can only succeed as part of a larger local and global social struggle for material redistribution and cultural recognition' (p. 183). Because the fates of individual schools and their communities are inextricably linked (Warren, 2005), school reform has to proceed in tandem with reform to the political economy and society at large. Supporting this argument, Anyon (2005) asserts that failing public schools in United States cities are the logical consequence of an unjust macro economy and the federal and regional policies and practices that support it. They cannot be blamed exclusively on schools, teachers, principals and urban students, as many of the ideologues of the right would have us believe. In essence, it is a case of 'macro economic mandates trump urban educational policy and school reform' (p. 2).

Berliner (2006) also concedes that efforts which focus solely on teacher quality, curriculum change and school organization are unlikely to make substantial difference to the alleviation of educational inequalities. Since schools and families are generally situated in neighborhoods that are highly segregated by social class, the bigger challenge envisaged by Berliner is to set about 'building a more economically equitable society' (p. 988). Families in economically depressed areas suffer from a myriad of social problems including low incomes, financial insecurity, increased levels of homicide and domestic abuse, a higher incidence of physical and mental ill-health, lower life expectancies and a much greater proportion of children with multiple and severe disabilities (Thrupp, 1999). These problems cannot be solved through community-oriented schooling, but require more far-reaching policy reform in public housing, transport infrastructure, wages and employment conditions, health services and family support programs (Anyon, 2005).

Studies in the Wirra Wagga and Bountiful Bay communities in Australia have also shown the potential benefits and limitations of community-oriented schooling in addressing educational disadvantage. As described previously, neighborhood renewal in Wirra Wagga involved a high degree of cooperation and trust amongst resident groups, government departments and local schools that have led to a common vision for schooling and a more integrated approach to the delivery of human services. Although the idea of extended schooling was far less advanced in Bountiful Bay, a major emphasis on community-based learning, civic engagement and school–community partnerships had led to improved school retention rates and higher levels of student engagement. In both communities a core of socially engaged teachers had transformed the physical spaces in schools to a welcoming environment where students were treated with respect and dignity, and classroom doors were opened to the outside world. These teachers contested the prevailing deficit views of young people in poverty and worked to provide rigorous and challenging learning opportunities. Yet the constraints to transformation in a hostile policy environment were undeniable. Teachers in Bountiful Bay had to navigate a pathway between state, district and school accountability requirements and their own knowledge of what really works for the most marginalized students. Many innovative and engaging programs were highly dependent on the goodwill and generosity of teachers, residents and local sponsors. In the case of Wirra Wagga, the long-term viability of community-oriented schooling appears to be highly contingent on ongoing funding for neighborhood renewal and significant improvements in economic and social conditions within the community. The harsh reality is that schools alone cannot alleviate the escalating levels of youth homelessness, poverty and welfare dependency in Australia.

We have suggested that critically engaged forms of schooling typically appear as 'pockets of hope' in a vulnerable policy landscape. However, as de los Reyes and Gozemba (2002) show, democratic classrooms exist in some of the most educationally desperate cities. In particular, Deborah Meiers' Central Park East public school in Harlem, New York, stands out as a source of inspiration for those seeking to transform inner city schools. Not surprisingly, critical educators who challenge the inequitable policies and practices associated with neoliberal reforms become easy targets of the right wing critics. In these circumstances, it is crucially important that they build alliances with colleagues, administrators and citizens committed to practices of freedom, justice and equality (Anyon, 2005). Because the task of reforming education cannot be separated from the larger goal of building a more equitable society, critical educators also need to become community activists who:
– link educational issues to community concerns, such as employment, wage justice, housing and public transport
– reject deficit views of working class students and their communities
– engage students in social and political activities designed to make for a more just society—that is, to promote civic activism
– act as advocates for the community and contribute to rebuilding programs
– work collaboratively with labor unions, professional associations and social movements to defend public education and tackle social injustices, such as racism and discrimination against gay and lesbian people.

Transformative schooling of this kind is intimately connected to community building. When Myles Horton formed the Highlander Center in 1932 he created a

space in which grassroots activists from around the world could share their experiences and work together to build democratic communities and a better world. Horton held the view that the poor and the most marginalized had a capacity to take control of their lives and circumstances with the support of social activists. Education, local empowerment and community building which were always at the center of Horton's approach live on through the work of Helen Lewis. In *Rebuilding communities: A 12 step recovery program,* Lewis presents a democratic pedagogy to prepare students to become critically engaged citizens (de los Reyes & Gozemba, 2002, p. 208). In summary, Lewis advocates the following steps for organizers seeking to rebuild communities:
– Understand your history; share memories
– Mobilize, organize, revive community
– Profile and assess your local community
– Analyze and envision alternatives
– Educate the community
– Build confidence and pride
– Develop local partnerships
– Strengthen your organization; develop shared leadership
– Collaborate and build coalitions
– Take political power
– Initiate economic activity
– Enter the local, regional, national and international planning processes.

Although the idea of a recovery program hints at a deficit view of community, the course of action proposed by Lewis illustrates the importance of collective political action, indigenous leadership and economic empowerment in rejuvenating communities. Schools which foster belongingness, inclusive relationships and a sense of community have the potential to contribute to this goal through social and cultural networks that extend into, and strengthen, local communities. However, educators need to be guided by a local view of what is needed, rather than a needs-oriented or deficit approach which says 'we know what's best for kids in poor communities'. What this amounts to—as we saw in Wirra Wagga—is a willingness on the part of administrators and teachers to engage in authentic dialogue with parents, students and residents to develop a shared vision of schooling that is respectful of the culture, histories and experiences of local communities. At the same time, educators need to be conscious of the fact that 'the problems of school are deeply rooted in the conditions of society' (Shor & Freire, 1987, p. 129), and cannot be solved solely by local initiatives alone. Community-oriented schooling may not be a panacea for overcoming entrenched inequalities but it is surely an important starting point in addressing the most immediate and damaging effects of student alienation and disengagement.

## CONCLUDING REMARKS

We began this chapter with some sober reflections on the complicity of governments in sanctioning racist policies that resulted in immeasurable harm and suffering to indigenous Australians. The broader point we wished to make was that the public policy environment often sets limits to what can be achieved in transforming existing social and economic inequalities. In this context, we drew attention to the manifest failure of authoritarian solutions to the problems of school retention, student engagement and educational disadvantage imposed by neoliberal and neoconservative governments in the form of centralized curriculum and high stakes testing regimes. Reclaiming educational policy amidst a 'discourse of deceit' is fraught with difficulty, but as we have shown in our Australian and overseas studies, schools and teachers still have a degree of freedom to develop organizational structures and programs that promote more inclusive, community oriented and critically engaged forms of learning for young people. These 'pockets of hope' or 'enclaves of resistance', point to the possibilities of transformative schooling when teachers and communities are placed at the center of education policy.

In challenging the prevailing approaches to school reform, we acknowledge that the goals of schooling are inseparably linked to the broader goals of building more equitable communities. This demands a new kind of politics based on relational power, trust and solidarity with the parents, students, teachers and residents who have the greatest investment in the community. From this perspective, school and community activists, rather than politicians and educational experts, are the drivers of change and the owners of the educational vision for the community. The theoretical and practical possibilities of 'relational power' will be explored more fully in the next chapter when we discuss the experience of community renewal in Wirra Wagga against the key ideas of the Alinsky tradition of community organizing.

CHAPTER 3

# RELATIONAL SOLIDARITY: HARBINGER OF A PARADIGMATIC SHIFT IN SCHOOL AND COMMUNITY RENEWAL

## INTRODUCTION

... genocide is what supplanting societies do. People moving onto the lands that are already occupied seek to make the original inhabitants disappear. (Day, 2008, p. 70)

This somewhat provocative comment in a recent article entitled 'disappeared', was made in respect of the Australian government's long overdue apology to the indigenous people of the country for the forcible removal of part-Aboriginal children from their families over the period from 1920 to 1970. In many ways, what occurred in that instance is deeply reminiscent of what has been happening to the work of schools and teachers in disadvantaged communities for several generations, and it is accelerating and going on largely unopposed. Our reason for invoking the notion of genocide here is to put the spotlight directly on the uninterrupted and totally inappropriate invasion of managerialist and policy discourses into schools and communities. While such policies in and of themselves may not have directly resulted in the death or extermination of the inhabitants, it is nevertheless the case as with any 'supplanting societies', that the intent is to 'drive the original inhabitants off the land by policies of forcible expulsion' (Day, 2008, p. 70). To pursue the issue of genocide a little further, it is possible to destroy indigenous inhabitants 'without direct and deliberate killing. It can be the inadvertent consequence of invasion, such as when deaths are caused by the unintentional introduction of new diseases—as occurred following the European invasion of the Americas, when diseases killed up to 90% of the indigenous people in some areas' (Day, 2008, p. 70). The point that Day is making is that such invasions and the subsequent 'disappearance of people is intentional, and genocidal in purpose'.

The incursion of what Adorno (1994/1974) called 'alien' and 'interloper' discourses, in our case of business, management and the military into schools and social policy discourses more widely, has been 'uncouth', 'arrogant' and 'improper' (p. 23). This kind of discursive assault is what Saltman (2007) refers to as a kind of 'smash and grab' form of privatization of schools and communities in the most disadvantaged settings, in a context where full frontal attempts at privatization have demonstrably failed. It is not that such failed attempts have abated, but rather that they have intensified in a situation of massive disinvestment in public education, around major strategic back-door forms of privatization that use marketized and management discourses as the way of capturing the hearts and minds, and hence the practices of schools, through consumerist notions of so-called choice, diversity and partnerships.

Our reason for starting this chapter in a somewhat dramatic way is to make the point that something of enormous value is being lost and obliterated in the drive to eliminate the notion of public schooling, and it is going on largely unopposed and with the most devastating of consequences for communities already put at a disadvantage.

The starting point for this chapter is, therefore, an endorsement and acknowledgment of the salient if somewhat belated recognition noted by Portelli & McMahon (2004), that relationships are a crucial part of all aspects of education. We could be forgiven for failing to see this stunningly self-evident fact, given the policy trajectory in recent times in schooling that have had to do with everything other than relationships—some might even argue that such policies have been anti-relationships. There can be no denying the burgeoning literature in recent times either, around educative relationships, not to mention the emergence of a healthy and no doubt very profitable consultancy industry as well, around the restoration of torn and damaged relationships for many young people in schools. It is without question, that there can be no education without relationships (Bingham & Sidorkin, 2004; Sidorkin, 2002), and that schools are at essence relational organizations (Smyth, 2007a). What is much more contestable is the nature and intent of relationships in education, and the valued social purpose to which they are committed.

In this chapter we elaborate and extend the notion of activism and the socially critical commenced in chapter two, and show that an alternative to the neoliberal discourse of deceit exists and it is embedded in a set of relational politics that have a capacity to challenge and supplant false and misleading logics. The purpose of this chapter is to explore a view of relationships that goes beyond the somewhat narrow humanistic and psychologistic view of learning as being dependent upon caring, trustful and respectful relations between student and teacher—that much is not in dispute from us, but we argue that there is more, much more to this.

We find McMahon & Portelli's (2004) three discourses of student engagement, and the view of relationships implicit within each, to be a most helpful starting point, and we want to build on their work in our discussions of the place of relationships in an analysis of school and community renewal. Their framework or heuristic encompasses—the 'conservative or traditional conception' (p. 61), the 'liberal or student-oriented conception' (p. 65), and the 'critical-democratic conception' (p. 69).

At essence here are a set of quite different conceptions of democracy that go to the heart of the way people relate to one another and to knowledge and ideas. At core is the distinction, Portelli & McMahon (2004) argue, between two competing views of democracy—in the first instance, as a form of government, which is a fairly detached, procedural and distant, or on the other hand, as a way of life. The former collapses down to 'protectionist, or minimalist, or managed/market democracy' (p. 40), while the latter is characterized by a much more embodied, reconstitutive or transformative process. Thus, a critical view of democracy, is much more concerned with and takes seriously issues of 'community', 'equity', 'creativity' and 'difference' in a context of inquiry that eschews the separation between thinking and action.

When we draw these wider ideas into conversation with educational disadvantage, the premise we start from in this chapter, indeed in this book, is that no amount of external leverage on its own can change educational disadvantage, and that three inter-related conditions of people-centered 'capacity building' (Eade, 1997) are necessary. The first condition is a respect for the knowledge, language, class location, culture and experiences of communities of disadvantage; the second, an understanding that 'awareness, learning, self-esteem and the capacity for political action are mutually reinforcing' (Eade, 1997, p. 11); and the third, a realization that people who are placed at disadvantage have the right and, more importantly, the capacity to challenge authoritative 'solutions' to their problems (including the application of resources) that may not be in their interests, and to supplant such imposed solutions with better alternatives. What we seek to do in this chapter is to get up close and map what occurs when disadvantaged communities and their schools embark on a neighborhood and community renewal program that amounts to developing action plans to rejuvenate their community as well as its schools.

The central theoretical idea we want to pursue in this chapter is the notion of *relational power* which refers to the building of trust with a range of groups in schools and their communities around a common vision of how schooling can work for all, including those most marginalized and excluded. It is about using the capacity of 'social power' (Speer & Hughey, 1995) that inheres in relationships to begin to address and re-dress social and structural inequality in terms of who succeeds and who fails. Relational power really amounts to a 'set of resources' that draw upon 'trust and cooperation between and among people' (Warren, 2005, p. 136), and that acknowledges that learning involves 'the power to get things done collectively' (p. 138) by confronting rather than denying power inequalities. This means going beyond stigmatizing students and families from the most disadvantaged backgrounds as 'bundles of pathologies' (Warren, Thompson and Saegert 2001) to be 'fixed up'. It means going beyond a 'social services' mentality of problem-fixing among individuals and families, to the 'intentional exercise of power' (Speer, et al., 2003) through a 'social change' approach. The chapter draws upon notions of 'organizing for power' and Saul Alinsky's community organizing approach of 'indigenous leadership' as a way of analyzing and exploring 'individual, organizational and community strengths with minimal control by professionals' (Speer, et al., 1995, p. 57). What we are referring to is the potential for democratic transformation in/through relationships— particularly the way in which such relationships provide the 'space for challenge' (Bacchi, 2000) within which to confront and supplant dominant and authoritative discourses.

When we talk about pursuing or initiating change in disadvantaged or working-class schools and communities, whether we realize it or not, we are implicitly

CHAPTER 3

endorsing a particular way of framing and acting on the world. Schutz (2008) argues that how we think about and act in respect of school or community reform, is inextricably connected to the kind of sociological perspective we wittingly or unwittingly bring to it. Something we have been inculcated into believing as researchers, and as a consequence leaching out of educational research, is any sense that learning and the wider contexts in which it occurs, might be powerfully informed by notions of social class. Schutz's (2008) argument is that there is an in-built middle-class bias in the way we think and talk about schooling and education. For example, we can see this in notions of meritocracy, the emphasis on individual forms of achievement, team and group-building, dialogical forms of collaboration, and rational, expert reliant data-driven approaches. This kind of middle class perspective, even when couched in the most enlightened form, amounts in an ideal-type to what Schutz (2008) labels 'discursive democracy'. There are forms of cultural practice, habitus or bundles of dispositions resorted to that are consistent with the way some social groups makes sense of the world, and that are alien, inexplicable, or inhospitable to other groups.

Schutz (2008) says that if we examine it historically the middle class has become 'an odd kind of class, maintaining a coherent collective identity through a kind of studied independence' (p. 410). He explains what he means by this by invoking Blumin (1989), who says that middle class formation emerges out of and 'binds itself together as a social group through the common embrace of an ideology of social atomism' (pp. 9–10). It is this enduring impersonal approach to relationships that enables the constant 'shift [in] relational ties [necessary to] work closely with relative strangers' (Schutz, 2008, p. 410). In other words, there is an in-built bias towards 'participation as an act of choice' and the notion of 'constant recreation of communities' (p. 428). All of these are features that translate into the way the middle class engages in child-rearing (Lareau, 2000; 2003), and that have a profound effect on reinforcing the way their off-spring experience success in the middle class institution of schooling.

On the other hand, if we pursue an ideal-type perspective on the working class, it is quite different—it tends to coalesce much more around what Schutz (2008) labels 'democratic solidarity' that has more of an activist and collectivist flavor to it. According to Schutz (2008), a working class orientation is much less disposed towards 'extended rational dialogue' (p. 417) and is more inclined towards forms of 'straight talk' and direct resolution of conflict (p. 416), in ways that eschew abstraction, that involve practical or pragmatic action, and embody a style that has little time for protracted or elaborated forms of negotiation. If there is discursive aspect, it tends to reside in speaking of experiences, or story telling. The effect is that the working class tends to resort more to webs and networks ' to get through hard times' (p. 415), rather than draw upon personal or material reserves and resources, and to see membership of its social group less in terms of choices and more in terms of embedded 'networks' (p. 429), such as extended families, in which identity comes from being known and respected (p. 429), rather than from individualized and detached processes of identity formation. Issues, from a working class perspective, tend to be framed much more in terms of 'power [that has to] be wrested from others' (p.429), than abstract niceties to be worked out dialogically. The overall effect can appear to be, and indeed is, one of informal hierarchy in which 'individual voice' can appear to be suppressed (p. 430).

In effect what Schutz (2008) is saying is that the middle class institution of schooling, for that is what it really is, has a strong ideological preference towards an idealized discursive form of democracy, at best, and this may rest uneasily with the equally idealized working class ethos of democratic solidarity—indeed, the latter may rub somewhat abrasively against the polite and negotiated norms of the former. Both idealized forms have important implications for the way in which children placed at disadvantage learn, the way their families and communities embrace the notion of schooling, and the basis upon which schools and communities approach change.

## THE POSSIBILITY OF A RELATIONALLY-LED BACKLASH

The notion of the relational seems to be becoming something of a rallying point for schools and communities besieged with an agenda of 'economic instrumentality' (Stronach & Piper, 2008, p. 6; see also Smyth, 2007a; Smyth & Fasoli, 2007; Smyth, 2007b).

We can find evidence of this in several quarters, some of them somewhat unexpected. For example, Stronach & Piper (2008) undertook a study of the celebrated exemplar of 'free schooling', Summerhill School in England, in a context of government attempts in 1999 to close it down. The attempt back-fired spectacularly (Vaughan, et al., 2006), and what got to be exposed was the sophisticated complexity of how the school had developed a way of living what Stronach & Piper (2008) labeled the 'relational touch'—a process:

> ... wherein Summerhill learned to relate to themselves, to others, and to intuit boundaries. (p. 28)

To put it another way:

> People learned to read each other, and hence themselves in a kind of social dialectic: in such interaction, varying degrees of relational touch were negotiated. (p. 23)

It was as Stronach & Piper (2008) put it, a delightful case of an 'inversion of the audit touch' (p. 7) which is currently bearing down upon schools with such damaging effects on the social fabric of schools as relational cultures. It is something of a delightful irony that a small school that has long been pilloried by a panic-stricken media as being an extreme case of anarchy and chaos, should be one that it is being held out an exemplar of how students and teachers might negotiate relationships—in this case, on almost everything, with 174 'laws' currently in place, that have been negotiated into existence on a case-by-case basis. The school has become something of a *cause celebre* in having developed the means with which to push back into the stupidity of mechanistic reforms, developed at a distance, and imposed upon schools in a one-size-fits-all way.

## CHAPTER 3

The problem of reforming schools in communities of disadvantage is that the process has largely been hijacked by an ideology of technicism—which is to say, the view that school reform is simply a technical problem — inserting more competent and enthusiastic teachers; raising standards; making and holding schools more directly accountable for delivering on achievement and outcome targets; ensuring that parents maintain pressure on schools to deliver quality outcomes by requiring them to exercise school choice; inserting a cadre of 'super' principals to ramp up leadership and fix the problems; and, paying teachers according to results by means of performance-related pay. The problem with all of these approaches when applied to communities of disadvantage is that they assume a particular logic, or what Oakes & Rogers (2006) call the flawed 'logics of merit and deficit' which, in the end, 'leave the prevailing norms and politics of social inequality untouched' (p. 159). The argument put by Oakes & Rogers (2006) is that in order to bring about change aimed at making schools in disadvantaged contexts more equitable, we have to 'disrupt... the logic of schooling that creates and sustains inequality', and that means engaging with 'larger social struggles' (p. 158). In other words, upsetting the three 'powerful cultural narratives' that operate to frame how it is that people make sense of schooling— 'the logic of merit, the logic of deficits, and the logic of scarcity' (p. 158). As they put it:

> The first assumes that young people compete for schooling advantages with their talents in a context of equal opportunity. The second presumes that low-income children ... and their families are limited by cultural, situational, and individual deficits that schools cannot affect. . [And that] the combined effect of these narratives is compounded today by a logic of scarcity—the belief that our society can afford only limited investment in public life and public education. (pp. 158–159)

Where this line of reasoning is taking us is in the direction of acknowledging that technical approaches to school equity reform, by which we mean a focus on structures, forms of governance, pedagogical practices, and the like, fail because of an inherent refusal to understand that 'privilege and exclusion are not discrete problems', as Oakes & Rogers (2006) put it:

> ... no matter how hard people work at them, the usual approaches to school reform... are simply not efficacious enough to counter the multiple forces that maintain the unequal status quo among and within schools. (p. 15)

Bringing about equity reforms in schooling is not only about devising and implementing better formulae for distributing resources and practices that enable schools to operate in the interests of the least advantaged, they also involve deconstructing the cultural and political processes that sustain and maintain privilege and that 'preserve advantages for wealthier and more powerful communities' (p. 15). Disparities among and within schools need, therefore, to be seen 'as much a cultural and political problem as a technical one' (p. 15). The consequence of not having a more expansive view of reform is to resort to diminished solutions that are likely to be quite ineffectual. When we lack this 'social or political critique of the logic of schooling' then we end up:

> ... assign[ing] problems to whatever deficit seems most closely attached to a problem. Terrible facilities? The kids do not take care of them. Lack of qualified teachers? The kids are not rewarding to teach. Low scores and behavior problems. Parents do not care. (Oakes & Rogers, 2006, p. 163)

## A RELATIONAL POLITICS FOR SCHOOL AND COMMUNITY ACTIVISM

This brings us to the salient point made by Boyte with Gust (2003) that in order to transcend narrow impoverished technical views, we need a 'different kind of politics'—one that is at the same time bolder, more 'savvy' and capable of transforming 'an increasingly materialist and competitive culture' and confronting the challenges of 'a turbulent and interconnected world' (p. 1).

Elsewhere we (Smyth, Angus, Down & McInerney, 2008) have invoked Evans & Boyte's (1986) notion of 'free spaces' as a useful category for describing new sites and ways in which individual and institutional lives 'can act with dignity, independence and vision' (p. 17). This is a stance Boyte (2002) argues that is based on 'the assumption of plurality, widely owned by citizens, that is productive', but more importantly, is also based in 'a deep respect for ordinary citizens that is sorely needed today among intellectual and professional groups' (p. 1). Oakes & Rogers (2006) express this in terms of:

> ... seek[ing] to connect 'ordinary citizens' with 'experts' as long as expertise does not take precedence over 'civic intelligence' to impose professional solutions on communities and their families. (p. 164)

What Boyte (2002) is arguing for is social capital, but a version of it that is much more reminiscent of the way it was envisaged by John Dewey, in many respects its original architect. Dewey's view 'had a critical and feisty edge largely lacking in its current usage' (p. 3). What Dewey was proposing was a view of social capital that is much more up to 'challeng[ing] the logic and dynamic of private capital and the deification of the marketplace' (Boyte, 2002, p. 3). While acknowledging our enormous debt to Dewey especially for the way he so cogently argued for the ideas, perspectives and intelligence of 'ordinary people', Boyte (2002) admits that Dewey did not have all the answers and was 'limited by his time and his context' (p. 1). Notwithstanding, our current context of rampant materialist consumerism has evacuated any true sense of politics from contemporary culture, and what has been left in its wake is 'a thin and sickly conception of citizenship', a conception of the 'citizen as an apolitical volunteer', and a view of the 'policy maker as expert who purportedly 'knows best'' (p. 2). Boyte's (2002) call is a clarion cry to put politics back into 'all our civic and economic environments, but with a deeper, grittier, and also a wider sense of politics than Dewey's' (p. 1).

CHAPTER 3

Part of the impetus for the renewed push in this direction is coming from what commentators like Boyte argue is the corruption and disappearance of the notion of politics in our lives, and the imperative to restore it. By this Boyte (2002) means, the disappearance of 'horizontal civic relationships' and its replacement by 'vertical state-centered relationships' (p. 13). Putting this in some kind of historical context, he says:

> In the fifties and beyond, the professionalization of mediating institutions such as political parties, unions, schools and universities eroded the everyday experience of politics through which people learned skills of dealing with others unlike themselves, and developed some sense of their productive contribution to the larger democracy. (p. 13)

The version of politics embodied in elections, political parties and the 'over-promising' that comes with political leaders declaring themselves to be 'in charge', brings with it a mentality of a subservient 'client' relationship around 'delivery' and 'service', in which the only issues that get aired are 'distributive questions [of] who gets what, when, how?' (p. 3). The reality is that as we get to increasingly be defined, even referred to, as 'clients', what comes with it is the expectation that we will acquiesce and be 'served' by self-proclaimed experts. We have lost the collective skill, will, desire and imagination to be active citizens working at understanding the obligations inherent in what it means to have human relationships. We have lost the power to act as political agents 'in the deepest meaning of the word political' (p. 3).

We will not dwell any further here on the theory or philosophy behind Dewey's notion of 'social intelligence' or his ideas of the 'social quality' of knowledge production, except to say that we endorse Dewey's basic premise that 'all knowledge... is social knowledge' in the pragmatic sense of being 'the product of an interplay of experience, testing and experiment, reflection and conversation' (Boyte, 2002, p. 7). To put this another way, 'knowledge power is increased through sharing transactions' (p. 7)—and we have discussed this in detail elsewhere (Smyth, 2008).

HOW THEN, DOES 'A DIFFERENT KIND OF POLITICS' (BOYTE WITH GUST, 2003) PLAY OUT PRACTICALLY?

As a way out of the theoretical terrain we have been sketching out above, and as something of a conceptual bridge to some of the ideas on school and community renewal we have been working on in an Australian context, we would like to flesh out some of the ideas Harry Boyte (HB) canvassed above, through some extracts from an interview he had with Susan Gust (SG)—a neighborhood leader and community activist in Minnesota, and the person Boyte attributes with first using the term ' a different kind of politics'.

At the time of the interview, Susan owned her own construction and community development business in Phillips Community, Minneapolis, USA. Harry Boyte, long time political activist and professor of politics at University of Minnesota, is talking to her about some of her experiences of 'civic engagement work' that she had been doing, some of it with the University of Minnesota. Susan responds by speaking of how she starts out by visualizing issues physically:

> I often have to visualize things to understand them. Winston Churchill has a great quote, 'We shape our buildings and thereafter they shape us.' (p. 1)

Susan finds that dealing with the 'physicality' of things, as she calls it, helps her to deal with the 'seams ... [and] the border between you and the world'. She goes on to give an example of what she meant though community work she had been doing with the university:

> Relationships would start to happen, not one way but two ways. The university would start to see communities not just in terms of needs, 'these disenfranchised people, these poor people,' but also from the assets, the riches. There would start to be interdependency. How do we see each other as constituents of maintaining the community life? The civic life? (p. 2)

She went on to describe a fight Phillips Community took on to prevent a garbage transfer station being located in the community, and of the lesson learned in how to select an issue in a cross-cutting way and how to present it in a way that united interest groups:

> One of the things we learned as resident activists was that we needed to choose issues that would cut across the race and class lines that often keep us separate. So we chose to focus on children, raising healthy children—'cause everyone is concerned that we won't or can't, making their taxpaying job more difficult—so who is going to stop us when we frame our activism around 'taking responsibility' as parents to provide a healthy and safe environment for our kids? (p. 2)

HB: Is that what you meant when you talked about a different kind of politics... ?

SG: Yeah. We have to be in relationship with each other... The thing that can make real change, really fast is being in relationship with each other. I don't mean just being diverse... I mean being truly in relationship...

> Before this garbage transfer fight, I had only worked on 'big issues' like the Vietnam War, civil rights. I started to see the importance of this neighborhood thing. I could feel it. These big 'isms' of the world, they all happen down here. (p. 3)

Susan went on to talk about how in the fight over the garbage transfer station the community hired a consultant who used a typical 'Alinsky style':

> He taught us that we had to pick our issues and they had to be winnable; they had to cut across race and class lines. And you needed a clear target, an individual to be viewed as the enemy (p. 3)... We learned that research and facts could give us a lot of power of information AND credibility. We

CHAPTER 3

> learned a lot. We learned it was a relationship thing, this one through the love of children. (p. 4)

> As a community activist you need facts and you need them now... That research helped us sink their ship. (p. 5)

Susan regards the approach they were being taught as distinctively different from 'the charity approach' that requires a distant and unengaged connection, or as she aptly put it:

> ... serving us by fixing us when we're broken—so they don't have to do anything else, participate in other ways. (p. 4)

Harry asks a clarifying question:

> ... how important it is for people from the [u]niversity ... to shift from thinking of themselves as helpers, to thinking of themselves as members, as participants in a common work?

> SG: In the beginning, we never thought of them as potential collaborators... At first, we thought the academics were just trying to build their own resumes, bring more money into the university by using us as canaries in a coal mine. There were long, difficult conversations in which we came to realize the value that this research thing could play in adding to our credibility and increasing our opportunity to change public policy. It took just as long for the University folks to value our arguments, our participation and our ability to govern this research project. (p. 6)

Susan goes on to elaborate on the importance of 'rules', but ones that were largely oral:

> ... we established what have now become rules. We don't have them written down, so we have to speak the rules. Some of them were established through our conflicts. The fact that they're not written down means you have to tell each other the rules. It's a very important piece. You have to look at the other person. You have to see how the words affect them. You watch their face.

> One of the rules was, no titles. Another was, if we're going to have evening meetings there has to be childcare. People are coming home from work or school, even if they're not, they can't attend without doing something with their kids. Children are welcomed and acknowledged. It isn't like they are just sent off into another room

> [Another one is that] we try to have a celebration at least once a year that includes our entire family. At those occasions, we honor our families. We say, thank you for giving such and such a person time to attend these meetings. So, we recognize the other members of the family and thank them for making a contribution to our work by allowing their mom, dad, or partner to have two hours a month to participate... Another way that we decided to level the playing field was to eat or break bread together. (p. 7)

Harry then moves to concluding the conversation by checking out what he thinks he has heard about this different kind of politics:

> I've pulled out some themes from what you've said. Let me run through them, using this frame that this is a different kind of politics, and see if they're right, or if there are more. Okay?
>
> First ... you described learning [in which] the neighborhood is a place to do politics. You said you learned that big issues are locally embodied; they live in the world in local situations. (p. 8)

SG: Right

HB: [Second] ... that politics is about relationships, and people are complicated. You can't simply see a single enemy who embodies all the evil, or demonize people. Politics these days are so oversimplified in the way it characterizes 'the other.' So, it's about relationships with complicated, real people.

A third thing is that politics is about power. There are power interests in ... having a relationship with the university. That means a realistic assessment of power. This is what we call power mapping... [You] figure out who you need to be in relationship with. [You] name power, and are real about it. Things happen because [you] develop power, not because [you] wish it to happen.

A fourth thing that you're talking about is that everyone needs to have interests at the table, and have those recognized and respected. University people get certain kinds of compensation. Neighborhood people's interests need to be acknowledged.

And then the point that politics means we're all in it together. We're all participants. We're all members. We're not advocating *for* somebody else. We're *with* people, rather than simply advocating for the dispossessed, or *for* people.

Are those right? Are there others? (p. 9)

SG: Those are good. I would maybe say a couple in different ways. I think we get goofed up, because of our system being more of a representative democracy. We don't know how to describe everyday politics, politics that are about our own actions, not about people doing it for us.

HB: Do you mean a citizen politics?

SG: Yes, citizen politics... We need to get politics off of meaning just the voting thing, electing politicians. We need to have the representative democracy piece described to us so that we understand some of its down sides, how it doesn't fully work unless we participate as individual citizens. Otherwise, it is just somebody else doing it for us again. We become dependent, giving up some of our own power or the ability to make our own

CHAPTER 3

> choices. That limits our freedom. Then we blame politicians for making the wrong choices on our behalf.
>
> HB: But we still need a citizen politics.
>
> SG ... We need to be much more conscious as everyday citizens that our everyday actions and choices are often political with a small 'p'... (p. 9)

Whether we are aware of it or not, what is being rehearsed in this dialogue between Harry Boyte and Susan Gust, above, is what Alexander, et al. (1977) refer to in a book that was forging a new attitude in architecture, as 'pattern language' [We are indebted to Harry and Susan for drawing this work to our attention].

Alexander, et al.'s (1977) argument is that how things are patterned in the world affects how we live, interact and behave, but equally how we read and understand patterns gives us agency in further shaping structures. While Alexander was talking about physical constructions like buildings and towns, the same applies to the construction and re-making of social entities like communities and schools. According to Alexander, et al. (1977), 'people share a common pattern language' (p. x) otherwise we would not be able to co-habitate or improve the conditions of our lives. He says that pattern language has essentially the structure of a network—there is a sequence:

> ... from larger patterns to the smaller, always from the larger patterns to the smaller, to the ones which then embellish these structures, and then those that embellish the embellishments... (p. xviii)

Like any network:

> ... there is no one sequence which perfectly captures it. But the sequence... captures the broad sweep of the full network; in doing so it follows a line, dips down, dips up again, and follows an irregular course, a little like a need following a tapestry. (p. xviii)

Importantly, 'the sequence of patterns is both a summary, and at the same time an index to the patterns' (p. xviii). In other words, as Alexander puts it, patterns inextricably relate to one another: '... no pattern is an isolated entity. Each pattern can exist in the world, only to the extent that it is supported by other patterns' (p. xiii), and this is fundamental to the world:

> ... when you build a thing, you cannot build that thing in isolation, but must also repair the world around it, and within it ... (p. xiii)

Similarly, how we articulate social problems, how we problematize them, and how we explore possible 'solutions', also has a pattern language sequence, even when we are talking about something as apparently free-standing and autonomous as grassroots forms of organizing (Chetkovich & Kunreuther, 2006) for school and community reform.

We want to turn now to how this notion of pattern language came to be experienced, articulated and played out in a community and school reform approach, with a difference, in an Australian context we are calling Wirra Wagga.

## THE ARCHITECTURE OF A 'COMMUNITY VOICED' APPROACH TO NEIGHBOURHOOD AND COMMUNITY RENEWAL

Communities *put at a disadvantage*—our deliberately chosen language to avoid notions of victim construction and disparagement (Smyth, 2006)—invariably present with varying degrees of physical degradation. Physical facilities and infrastructure have been allowed to fall into disrepair through official neglect or because residents themselves have more pressing priorities around survival. In some respects, but by no means all, relationships among residents, between residents and their wider surrounding community, and between residents and official institutions, there are also varying degrees of relational untidiness.

In Wirra Wagga, a community located in a regional town in Australia that has been ravaged by almost 50 years of de-industrialization and the attenuated effects of globalization, one of the most prominent themes to emerge in the latest attempt to bring about improvement in the lives of the residents, was the need to engage in a very 'different kind of politics' from what had demonstrably failed in the past. What was clearly needed was deep engagement with a radically different style of thinking and acting that went beyond a 'client', service', and a 'welfare' mentality which had only served in the past to perpetuate a situation of dependence in which the members of the Wirra Wagga community were excluded from authentic control over how problems were framed, possible pathways to solutions, and ultimately denial of control over their own destinies. The best example we can find of a body of theory, practice and ideas that helps to explain what is going on and that holds out the possibility of an alternative is around what is known as 'community organizing', or what Boyte (2004) has shorthanded as 'everyday politics'. We will make a diversion here and return to the community of Wirra Wagga in moment.

The idea of community organizing that is theoretically central to our discussion has its origins in the neighborhood renewal and coalition alliance building activities of Saul Alinsky in Chicago in the 1930s in the Back of the Yards neighborhood of that city (so called because of its location in the slums and poverty afflicted stockyards area behind the Union Stock Yards). The legacy of Alinsky's work (originally published in 1946) through what he called 'people's organization' (Alinsky, 1989a), is very much alive and thriving today throughout the U. S. operating under the unlikely title of the Industrial Areas Foundation and affiliates (so named because of Alinsky's pioneering organizing work in the industrial areas of Chicago). It is continuing to have a profound impact, especially in parts of South Texas, because it provides a way of marginalized people gaining control over aspects of their lives (Warren, 2001; Shirley, 1997; Shirley, 2002) hitherto considered impossible.

While there is much to be gained from this work, it is only possible to give a brief glimpse here of it here and there are aspects of Alinsky's work that are somewhat problematic today, especially considering the dispersed grassroots community organizing approaches he was pursuing. Where his work has less credence and relevance is in its heavy emphasis upon the singular 'would-be hero-organizers' (Horwitt, 1989, p. 174) that is such a prominent part of his major work *Reville for Radicals* (Alinsky, 1989a). As Alinsky chronicler Horwitt (1989) put it:

> One could almost envision Alinsky's organizer flying in a Superman cape, swooping into a forlorn industrial community, ready to fight for 'truth, justice and the American way'. (p. 174)

Notwithstanding the shortcomings of this heroic formulation, the intent behind Alinksy's work is nevertheless still highly relevant today:

> ... to create a setting in which victimized people could experience and express their self-worth, power and dignity. (Horwitt, 1989, p. 174)

While it is not easy to present in cogent summary form a set of defining principles from Alinsky's often polemical and rambling writings, there are a number of consistent central commitments to community organizing that come through as indicated by Horwitt (1989):

- '[T]he centrality of native or indigenous leadership'. (p. 174)

- The crucial importance of representative organization

- The 'establishment of new norms of behavior, with an emphasis on collective action, cooperation and unity'. (p. 174)

- The role of outsiders in not making 'value judgments about a community's values, traditions and attitudes' (p. 175) not feeling 'superior to the people [being] organized'. (p. 176)

- Changing attitudes 'not by unilateral action, but by raising alternatives, by engaging community members in a kind of Socratic dialogue, and working with them to implement those alternatives in an indigenous community organization'. (p. 175)

- Implementation of priorities as a result of 'discussion, debate and negotiation'. (p. 175)

- Attempting to build a 'democratic communal life' in which 'trusting relationships would grow across boundaries'. (p. 176)

- Above all 'not forcing an alien, unwanted value system on people'. (p. 175)

Presenting such a complex body of ideas synoptically, means that we need to step back and look more broadly at the body and substance of Alinsky's work and legacy both in terms of his own writing (Alinsky, 1989a; Alinsky, 1989b) and those who have taken it up (Cortes, 1993; Cortes, 1995; Cortes, 1997), as well as those who have been commentators on his ideas (Boyte, 1984; Williams, 1989; Gecan, 2002; Sanders, 1970; Chambers with Cowan, 2004; Shirley, 1997; Shirley,

2002; Horwitt, 1989; Osterman, 2002; Warren, 2001; Warren & Wood, 2001; Thomson, 2005). When we do this, it becomes clear that there is a single overarching theme running through it all, namely that of power.

Maria Avila (2006), Director of the Center for Community Based Learning, Occidental College, Los Angeles, and a former community organizer with the Alinsky-inspired Industrial Areas Foundation, put it perceptively in these terms:

> Our society's predicament [in communities like Wirra Wagga] is such that it requires efforts to restructure the way we think, act, behave toward each other, [and] the way we act as a collective to restructure power and resources around us, in a strategic, slow, process oriented, but focused way. (p. 5)

Summarizing the essence of Avila's argument Boyte (2004) says that bringing about change through a community organizing approach requires a focus on 'culture change before structural change' (p. 144). We concur with Avila and Boyte that 'change is a profoundly relational process tied to organizing and power' (Boyte, 2004, p. 144). While our research is deeply informed by Saul Alinsky's ideas (Smyth, 2006) and activities of organizations like the IAF, our specific reading is more indigenous or home-grown and emerges as a hybrid from the specifics of an Australian context.

We should say something briefly here about the theoretical 'thinking space' (Crang & Thrift, 2000) that lies behind our discussion and analysis of what occurred in Wirra Wagga. One of us in particular has long been deeply affected by the inspirational community organizing work of Saul Alinsky and those who have carried on his work (see Smyth, 2006). In this chapter we are using Alinsky's ideas as a backdrop with which to make sense of what happened in Wirra Wagga, rather than present this as a community that consciously set out to use or implement Alinksy's ideas. In a sense what we are doing then, is a backward mapping exercise using some of Alinsky's ideas to understand and make sense of an instance. What happens when we do this is that we find traces of ideas, places of absence and silence, and places where new ideas are emerging. That was very much the case in this instance.

Our 'take' on the essence of Alinsky's community organizing ideas are that it emerges from and is encapsulated in four major philosophical and practical commitments, and in what follows we borrow from and extend some of our own previous work on this topic (Smyth, 2006, pp. 23–26). We turn to each of these now.

*1. Relational Immediacy*

Residents and parents of young people in low-income communities are most likely to 'buy into' reform processes, whether that be of schools or the wider community, when they can see it is likely to result in tangible and immediate benefits to their own life chances and those of their children. As Warren (2005) put it, they '… are more likely to begin their engagement in community and public life with the issues and institutions that most immediately affect them' (p. 158). The fundamental basis of community organizing is 'face-to-face relationships' (p. 158) or as Avila (2006) calls it 'conversations around questions that matter' (p. 7). In other words, it is about making connections between people and the issues that concern and worry them in their everyday lives. What is really occurring here is a 'relational-organizing' approach in which: 'Change starts through conversations ... [and] concerns [and] agenda for action emerge from these conversations and relationships' (p. 160), for example, around immediate concerns for 'safety'(p. 160). Although the language may sound somewhat off-putting because of its tones of indulgence and selfishness, Avila (2008) refers this aspect of the Alinsky tradition as 'self-interest', or as she put it:

> ... what people really care about and which is important enough for them to want to get deeply involved [in] over a long period of time. (p. 5)

The dual intent of the community organizing approach is to both engage people around issues that hold passion for them, while at the same time changing long term power relationships. It is 'the art of building relationships while still aiming to build collective power...' (Avila, 2006, p. 4). There is bound to be a level of discomfort in this, as Avila (2006) says, if '... we are to be real with each other, to show our vulnerabilities, our real passion, fears, pain and anger to each other' (p. 6). The challenge, she says is 'to put all this into a societal context, to create spaces where we can learn, reflect, and act together to create change, to restructure power relations' (p. 6). Actions, therefore, grow 'authentically from ... interests and ideas' and have the imprimatur of 'enthusiastic support', rather than being 'imposed from outside' (Warren 2005, p. 160). When this occurs, what is really happening is a process of building 'social capital and relational power' (p. 163). What gets spawned through this way of operating are 'initiatives that are strongly rooted in local conditions, interests and values' in which 'educators, parents and community members are committed and enthusiastic' (p. 167). The effect of this kind of participation is that it 'creates a sense of ownership of the change process and a commitment to making it a success'(p. 167).

*2. Investment in Indigenous Leadership*

Alinsky (1989a) argued that 'native leadership' is crucial to the wider re-workings of power implicit in this approach and it involves 'those persons whom the local people define and look up to as leaders' (p. 64). He argued that 'most attempts at community organizing have foundered on the rock of native leadership'(p. 65). Allowing and enabling local people to own and develop leadership is central to Alinsky's 'Iron Rule: never do for others what they can do for themselves' (Cortes, 1993, p. 300). In other words, outsiders cannot speak for others, and the best they can do is engage them in ways that teach them 'how to speak, act, and to engage in politics for themselves' (Cortes, 1993, p. 300). Implicit in this indigenous or native approach to leadership is what Warren (2005) refers to as a strong commitment 'to engage and train leaders to take public action for the improvement of their communities' (p. 159)— where leadership training is taken to have a loose and generative rather than a prescriptive meaning. What this means practically speaking, is regarding community members as 'change agents' rather than 'clients' (p. 163). In other words, '... not as recipients of services, but as public actors and change agents, capable of being leaders of their community' (p. 164). Shifting from a situation of 'seeing children, their families and their communities as problems to be fixed, toward an appreciation of their potential strengths and contributions' (p. 166).

What is being advocated is a process of investing ordinary people with power founded on a 'willingness to collaborate and compromise' (Warren, 2005, p. 160). This means moving away from traditional, hierarchical notions of management towards a collaborative model of fostering leadership. Warren (2005) says that: 'By paying more explicit attention to questions of power', what is created is 'relational power' that generates an internal capacity for cultural change. This is a view of leadership that requires an investment in careful and 'patient work' (p. 167), that moves beyond mere involvement of isolated individuals, to one of having a 'collective [view of] leadership' (p. 165) in which power relations are radically transformed.

*3. Interdependency*

Alinsky (1989a) also argued that power and change lay in numbers, and that power came from being able to organize large numbers of people to act on their own behalf. His single most important article of faith was:

... a belief in people, a complete commitment to the belief that if people have power, the opportunity to act, in the long run they will, most of the time, reach the right decisions. (p. xiv)

Alinsky was sanguine enough to realize that collectives of people could not operate alone and that there was a crucial need for dialogue with outsiders. His point is that there needs to be continuous 'dialogue between experts and [an] engaged community' (Warren, 2005, p. 167). Unlike the currently prevalent thin or diminished view of accountability, what we have here is 'accountability to an organized informal constituency' (p. 167). If we follow the lines of effect here, and connect them for our purposes to the instance of schools, then reforming communities in this way produces parent and community partnerships that 'build capacity for change' (p. 166) in schools in quite explicit ways. As Warren (2005) argues, it:

- Increases support parents give at home
- Brings support into classrooms and in-school activities
- Improves teaching by increasing teacher understanding of children's needs and community strengths

CHAPTER 3

- Creates co-ordinated action by teachers, parents and community activists for holistic child development. (p. 166)

*4. Painting a Bigger Picture*

The idea that school reform might be more constructively based on 'build[ing] relational power beyond the school' (Warren, 2005, p. 162), and that it is political work, is part of a wider set of understandings that to gain power it is necessary to have 'a broader agenda [of] addressing the needs of low-income families' (p. 162) which in effects means attending to the 'broader structural issues' (p. 159) that make things the way they are. In other words, ensuring that there is a broad-based organization and constituency that has 'a vision of education reform linked to the strengthening of civil society' (p. 168). The larger frame is, therefore, a deeply held conviction that problems in low-income communities are 'the result of fundamentally unequal power relationships in our society' (p. 167).

Against this background, our research in Wirra Wagga revealed a fascinating and consistent constellation of orienting concepts and elements that appeared to be central to the different kind of politics alluded to by Boyte (2004). We present these elements schematically below, and in what follows, we will elaborate on how glimpses of each were revealed to us through the voiced and narrative lives of community members, activist bureaucrats, teachers and young people in Wirra Wagga. We will employ the approach Green (2002) refers to as 'slices of life'.

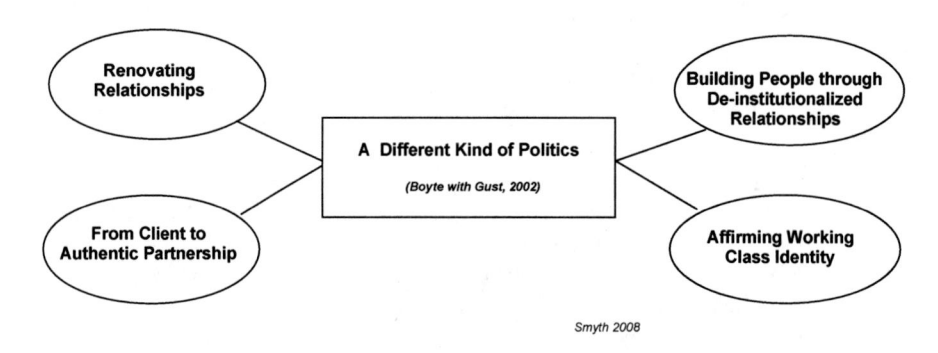

*Figure 2.1: Relational Power through Community Organizing*

RENOVATING RELATIONSHIPS AS WELL AS BUILDINGS.

Sally, who grew up and lived in the community, and at the time of the study worked as a communications officer in the community renewal project, was in no doubt as to the source of the problem, and the likely form this renovation might need to take.

> There are a lot of unfounded perceptions about Wirra Wagga—about the lack of pride in the community, high crime rates and safety concerns... [O]ur family has always been involved in the neighborhood and we've known about the strengths of the community. When people say that there are people that don't come out of their houses and that there is a transient population that's not accurate at all... People take more pride in their properties and they have fences, now that's changed [as part of the Community Renewal process], but the heart and the soul is the same. It's always been there ...

Her concern was with the way in which misperceptions and stereotypes get to be constructed, sustained and maintained, and how the effect is to laminate over and make invisible what are demonstrable community strengths and assets. As Warr (2007) put it, the cruelty of stereotyping lies in the way contrived images conceal and render strengths invisible:

> Stereotyping is a signature contrivance that effects the stigmatization of poor neighborhoods and the people who live in them because it dehumanizes personal circumstances and disregards the diversity of collective circumstances. (p. 9)

The way this 'territorial stigma' (Wacquant, 1999, p. 1644) operates is through 'discourses of demonization' that 'often have only tenuous connections to the reality of everyday life... (p. 1644)

As Sally put it:

> Unfortunately the whole community gets labeled because of the bad effects of one or two families. The media thrive on this... There has certainly been a perception that this is not a safe community and that we have police here all the time, but it's an insult to the community. The crime rate is not high and we don't have safety fences around our school. ... We hear all the talk about 'those low lives' and 'they can't do this and they can't do that'. Our children do get bullied and those sorts of things do happen. But this generation of children will tell anyone who will listen that they are from Wirra Wagga and maybe that's what this renewal project has done. It's given them pride.

What Sally is alluding to in the latter part of her comment is the way in which the community renewal process provided a much-needed circuit-breaker to this debilitating cycle. According to Warr (2007), stereotyping leads to the perception among both insiders and outsiders that communities like Wirra Wagga are 'problem places for problem people' (p. 17) and in a very real sense 'no-go' zones. This territorial faction 'heightens their susceptibility to develop negative reputations for being unpleasant, and even dangerous places... deceptive mixtures of experience and perception, fact and fiction' (p. 17).

The debilitating effect, says Wacquant (1999) is that this can weaken 'communal bonds' (p. 1644) and social networks, and as Warr (2007) points out: '... in the absence of positive narratives of place, some residents feel that their best chance of combating (seemingly) negative influences is to remain aloof from others in the area' (p. 17). What this fuels is:

> ... a retreat into the sphere of privatized consumption and strategies of distancing ('I am not one of them') and that further undermine local solidarities and confirm deprecatory perceptions of the neighborhood. (Wacquant, 1999, p. 1644)

What this undermines, limits and regulates is the 'potential social solidarity in which residents [can] collectivize and mobilize in order to challenge and resist the demonization of their neighborhood' (Warr, 2007, p. 17)—something that has clearly begun to be turned around through the renewal process in Wirra Wagga.

One of the tests of the authenticity of outsiders who were trying to bring about change in Wirra Wagga was around whether or not they were authentic, and the locals interpreted this in two ways; first, whether tangible results could be delivered; and, second, whether locals were genuinely invited to participate in constructing their own futures. Giving residents a way out of the stultifying stereotypical categories that had been constructed for them, required actions that went beyond yet more outsider talk, what residents called 'government speak', that had failed to deliver them anything in the past. In the case of Wirra Wagga, residents made it clear that they wanted immediate physical improvements to their housing, and public spaces, and that they wanted a form of participation in this that was better than the counterfeit versions they had experienced in the past.

Speaking about how this happened Sally said:

> I think without the visual things it's harder because the government comes to us and says that this is what we are going to do for you, but [we] never see where the money has gone. In the community they said that 'yes this is another government project and nothing will happen and we won't have a say'...

> Over about 18 months we had a lot of meetings and we were all burned out. There was a lot of talking and not much happening. The people needed to see things happening in their community. Some of the things that have made a difference are the park, the shops and the fences which have given privacy—you don't have the next-door neighbor driving across your lawn.

The broader concept behind what is occurring here is the construction of a counter narrative to the process of 'othering'. Dimitriadis (2008) defines 'othering' as a pathologizing process 'by which a group or individual is marked as fundamentally different from what is perceived to be normal or mainstream' (p. 1). Lister (2004) also highlights the demarcating and differentiating way in which othering produces lines of separation between 'them' and 'us'. It is most pronounced in the way it works where 'inequality is the sharpest' (p. 102) and where people have the least voice. The discursive shift that was occurring in Wirra Wagga was from 'othering to respect', and we will explain more about how this was occurring through the stories of some of the other residents.

## BUILDING PEOPLE THROUGH DE-INSTITUTIONALIZING RELATIONSHIPS

It would be hard to find a better example anywhere than Warren Kane—a fairly newly arrived resident who came to Wirra Wagga after a lifetime of crime, drug dealing, substance abuse, and imprisonment. He has become something of an icon in the local community and beyond, as a spokesperson for what is possible when people not structures or bureaucratic processes become the focus. Warren is an illustration of someone who has undergone a dramatic transformation—from self-confessed angry outcast, to outspoken and enthusiastic spokesperson for a new relationally-focused approach to neighborhood and community renewal. The turnaround for Warren came when he realized, for the first time in his life, that there were people in the world who were prepared to accept him for who he was rather than stigmatize him because of his colorful past. Warren was in no doubt that re-building how people related to one another was also crucial to turning around and rejuvenating a damaged community. He was emphatic about the need for a changed mentality, and cited his own case:

> I found that the people here accepted me for what I was, not what I looked like and all the drugs I did in the past... for the first time in 36 years, I thought, I could do this without medical help...

> I could see that this [community renewal] program was going to work because these people just accepted me. I thought they might think 'what is this going to be like with a junkie on the committee'.

Warren's case is particularly illustrative because he came to this community with a lifetime of having only ever experienced institutionalized relationships, what this meant in terms of loss of power, and always having to respond to other people's orders and agenda. He admits to being very confused, even to the point of being angry, the first time he was not given answers in the community renewal program, and when his opinion was sought:

> At the beginning I used to get angry with the women at Community House. Whenever I asked a question they never answered it; instead they sent me away with more questions for myself. They never told me to do anything. I was used to being told to do everything, even go to the toilet when I was in jail.

Being treated with respect, having his opinion sought, and giving him the opportunity to have a measure of control over his life, and the wider community of which he was a part, represented a sharp break with past experiences for Warren. No limits or constraints were proscribed, nor were there any pending retributions or reparations, according to how he responded—he was being given the space within which to bring something of himself, his own personality and humanity into a situation to help improve it. He was understandably confused.

Usually when the term de-institutionalization is used it refers to the process that began in the 1970s in which mental health systems moved from long-term institutional care for mental health patients to community-based forms of treatment. The sense in which we use the term de-institutionalized relationships is broader than this medicalized use of the term, as well as being somewhat metaphorical and sociological. What we mean by de-institutionalizing relationships is freeing people from having to respond within relationships that bring with them certain aspects of an existing state of affairs, characterized by a 'service' or 'master/client' connection. We regard these as prima facie instances of where a formal hierarchical structure predisposes one party to respond in a subservient, dependent or submissive way.

Warren used the example of how residents were forced to respond to the Department of Housing and how it framed up the relationship, and how this was in marked contrast to what happened when the community renewal program brought with it a humane, face-to-face, on-site approach:

> They [the instigators of the community renewal project] wanted the residents to have the input and make the decision. They put a face to the department of housing that made this possible. When there was razor wire around the office of housing it was a case of us and them. Then it just all seemed to come together... but its not just bricks and mortar, it's about people... 'Consult us don't insult us' we said.

It is crucial in trying to explain how this different kind of relational politics worked, to not under-estimate the importance of participation *as* power and how deeply this is implicated in the lives of people in poverty.

## AFFIRMING WORKING CLASS IDENTITY

One of the ways in which the stereotypical stick-figure portrayals of people in disadvantage can be punctured, is through revealing the myths that serve to prop up this view. But first, we need to say something about this dominant or prevailing view. In the U.S. at the moment, and other affluent countries are not unaffected by viewpoints constructed in that country, the dominant voice on class and poverty is presented by self-styled entrepreneur and for-profit spokesperson Ruby Payne (1998/2005; 2002). The irony as Gorski (2008) notes is that she is 'peddling poverty for a profit'. Payne's line to educators is that teachers need to understand the 'culture of poverty' in order to equip students with middle class values so as to succeed in the middle class institution of schooling. What is especially troubling about Payne's perspective, not to mention the fact that it has no scholarly basis to it, is that it is deeply insulting to and disrespectful of the people it is supposed to be benefiting—those in poverty. The way this works, as Gorski (2008) put it, is through the deficit view presented of these people. What is required is to 'fix the value systems and attitudes [or as Payne calls them the 'mindsets'] of economically disadvantage people, rather than fixing the conditions that require the existence of poverty' (p. 135). This is an approach, Gorski (2008) argues, that can lead to the 'demonization' of the poor and ultimately 'the elimination of programs that support them' (p. 135). This kind of caricature deficit presentation is one that reifies and homogenizes the stereotype.

Speaking of the Australian context, Peel (2003) describes the way in which poverty knowledge is constructed:

> ... we are encouraged to focus on what is wrong with poor people, and on their bad decisions, rather than on what might be wrong with the context in which those decisions have to be made. (p. 23)

Clearly, we need what O'Connor (2001) refers to as 'a genuinely different kind of poverty knowledge' (p. 7)—one that is in her terms more concerned with 'the problems of political economy than the behavioral problems of the poor' (p. 7). Peel (2003) says that this would mean focusing less on the 'magnitude of the threat that [poor people] pose' and 'their own culpability for poverty' (p. 24), and putting the emphasis more on the complexities of how people in these circumstances understand and experience poverty and the conditions of injustice that produce it, in order for them to participate more fully in crafting remedies that might better address what needs to be done. Studying poverty from the inside out, involves holding back on rushing to judgments, and focusing instead on what these people want to say, what they see as happening, and what they hope might yet happen, to paraphrase Peel (2003, p. 4). This will necessitate listening to stories of anger, frustration, and pain, but also to accounts infused with heroism, hope and optimism. It means revealing accounts that have hitherto been hidden, of people living 'at the sharp end of [economic] reshaping' (Peel, 2003, p. 3). Peel's account of such people is one that portrays them in many instances as 'supportive of each other, more generous and resilient, and more willing to sacrifice for others' (p. 40). As one of Peel's (2003) respondents put it: 'The people here, they're pretty genuine. We care about each other. They are not false' (p. 40). What Peel was describing was a kind of inversion of the popular view in which these people were in effect saying:

> When you're sure most people think you don't count for much its all the more reason to make yourself count. (p. 41)

Peel's (2003) stories of 'battlers', or as he calls them, 'the class who used to have work' (p. 45), are of people who pride themselves 'on their ability to discomfort outsiders and take a good deal of enjoyment in stories of 'mean streets'' (p. 25). In other words, he is keen to puncture single dimension stereotypes, and in the process reveal something of the depths and complexities that reside in the relational nature of working class identity.

Brigid, an informant in our research, in her transition from 'feisty critic to powerful ally', as we describe her elsewhere (Smyth, Angus, Down & McInerney, 2008), presents in precisely this way. She was a local public housing resident who became involved in the community renewal project almost by accident through an altercation she was having with the Department of Housing. During a visit to her house by the local community renewal project manager, Brigid's self-taught skills in computers became the point around which to defuse the tension over her housing

## CHAPTER 3

issue that led to her establishing a computer club which engages young people who have dropped out of schools (from ages 8-20) in rebuilding and repairing computers.

> I got involved in the renewal program through a dispute with the department of housing. I'm in public housing and proud of it. I had a window you could stick fists through and when I couldn't get any action from the department I took it all the way to the premier [of the State]. I took on the government on the radio and it closed three times from all the calls. I then met Carol from the Community Renewal Center and in our discussion about the problem she said she had 60 computers that she didn't know what to do with. She knew I had some computing skills and when she came to check the house she asked if I could share my knowledge with the community. So that's how we met. We make a good team. Everyone thinks everything is roses, but it only gets changed because it isn't roses. I'm now running computing classes in the shopping center. Information technology scares people—so we call it a computer club.

Brigid's case is illustrative of someone with an abundance of informal knowledge, garnered from her working class upbringing, and of how this might be used to considerable effect. She used it not only in addressing one of the most significant ways in which poor people are marginalized in not having access to information or the technical means with which to acquire it, but equally she demonstrated to young people who had excluded themselves from school, how formal education and access to knowledge and information need not be an irreversible or normalized state of affairs. Brigid is also indicative, as Peel (2003) has noted, of a working class person who has 'a very acute appreciation of how power is used, most especially of what happens to ordinary people when it is used badly' (p. 43). In Brigid's case, she refers to how her young charges in the computer club have been caught up in the power games of schooling, with many of them ending up with her because they have spoken back to the institution of schooling. She also shows how her savvy working class background is not going to allow her to get caught up in further damaging these young people through those same kind of power games:

> It's the kids' choices that they are here with me. I don't have to put up with their crap. I'm not their teacher. I've lived here since I was one year old so I know the community. I've got respect... I know what it's like to have $2 in your pocket. What I'm doing is helping these kids—to stand up for them... A lot of kids just need confidence... No one is the boss [here]. The social aspect of the club is huge. Kids develop confidence and pretty soon they are holding their heads up. People feel comfortable coming here.

Coming through in all of what Brigid is saying is a strong sense of advocacy, of pride in working class culture, and of being able to speak from a position of first-hand experience of what it means to not only work with what you have but to also learn how not to be exploited even further. There is within her comments a strong sense of affirmation of what is to be celebrated, and what is possible and achievable, from within a working class identity. As he put it:

> I've got two young kids no other family and I've had some spells in the hospital. I'm ok as long as I can walk—if you are not on your hands and knees dragging yourself across the floor it's a bloody good day. So far as my computing goes, I'm mostly self taught although I learnt a little from my uncle. I can't have three computers in my house and have the money to fix them... When people come in and say they need a computer the first thing I ask them is what you need it for... Too many people get ripped off by service providers. There's just not the money in this community so people have to learn to build their own computers.

Probably the most salient lesson to be taken from Brigid's story is how working class identity is an asset, a strength, a positive attribute in a complex web of relational power to be used in community organizing to bring about a much-needed shift from dependent 'client' at the margins of society to powerful 'resident' operating from the center.

It is the transformation from 'client' to 'active partner', but this time from the vantage point of outsiders who have to reinvent themselves, that we want to turn to now.

## FROM CLIENT TO AUTHENTIC PARTNERSHIP

There is no point in under-estimating the magnitude of the task involved or the difficulties likely to be encountered along the way in turning around inter-generational disadvantage in communities like Wirra Wagga. There is also little to be gained either from over-romanticizing what is possible using all the strengths and assets from within the community, and the massive effort still required to bring about long term sustainable change. The complexity of the kind of transformation necessary requires much more than either insiders or outsiders can bring to the task—even when they work together with the best of intentions and in the most harmonious ways, and things go swimmingly well. The task will still be monumental in terms of the extraordinarily levels of conception necessary, and the remarkable reserves of strategic understanding required, and the vast amount of patience and sensitivity necessary to pull it all off. In the case of Wirra Wagga the joint effort was a long way from achieving that lofty and elevated aim, but a modest aspirational beginning was underway.

The starting point for the kind of turnaround necessary has to be a dramatic transformation in the way outsiders think about and act towards the people who inhabit settings like Wirra Wagga—'the residents' as they prefer to call themselves. The notion that they are 'clients' to be 'serviced' by outside agencies is a concept that while it may appear to be an accurate depiction from an outsiders' perspective, is a label that is anathema to the residents. It smacks of a paternalistic relationship which they regard as being grossly unequal because of the way it

CHAPTER 3

portrays and presents them in a deficit/dependency light—something they find hard to accept and difficult to live with in a context of trying to improve their own lives.

There is a story to be told as well here from the position of the 'street level bureaucrats'—Lipsky's (1980) term for the outsiders who are working with residents to try and fashion workable forms of community ownership. Street-level bureaucrats work in contexts with high levels of uncertainty and unpredictability, generally with inadequate resources, and where deliverables are notoriously difficult to measure. Because of this endemic uncertainty, street-level bureaucrats tend to have 'high degrees of discretion and relative autonomy' (p. 13). What they are trying to achieve is too complex to be amenable to programmatic formulae, and the nature of the work requires high levels of human interaction in ways that make these people 'de facto policy makers' (p. 24) in the way they have to creatively resist organizational pressures while making it up with their 'collaborators' as they go. What they are enacting is a very delicate balancing act in moving adeptly between dilemmas, contradictions and paradoxes, while exercising just the right amount of leadership, orchestrating outcomes, and facilitating genuine community ownership—all of which is no mean feat.

The defining and extremely unsettling question here is: 'in whose interests?'. By that we mean, when we peel back all of the polemic, the politics, and the jargon that come with the apparatchik of outside interventions, who really benefits? Is this yet another instance of paternalistic outsiders using communities like Wirra Wagga to advance their careers, working with residents in the nicest and most polite ways, but nevertheless still defaulting to their middle class persona? Are we dealing with yet another well-meaning instance of what Gorski (2008) in his blistering critique of Ruby Payne's 'culture of poverty', calls 'peddling poverty'? (p. 142). If not, how do we know this? These are not questions to which there are easy or definitive answers. They are certainly unanswerable in the current study, but the fact that we have been provoked into even asking them is in no small measure indicative of the fact that what were encountering in Wirra Wagga was 'getting at us'. At a deep level, it was unhinging us.

Carol, the community renewal co-ordinator, was at pains to convey to us that she regarded her work from the start in Wirra Wagga as seeking to be very clear about the issue of community ownership of ideas, processes and decisions:

> It's all very well to have visions but it was up to the residents to have the light go on. We could tell them the repercussions, but the rest came from them. They had to reach the decision themselves.

Clearly, there is a lot of complexity here in how a community with a history of having been stereotyped, often in ways that amounted to self-belief by some residents, moves to challenging these portrayals and asserting instead a positive identity of 'who we are'.

There can be little doubt either that the role of outside agencies requires them to work against their own ascribed and inscribed 'expert' status by continually challenging and working against their training and upbringing. This can be extremely uncomfortable and amounts to what Shweder (1986) claimed good ethnographers do when they enact a kind of intellectual 'exorcism' —forcing oneself 'to take the perspective of the other' and as a result being 'wrenched out of our self' (p. 38). They need to be profound listeners, which involves more than becoming mute. Invoking Fiumara's (1990, p. 86) notion of 'radical listeners', Giles (2001, p. 132) says being a radical listener involves outsiders becoming 'aware of the undertow dragging [them] towards benumbment' (Fiumara, 1990, p. 86). Put another way, it means responding to the tendency to be psychically closed down and drowned out by words and the attendant meanings that attach to our thinking. Radical listeners are people who cultivate a sense of 'how language enters [their] thinking' (p. 133) as they develop reflective ways of seeing these as 'the enemy' 'drowning out and suffocating... the words of others' (p. 133).

An illustration of what radical listening means can be seen in Carol's view of what constituted community identity-building. In this community, outsiders working with the community don't speak *for* the community, as Carol put it:

> We have a very clear understanding with this community that we won't stand up and represent them. One of the first things that happened [at the beginning of the community renewal process] was all the 11 secretaries [the most senior bureaucrats] of all the [government] departments came here as part of a whole of government approach to community renewal. The residents presented them with all the things they wanted and outlined the things that were wrong. They owned it [the community renewal process] from day one and they would never let us talk on their behalf. It's a normal community. No one could stand up in [my community] and speak for me.
>
> Community renewal is from the bottom up and from the top down and we are the bit in the middle. We pick out people that we think can do it and they do a few things and before you know it, that person becomes a bit of a voice for the community. One of our biggest challenges was getting other residents to take part in things.

Placing the emphasis squarely on residents owning the community renewal process serves the dual purpose of both demonstrating skills they did not acknowledge themselves as having and advancing leadership skills in the community, while at the same time providing tangible evidence with which to debunk or puncture simplistic outside-held stereotypes. In Carol's words:

> The more people we take outside, and people don't see that they have two heads and horns [sentence incomplete]...and getting people to come inside here to Wirra Wagga... Some people embrace the term Wirra Wagga-ite, and the sense of a little bit of defiance that goes with it. Some people just consider themselves to be ordinary, and there are others who have taken on the victim role. That's the hardest thing we have had to do is to take them out of the victim thing.

A major part of the image and accompanying stigmatizing problem, stems from the high level of dependence on government financial assistance among residents. Just because 98% of the people in a community are cardholders and 46% of the houses are government owned, and practically no one in Wirra Wagga earns income from wages, is not to say that this is not a robust and proud community with an identity of itself. According to Carol, the government lost out when it tried to ride over the community by attempting to change its name:

> The community is clearly defined. If you live here you can't escape it. They tried to rename it before the renewal program was set up, but the people wouldn't have it. I think it's to do with the social fabric that has built up over the years.

That is not to say that everyone necessarily agreed with what was being attempted through the renewal process, or that they were not understandably suspicious of a takeover, given the previous history of outside agencies in this community. There was no shortage of either of these perspectives. Notwithstanding, what seemed important was the way in which Carol and people like her were seeking to foster what Boyte (2004) calls new 'horizontal political relationships' (p. 43)—and the starting point for this was residents believing in their own capacity for improvement. Achieving even a small modicum of success in this constituted a major step forward in light of the history of 'social service bureaucracies and professionals who, in the name of doing good, infantilized lower classes' (Boyte, 2004, p. 41).

In contrast to past ineffectual efforts to either do things _to_ or _for_ disadvantaged people, the way Carol envisaged her job was as acting as a kind of bureaucratic insurgent— using power and knowledge of how the system operates, to work for the local community. As she put it:

> One of the best skills I bring to this community is that I was a corporate human services manager. I know what I can get away with and what I can't and I know about the paper work.

Part of the process for people like Carol is to recast the role of the outsider in authentic ways, and trust has to be earned, as the following incident indicates:

> You have to be really honest with people in this community. They have big bull shit detectors. When we first started our community discussions we tried to make people feel at home and we provided plates of sandwiches and drinks. To begin with it seemed a brilliant idea because it brought in the people. We were honest with them and we told them we would feed them, but then we started hearing things like 'How much of our 3 million dollars [the community renewal grant] is left?' So we pulled back on the food, and then we changed the meeting times.

This involves conveying in very tangible terms that the basis of the relationships is not a master [sic]-client one, but a true partnership. There are resonances here in the residents' comments of what we spoke about in the opening part of this chapter when we invoked Schutz's (2008) defining hallmarks of working class identity, namely—'straight talk', 'direct' ways of resolving conflict, eschewing 'abstractions', a tendency to rely on 'webs and networks' in difficult times, and generally the sense that 'power' was something that had to be taken rather than won over through the force of argument. As Carol put it, the importance of affirming working class identity among the people she worked with in the community meant acting in ways herself that punctured the myth of the necessity for vertical relationships:

> It's an important process to sit down with these people. Sit down and eat an apple with them, and they get confused, especially if they think that you are up here [pointing upwards]. We said we were going to call ourselves bureaucrats, but we're going to turn it into a nice word.

A major aspect of working in this way is knowing when your job is done, and the tricky business of making a dignified and honorable exit in which power is truly handed over:

> I think I still have something to give to the community and I have to be big enough to step aside when I think I have reached my use by date.

What we see being enacted in Carol's story of a self-confessed re-constructed bureaucrat, is what might be termed a thickening of the concept of engagement around what Portelli & McMahon (2004) appropriately label a 'critical-democratic conception of engagement' (p. 40). By this they mean moving beyond a thin view of engagement that collapses down to a 'set of techniques, strategies or behaviors that are meant to be universally replicable regardless of context' and that result in what Martin (1992) describes as 'spectator citizenry' (Portelli & McMahon, 2004, p. 40). Martin (1992) argues instead for 'critical spectators' (p. 171) who are not detached and captivated in seeing and living the world though the eyes and thoughts of others, but rather active critical residents/actors/participants who have learnt 'to know when to question something, and what sorts of questions to ask' (McPeck, 1981, p. 7).

## CONCLUDING REMARKS

In this chapter we have argued with some passion that the official policy discourses around both school and community renewal are having devastating effects in contexts of disadvantage. These alien and totalizing discourses are producing a state of benumbment, and the only real hope of reclamation is claimed to be around what Boyte with Gust (2003) term a 'different kind of politics'. The relational version of politics we propose is embedded in an activist set of views that involve a fundamental reworking of notions of power. In pursuing this we have drawn from the colorful legacy of the work of Saul Alinsky and his more recent adherents, to help us flesh out what such a relational framework for community organizing might look like. We have used this to advance some thinking and draw out some of the early traces of this approach in an Australian community undergoing a 'top down and bottom up' form of community renewal. The example is very much a case of unfinished business, which not surprisingly is consistent with this kind of genre.

In chapter four, which follows, we strike at the heart of the neoliberal project by exposing how the flawed logic of the school effectiveness movement has distorted, distracted, deflected, and deformed relationships. We use the ideas of relational politics explored in the current chapter to present an alternative imagining for 'doing' education that goes beyond the domesticating managerialism of the school effectiveness movement. We present an alternative that we believe is more attentive to the notion of agency, and that provides the space necessary for actively challenging the constrained and constraining views imposed upon marginalized and excluded communities.

CHAPTER 4

# TAKING A STAND AGAINST SCHOOL EFFECTIVENESS: PURSUING A PEDAGOGY OF HOPE

INTRODUCTION

We all want schools to be effective and efficient places. We would all like schools to be better than they are now. Indeed, the purpose of this book is to provide evidence and insight into the ways in which schools can be better places for more young people to learn in. We demonstrated in the previous chapter that educative processes require engagement—between teachers and students, schools and communities, and in multi-directions among educators, education officials, parents, young people and community members. In other words, education is, first and foremost, a relational (and certainly not a managerial) enterprise. Only through such engagement, we argued, can local schools and local communities in areas of social and economic disadvantage find space to challenge the political and education policy environment which is dismissive of their particular needs, knowledge, cultures and aspirations. We want schools to improve their relationships with students, families and communities in ways that can enhance educational outcomes for all young people, particularly those who are currently at an educational disadvantage. We argue, however, that what has become known as the 'school effectiveness movement', or the 'official school improvement paradigm' as it is sometimes called in England and Wales, does not work to the benefit of very many young people and is a distraction from, and actually impedes, the kind of educational reform this book is about. In fact, we argue that the effects of so-called 'school effectiveness' are anti-democratic and ultimately anti-educational.

Our critique of school effectiveness, despite its wide acceptance in education circles and, particularly, within education policy, is, therefore, very important both politically and educationally. We believe that one reason for its wide acceptance is that it seems, on the surface, to be useful and practical, but we argue that it is deceptively simplistic. We think there are many grounds upon which criticisms of school effectiveness are necessary, but we want to do much more than just simply attack this movement. We want to offer a different way of thinking and talking about school improvement, particularly in relation to schools that work with communities that for a range of reasons might be regarded as disadvantaged.

In this chapter we consider the emergence of the school effectiveness movement, which rose to prominence during the 1990s, and which, at this early stage of the 21st century, has come to typify the managerial, neoliberal policy environment that exists in education in many countries. We identify and challenge many of the assumptions and values that underpin prevailing concepts of school effectiveness, and, through such examination, point to the many weaknesses and misconceptions of the movement. In particular, we question the positivistic, scientific methodology that its advocates claim characterizes school effectiveness research. We conclude by summarizing some of the very strong evidence that school effectiveness thinking restricts the professionalism of educators, results in pedagogies and curriculum that is extraordinarily narrow, and promotes a conservative and backward-looking conception of the appropriate relationships between schools and their communities. Our aim is to demonstrate that contextual imperatives need to be incorporated into good teaching for all young people. We argue that this requires forms of teacher professionalism that are far more relational and more participative than those envisaged within the standardized, managerialist 'school effectiveness' agenda.

THE CONFUSED ORIGINS OF 'SCHOOL EFFECTIVENESS'

Despite its prominence, most advocates of the school effectiveness movement seem somewhat confused about its historical emergence and its possibilities. Almost all its proponents trace their work back to what they see as the defining break of school effectiveness research from the mainstream sociology of education in the 1980s (Angus, 1993). They are generally critical of the fact that, from around the 1970s onwards in Western countries, major studies of the relationship between education and disadvantage have been conducted that resulted in findings that social circumstances and family backgrounds are the main predictors of success or failure in schooling. This type of research characterized the sociological work of the period, and the results certainly provided bad news about the capacity of traditional schools to contribute to greater social equity.

The school effectiveness movement simply rejected the unwelcome conclusions of these major studies, such as those conducted by Jencks, et al., (1972) and Coleman (Coleman, et al., 1966), which demonstrated that most of the difference in the educational attainment of school children was caused by social and family reasons rather than by good or bad teaching in good or bad schools. Since that time, school effectiveness researchers have stolidly maintained that there is, in fact, a substantial, independent contribution that 'good' (i.e. 'effective') schools, compared with 'bad' (i.e. 'ineffective') schools, make to the academic achievements of their pupils. They have been determined to establish that Coleman, in particular, was wrong—that, in the words of the slogan of the school effectiveness movement, 'schools make a difference' (Brookover, et al., 1979; Mortimore, et al., 1988; Teddlie & Reynolds, 2001; Reynolds & Teddlie, 2001). Coleman and Jencks have thus become regarded as villains in a tight and selective tradition of school effectiveness research and commentary which is internally focused, self-referential and has its own set of cultural markers—heroes, villains, sagas and legends—but little theoretical development or social perspective.

The stance of most school effectiveness proponents is to criticize the findings of Coleman and Jencks and to simply assert that particular schools *must* influence the educational outcomes of pupils, even when such influence is compared with the massive influence of factors beyond the school such as family background and all that 'family background' stands for. The classic studies have been dismissed, it seems, largely because their findings are deemed to be too 'pessimistic'. They are characterized as being typical of 'seventies pessimism', which school effectiveness advocates argue has been responsible for an unwarranted concern among education academics with the nature of society and the lives of young people outside school (e.g. Reynolds & Teddlie, 2001). Instead of worrying about such social issues, school effectiveness researchers maintain that the focus of research attention should be on the tangible factors that are characteristic of the everyday internal dynamics of schools and classrooms. The argument is that school principals and teachers are able to understand and manipulate such internal factors, and therefore can feel optimistic about contributing to better performance of students in their school work.

Accordingly, the major contributors to school effectiveness research typically, and proudly, maintain that the movement has been successful in improving 'the prospects of productive educational change by combating some of the pessimism that was the product of [critical education researchers] in the 1970s and 1980s. It is precisely this presumed 'relevance' and 'optimism' that has made school effectiveness into perhaps the most widely used body of knowledge in education by practitioners' (Reynolds & Teddlie 2001, p. 103). The chief apologists for the school effectiveness movement go on to explain:

> We have convincingly helped to destroy the belief that schools can do nothing to change the society around them, and have also helped to destroy the myth that the influence of family background is so strong on children's development that children are unable to be affected by school. 30 years ago there was a widespread belief that 'schools make no difference' (Bernstein, 1968) which reflected the results of American research (e.g. Coleman, et al., 1966; Jencks, et al., 1972). (Reynolds & Teddlie, 2001, p. 103)

The Bernstein reference cited here is the brief but very powerful essay titled 'Education cannot compensate for society', which was actually published on the 26th of February, 1970 (not 1968), in the journal *'New Society'*. And it should be fairly obvious that the claim that 'schools cannot compensate for society' is a very different one from the claim that 'schools make no difference'. Such strenuous claims and mistakes made by Teddlie and Reynolds perhaps indicate the level of their determination to distance themselves from the sociology of education generally and from the work of critical scholars in particular.

The very purpose of school effectiveness research is typically defined by writers such as Reynolds and Teddlie as identifying 'school level' factors that are associated with student learning outcomes which seem to exceed statistical expectations given a student's family background. This is the 'school effect', over and above the 'family effect'. Yet, after decades of school effectiveness research, the size of this 'school effect' identified by the researchers is, it transpires, about the same as that identified in the 1960s by Coleman and his team of researchers, who, all those years ago, put it as contributing about 15% of the effect on a pupil's school achievement compared with about 85% of the effect being due to family circumstances (Teddlie, Reynolds & Sammons, 2000). It could be concluded, then, that the 'school effect' is simply that which is left over after accounting statistically for background and attainment at an earlier age, or, as Murphy (1990, p. 83) puts it, 'another name for what cannot be explained, not for what has been discovered'. The quality of the earlier critical work that is so cavalierly dismissed within school effectiveness networks, therefore, needs to be considered on its merits.

The Coleman and Jencks studies in the USA were massive and involved substantial research teams in groundbreaking studies that clearly demonstrated strong connections between class and race and school attainment. Such findings were consistent with those of Bowles and Gintis (1972), who concluded on the basis of extensive statistical research that schools relate directly to the needs of the economy in that they tend to sort students according to their social class and their capacity to serve the needs of the labor market. Similar conclusions were drawn at around the same time, through a mixture of research methods, by sociologists such as Bourdieu (1971; Bourdieu & Passeron, 1977) in France and Bernstein (1970; 1971) in England. The radical work of this era made it clear that schools collaborated with other institutions in society in the 'microtranslation of macrosociological patterns' (Collins, 1981, p. 161) by concealing power relations and assuming that the culture authorized by the dominant class is neutral, accessible and appropriate for all children. When it comes to education, such cultural assumptions are demonstrably correct.

The critical researchers mentioned above made it abundantly clear that students of non-traditional cultural backgrounds (including cultures of class and race) tend to struggle in comparison with students from middle class, or dominant, cultures. Later, more detailed work (e.g. Angus, et al., 2004; Anyon, 1997; Willis, 1977) illustrated that subtle and largely unrecognized processes of advantaging and disadvantaging certain types of children occur in schools because of the general preference of schools for practices, norms and values that are, in the main, consistent with the habits and dispositions of middle class families. These insights, although they may have been expressed in a somewhat crude and reductionist manner in some cases, helped educators to understand schooling as a social, political and cultural process that is far from neutral. It is precisely this fundamental lesson that is ignored in the currently dominant perspective of school effectiveness.

As a result, school effectiveness researchers and writers tend to explicitly eschew any sociological perspective in favor of a pragmatic and largely unreflective concern with identifying statistical correlations between various school-level factors (the usual, predictable ones such as 'direct instruction' and 'strong leadership') and narrowly defined and measured student outcomes. The most common outcomes employed are student performances on standardized tests. Following this logic, as Thrupp (1998, p.196) explains, 'the quality of student achievement is seen within the school effectiveness logic as the result of school policies and practices, and any reference to broader sociopolitical factors is ruled out as an excuse for poor performance'. The upshot is that, within what Thrupp (1998, p.196) calls the 'politics of blame', schools and teachers who subscribe to school effectiveness dictates have nowhere to hide if they or their students are declared to be underperforming. They are the ones who are supposed to have ensured that the correct 'effectiveness' factors were in place. The assumption is that if such factors *were* in place then the school *would* be effective. This kind of approach concerns us greatly because it seems to imply that 'school effectiveness' is more concerned about the culpability of individual students, schools and, particularly, teachers than with redressing educational injustice and inequality. The logic assumes that it is individual teachers who are to blame for schools that perform 'poorly'. As Rassool and Morley (2000, p.240) explain this point:

> Teacher autonomy has been reduced [through school effectiveness measures] and new regulatory processes have been introduced to scrutinize teachers' work. As a consequence, educators have had to negotiate a litany of changes: new managerialism; new forms of assessment; new partnerships, e.g. with school governors, employers and parents. Teachers are held responsible for alleged falling educational standards plus a range of social ills such as youth crime, violence, young people's alienation and disaffection. Paradoxically, teachers are both burdened with enormous social responsibility, while simultaneously being constructed as professionally wanting.

Such has been the influence of school effectiveness thinking at the classroom level in many countries, particularly English-speaking countries, that not only have processes and practices of teachers' work been affected, but so have the ways in which teachers and principals think about the very nature of teaching and learning. This point is critical. Their positions have, in many cases, been altered to become more timid and more conservative. Their perceptions are necessarily shaped by the presumed need, expressed by school effectiveness writers, for continuous monitoring and auditing of student results. The emphasis on improving performance on standardized tests reinforces an outdated notion of teaching as merely transmission. Cochran-Smith and Lytle (2006) suggest that there are three particularly problematic influences on teachers as a result of this perspective. They are:

> ...[1] the heavy loading of responsibility and accountability on the shoulders of teachers without acknowledging the need for policies that deal with school cultures and complex societal problems; [2] the distorted and highly reductionist conceptions of teaching practice and the work of teachers; and [3] the explicit narrowing of the purposes of teaching and schooling, which results in an impoverished view of the curriculum and the broader social and democratic goals, processes, and consequences of education. (pp. 679-680)

The logic of school effectiveness, then, results in the work of teachers being reduced to the kinds of tasks that can be readily measured and which are regarded as 'effective teaching'. The assumption is that 'best' teaching practice and mechanisms for delivering 'quality instruction' are generated by experts outside of the school; and that they can be imported directly into schools and classrooms by committed teachers who are willing to become 'effective'. Local knowledge, locally generated and shared good teaching and learning practice, and curriculum and methods that might have been developed for their relevance to local circumstances, are likely to be put to one side and disregarded. School effectiveness advocates maintain that it is teachers who 'make the difference', but only if their teaching incorporates the correct school effectiveness factors. Webb (2005) suggests that the emphasis on accountability through the use of student test scores 'provide[s] the only kind of visibility that enables policy-makers to hold educators accountable. This form of visibility—data surveillance—compels educators to comply with state and federal standards through threats of sanctions and promises of rewards' (Webb, 2005, p.194). The 'high stakes' associated with such accountability and measurement bring teachers to 'the point where power reaches into the very grain of individuals, touches their bodies and inserts itself into their actions and attitudes, their discourses, learning processes and everyday lives' (Foucault, 1980, p. 39). We are not arguing here that every teacher is in thrall to school effectiveness thinking, but we are arguing that such thinking has had a conservative and restrictive effect on teacher professionalism as a whole.

Those who are engaged in school effectiveness research tend to be proud of their pragmatic and narrow approach to school reform. Teddlie and Reynolds (2001, p. 70), for instance, assert that they have confidence that 'the "narrow agenda" of pragmatists working in [school effectiveness research] is more realistic at this point in time than the "redistributive policies" of the critical theorists'. These authors maintain that scholars like themselves are . . .

> Pragmatists, working within the [school effectiveness research] paradigm, [who] believe that efforts to alter the existing relationship between social class and student achievement by bringing about broad societal changes are naive, perhaps quixotic. We prefer to work within the constraints of the current social order. (Teddlie & Reynolds, 2001, p. 71)

But what sort of logic is really being presented here? It is one thing to attempt to discover ways in which schools can, as it were, 'succeed against the odds' with children who are the victims of various kinds of disadvantage; but it is quite another thing to argue that the multiple forms of educational disadvantage, and the many social causes that lead to the conditions of disadvantage that exist in and around schools and which permeate our society, are irrelevant to considerations of educational reform. Yet this latter position is exactly what most school effectiveness researchers seem to advocate. We believe that such a proposition must surely appear preposterous to anyone with even a passing knowledge of the different social, economic and cultural contexts of different schools in different neighborhoods. For us, given that our beliefs and assumptions about the social world and educational reform differ so markedly from those of school effectiveness researchers, we have to admit to being somewhat puzzled about the enormous and pervasive influence of school effectiveness research in educational policy, educational management and educational 'reform'. Some of its limitations are quite stark.

For instance, the factors identified by school effectiveness researchers are entirely predictable. There are no surprises. All are conventional aspects that have long been associated with traditional, stereotypical, well-managed, safe, predictable, standard, unimaginative, boring schooling. One of the most influential overviews of school effectiveness research is that compiled by Sammons and her colleagues (Sammons, et al., 1995) on behalf of the Office for Standards in Education in the UK. This report examined school effectiveness work in a number of countries including Australia, UK, USA, Canada and the Netherlands. It continues to have important status internationally, particularly in English speaking countries. This report specified eleven categories of school factors that were identified as being the main contributors to 'school effectiveness'. These are: professional leadership, shared vision and goals, a learning environment, concentration on teaching and learning, purposeful teaching, high expectations, positive reinforcement, monitoring progress, people's rights and responsibilities, home/school partnerships, and a learning organization.

A huge problem we have with such lists of factors is that, even if there is some correlation or connection between the factors identified and the effectiveness of schools in certain respects, no matter how such effectiveness is measured, that connection does not necessarily imply a direct cause and effect relationship. Moreover, such factors, the so-called 'characteristics of effective schools', are not at all precise and often lend themselves to a range of interpretations. The effects that might be claimed, for instance, from the presence of a characteristic such as 'a learning environment' can surely be only partial or impressionistic at best. What kind of learning environment? How is the learning environment manifested? What kinds of learning, about what kinds of things, characterize a particular place as a 'learning environment'? But such questions are not asked and the so-called 'effectiveness factors' are presented with such a sense of clarity, confidence and precision that one feels almost obliged to agree with them. They fit snugly with typical conservative prescriptions and mythology about what makes good schools. They tend to reflect bonds with the past rather than opening up options for the future.

Such gross over-simplifications in school effectiveness rhetoric, and the reduction of the enormous social and educational complexities of teaching and learning to conventional stereotypes, immediately raises a further host of broader and obviously relevant questions. For example:

> How adequate is the rational-technical approach advocated by school effectiveness in addressing the multileveled needs of all pupils in the educational system? How effectively does it take account of the differentiated educational needs within an increasingly fractionalized social world? How appropriately does it take account of historical relations, and the discursive impact of national and international economic policies on particular sociocultural bases in different societies? (Rassool & Morley, 2000, p. 238)

CHAPTER 4

By failing to address or even consider such questions, school effectiveness researchers concentrate on only a small fraction of the influences on educational success. Their approach is educationally dangerous, not only because it ignores so much that bears down on schools, teachers and students, but also because the broad acceptance of the school effectiveness framework across entire education systems must inevitably lead to the standardization of school procedures and force from the agenda the many more complex issues that schools need to deal with every day. Forced to the forefront is an overarching concern with narrow issues of standards and performativity. It is the classroom results of students and teachers, typically measured narrowly by their performance in standardized tests, that count. It is not the issues and problems of everyday life that must be dealt with inside and outside classrooms as part of the educational process. As we have already indicated, the tests define what is 'officially' important educationally. They do so not just in terms of defining the educational content, but also, and possibly more dangerously, by shaping the processes that are regarded as effective pedagogy. Given the range of such obviously problematic issues associated with school effectiveness, we must now try to unravel some of the reasons for its enormous influence.

## THE 'SCIENTIFIC' APPEAL OF SCHOOL EFFECTIVENESS

Much of the appeal of school effectiveness, apart from its echoes of a more predictable, more stable and simpler past, would appear to be its reassuringly positivist, quasi-scientific approach, which involves dealing with measurable data that are claimed to be in some sense related to so-called 'real world' issues in education (Rassool & Morley, 2000, p. 237). The results can be presented as tangible and pragmatic in that they are directly able to be operationalized in ways that, so the argument goes, schools that heed the school effectiveness prescriptions can indeed make a difference to their students' educational achievement. Most of us would wish it to be so, and we can see why such an assertion is highly attractive to policy makers. However, there seem to be many more glowing commentaries on, and summaries of, school effectiveness research than there are actual research reports that indicate any benefits of school effectiveness (Angus 1993). The commentaries seem too good to be true, and, as is typical in such situations, they *are* too good to be true.

As mentioned above, one of the most influential surveys of the field was undertaken by Sammons and her colleagues (Sammons, et al., 1995). In Australia, in the State of Victoria, this report is highly regarded by policy-makers for many reasons, not the least being its so-called 'evidence based' underpinnings, which are referred to frequently in an important policy document titled *School improvement: a theory of action* (Fraser & Petch, 2007). The basis of this document, which was sent to all government schools and principals in the State, is the eleven categories of school factors that Sammons and her colleagues (1995) identified as being the main contributors to 'school effectiveness'. *School improvement: a theory of action* (Fraser & Petch, 2007) has been distributed widely 'with the express purpose of describing ... the work that has been undertaken as part of the school reform agenda [in Victoria] since the *Blueprint for Government Schools* was launched in 2003' (p. 11). The document reflects upon the previous several years of perceived 'progress' in education in Victoria and foreshadows still greater achievements through the combination of effective leadership and school effectiveness. The educational approach that the document prescribes is based largely on 'The Effective Schools Model' (p. 11) described by Sammons and her colleagues, which are said to 'have an evidence-based correlation with improved student outcomes' (Fraser & Petch, 2007, p. 11). While there is reference in the document to 'children from disadvantaged backgrounds' (p. 15) and brief mention of 'equity funding ... that is deployed to benefit those students who are most at risk' (p. 15), the only specific reference to 'inclusive education' is in relation to a 'Program for Students with Disabilities' (pp. 15–16).

In other words, the theory of action presented in this official document is derived from the particularly thin empirical base of the school effectiveness literature, which, in a somewhat pseudo-scientific manner, concludes that particular recipes or prescriptions for teaching amount to 'best practice' that should become standard practice. These prescriptions, then, displace homegrown, possibly collegial, good practice that would have been developed out of the learnings and hard work of staff members and the community over the years. The school effectiveness prescriptions are presented to teachers and principals, in the name of 'quality', as 'authoritative directives to be followed, not ideas to be examined' (Hinchey, 2004, p. 6). Yet all of these school effectiveness concepts are clearly worthy of examination and critique when, as researchers such as Teese and Polesel (2003) show, the least 'effective' schools in Victoria (those with the highest rates of failure and early school leaving) are also those that have the highest proportions of students in the lowest socio-economic group. These authors explain that this relationship applies even when students at a 'poor' school perform better than would be predicted for young people of their low socioeconomic status:

> When a poor school is assessed as effective relative to the standard predicted by its intake characteristics—that is, at least as good as could be expected—this leaves open the question of why it is not better than a rich school. Failure to raise this second question is dangerous. It risks lowering expectations to a norm that is merely the relative position of the groups served by the school in the social universe of the school system. (Teese & Polesel, 2003, p. 199)

Such is the logic of 'school effectiveness' that differential achievement relative to social class is endorsed and accepted as simply part of a natural order. As Teese (2004, p. 14) points out:

> By focusing on the things that make an impact in socially comparable settings, [school effectiveness research] overlooks the gaps *between* socially different settings. This is a failing of grave consequence. For it blinds us to the depths of inequality which exist at all levels in our school system and it pushes us towards policies which promise only relative relief. (emphasis added)

The differences in achievement among socioeconomic status (SES) groups are huge. In Victoria, as Teese (2004) demonstrates, even though more than three times as many young people from low SES background as high SES background fail to complete secondary school, of those who actually do complete 37% of students from the lowest SES band receive grades in the lowest quintile compared with only 6% of students in the highest SES band. Moreover, only 9% of the lowest SES students receive grades in the highest quintile compared with 44% of the highest SES students. The inevitable conclusion to be drawn from such evidence is that there is a hierarchy of school performance and that schools in communities that are characterized by higher than average concentrations of disadvantage in any form are going to find it extremely difficult to raise their narrowly-interpreted academic results. As Teese (2004, p. 19) states: 'This is not the death of class: it is the death of opportunity due to class'. The obvious point that Teese and others make on the basis of such evidence is that school effectiveness factors provide little insight for school reformers into how to go about making the educational experience for all young people more democratic and equitable.

There is no doubt that *School improvement: a theory of action* (Fraser & Petch, 2007) portrays school effectiveness as a progressive educational reform. But the status of the 'evidence-based' school effectiveness research that it draws upon must be seriously brought into question when confronted by the evidence of researchers such as Teese and Polesel (Teese & Polesel, 2003; Teese 2004). *School improvement: a theory of action* paints schools as benign and politically neutral places in which teaching and learning are unproblematic. It presents a framework that, whether it is acknowledged or not, encompasses no alternative but conserving the status quo. We argue that these limitations are due in no small part to not only the narrow conceptualization of education that is articulated in the document, but also to the research methodology that underpins school effectiveness research, which, also whether it is acknowledged or not, is profoundly ideological.

## SCHOOL EFFECTIVENESS, AUTHENTIC SCHOOL REFORM, AND IDEOLOGY

The approach to research and problem solving within school effectiveness is proudly positivistic. Terry Wrigley, a former inspector of schools in England, maintains that . . .

> the positivism [of school effectiveness research] is not merely a methodological limitation; it is intimately linked with the moral reductionism whereby researchers can wash their hands of responsibility for the social impact of their work . . . The nature of the academic discourse leads to a self-concept on the part of its researchers as 'objective' or 'scientific' and [they are] thereby absolved from moral judgments. (Wrigley 2004, p. 238)

Such a research orientation is much more concerned with questions of objectivity and facts than with questions of worthwhileness and values. To be sure, the principal advocates of school effectiveness research such as Reynolds and Teddlie

(Reynolds & Teddlie, 2001; Teddlie & Reynolds, 2001) are quite comfortable in calling themselves objective, pragmatic and positivistic. According to Lauder and his colleagues, their approach is characterized by an 'abstracted empiricism' that is incapable of addressing 'policy, cultural, political and historical questions' (Lauder, et al., 1998) because these are inevitably value-laden, and positivists deal only with the facts of the matter. Schools, which are seen as detached from any social context, are regarded in school effectiveness rationality as discrete units of analysis for the matching of discrete factors against narrowly measured educational outputs. In a linear, additive approach to knowledge construction, first the knowledge must be identified or discovered by research, then laid out systematically and measured, and then practitioners can pick it up and use it rationally and unemotionally.

The particular problem here is that educational practice is conceived of in a narrow, highly functional and mechanical way. There is scant regard for the emotional work that is typically regarded as 'central to teachers' definitions of being a good teacher [which] is being challenged by the definitions of capability formulated in educational reforms' (Hebson, et al., 2007, p. 676). The current 'standards agenda' in education displays a 'technical, calculative, rational mode of policy making' (Mahony, et al., 2004, p. 435). Teaching and learning are regarded as technical, managed processes that occur within the black box of the school in a functionalist model of education; it is the bit that comes between 'input' and 'output', and is seen largely as a set of techniques, the 'core technology', for managing educational 'throughput'. It is assumed within school effectiveness thinking that the process of teaching can and will improve if it incorporates 'what works' in schools according to the results of effectiveness research.

In this framework, therefore, educational practice is to be imposed by effectiveness experts who will 'deliver' pre-specified instruction. The framework seems to have no place for curriculum that is constructed and negotiated by knowledgeable practitioners who might adapt their practices to what their tacit professional knowledge tells them is appropriate in particular contexts. There is a set of techniques that have been certified by school effectiveness researchers to 'work'; these are regarded as 'evidence-based best practice' (Fraser & Petch, 2007) which is to be employed by teacher technicians on malleable, docile pupils. In such ways, school inputs are expected to be translated into desired outputs and outcomes. A problem here, however, is that, as Wrigley (2004, p. 231) points out, 'the identification of outputs is problematic, as schooling has a multiplicity of outcomes'. And only a narrow band of outcomes is regarded as indicative of school effectiveness.

The school effectiveness model, such as it is therefore, assumes a positivistic, rational-empirical approach which entails the direct application of knowledge that is supposedly based on 'what works'. The extent to which it works is supposedly indicated by statistically significant correlations between specified factors and particular, measured 'outcomes'. There is little consideration in this approach of how or why particular factors might lead to particular results; it is enough that there is a statistical correlation. What counts as knowledge and explanation takes the form merely of pointing to connections that have been established empirically between whatever atomist factors that researchers have had the wit to identify and investigate. Angus (1993) explains the reductionism inherent in such an approach:

> The very purpose of school effectiveness research is typically defined as identifying factors that are associated with student learning outcomes which exceed statistical expectations given a student's family background . . . Family background, social class, any notion of context, are typically regarded as 'noise'—as 'outside' background factors which must be controlled for and then [statistically] stripped away so that the researcher can concentrate on the important domain of school factors. The school, the process of schooling, the culture of pupils, the nature of community, the society, the economy, are not seen in relation to each other. It is particular school practices and their direct connection with particular outcomes which is important. All else is 'simply' context and needs to be statistically controlled. (p. 341)

It is such connections, or correlations, that underpin the claim that school effectiveness is 'evidence based'. But, as Avramidis, and colleagues point out;

> It is imperative that research starts to problematize basic understandings of 'effectiveness' and adopts a more holistic conceptualization of the term. Here, a sociological perspective of school effectiveness challenges the technocratic view of schooling implicit in much of the school effectiveness literature, and the idea that the process of schooling can be divorced from the social, cultural and political dimensions of the local and broader context in which the school is embedded. (Avramidis, et al., 2002, p. 161)

There is in the positivist research tradition that is embraced in school effectiveness work, an overarching concern with concepts such as measurement, reliability, prediction and replicability. Within such positivist methodology, it is assumed that, through observation and precise measurement, social reality, which is regarded as external to and independent of the mind of the observer, may be rendered comprehensible to the social scientist. Put another way, 'there is a modernist, rationalist belief that the complexities of the social world can be measured and recorded with the appropriate instruments and technologies' (Morley & Rassool, 2000, p. 172). In the case of school effectiveness, this means that 'specific performance indicators are selected to illustrate effectiveness and individuals and organizations are graded in relation to these signifiers. The results then provide a reified reading, which then becomes a truth' (Morley & Rassool, 2000, p. 172).

Critical social theorists (including the authors of this book) have attacked the positivist research tradition because, through 'fact finding' and 'head counting', positivist researchers, such as those working on school effectiveness, produce huge amounts of statistical data but do not question the social circumstances out of which such data arise (Angus, 1986). Moreover, through accepting pre-specified, arbitrarily imposed categories for differentiating the data, such research fails to do justice to the complexity of social reality. This is precisely the case with school effectiveness researchers. That is, their quantitative, positivistic studies assume the existence of a natural, 'real' social order of the school, with an underlying educational value consensus, which is fixed and neutral. It is seen as simply *the* 'reality', the one and only reality. Assuming, then, that 'reality' is fixed and measurable, the positivist emphasis is upon the search for generalizations or laws that will somehow connect the factors that have been identified. This is thought to enable not only explanation of phenomena to be investigated, but also the prediction of social behavior and, therefore, the possibilities of social intervention and control (Bernstein, 1978; Fay, 1975). That is why governments and policy practitioners are so strongly drawn to such research.

Suffice to say, for now, that we want to emphasize that, by treating conventional activities and social circumstances as if they are naturally occurring entities, the positivist approach reifies the surface aspects of the entity it is studying. By 'reification', Lukacs (1971) explains that social arrangements are treated as if they were immutable things that must necessarily be the way they are. Conventional social structures and structural relationships would therefore be regarded as naturally and inevitably functioning the way they currently do. Obviously, this approach is inherently conservative. It is also heavily functionalist. The key point that follows, and one that is critical to our argument, is that school effectiveness research, which reifies traditional school and classroom arrangements and conservative student-teacher interactions by treating them as neutral, cannot be ideologically neutral itself. Such research must implicitly endorse existing arrangements and, therefore, lend support to the status quo.

Positivist (or quasi-positivist) research like that employed by school effectiveness advocates, as we have argued above, is necessarily and profoundly conservative and has the effect of legitimating entrenched stereotypes, conventions, behaviors and beliefs. Such stereotyping appears in schools as a result of school effectiveness research. Managerial relationships in schools are likely to be seen as functional and not political relationships, and the priority given to student control can be seen not as coercive but natural and necessary. For example, this kind of research, according to critical social theorists like Fay (1975), disguises inequity because, within the positivist approach, 'those who are in a dominated position cannot come to see that they need not be in this position, that there are viable alternatives to their situation' (Fay, 1975, p. 64). Unmasking the ideological content of research is, therefore, Fay (1975) argues, 'not just an exercise in philosophical analysis, but a move to open up the possibility for a social order along quite different lines from our own' (p. 64). From our point of view, it is extremely important to be aware of the ideological messages that are incorporated in school effectiveness thinking.

For one thing, school effectiveness is profoundly conservative in an ideological sense because it is presented by its adherents as a self-contained, internally logical, value-neutral set of common sense, objective parameters for seeing and understanding education and educational reform. As in positivism more generally, school effectiveness assumes that there are universal truths to be discovered and that there is actually one best, context-free, scientific way to go about education, school reform, and raising the achievement of individual students. Such a 'scientific' approach to education, its advocates claim, can be empirically demonstrated and measured, and then applied in ways that do not disturb the conventional and natural order of the school. Educational problems are assumed to be amenable to remedy from within the internal logic of school effectiveness because it is claimed to represent a neutral and non-political (because it is 'evidence-based') rendition of the 'reality' of 'what works'. The presentation of problems in such a taken-for-granted manner has ideological implications. Ball (1995) is particularly adamant on this point. He argues that:

> ... effectiveness studies developed a technology of control which enables the monitoring and 'steering' of schools by applying 'neutral' indicators ... Thus, significant discursive and disciplinary work is done by effectiveness research, which is even further reaching in its implications when linked to notions of accountability, school review and school development planning. (Ball, 1995, p. 261)

In other words, because of the general acceptance of its positivist ideology, the education policy environment which is currently characterized by school effectiveness logic, is one in which 'what counts' as problems is defined by and within the internal logic of its own discourse, which, as we have established, is a discourse of educational control, surveillance and performativity. Problems are framed by, and within, the internal logic of means-ends positivism and school effectiveness. This means, in effect, that the kinds of problems that are actually selected for analysis within a school effectiveness perspective are ones that fit the existing, pre-conceived solutions (not the other way round), and, in the case of school effectiveness logic, as we have argued above, 'solutions' are conceived of in the limited terms of the nominated 'factors' that are presumed to have been 'proven' to contribute to school effectiveness.

This kind of promotion of 'taken for grantedness', normality and neutrality about school effectiveness is ideological in a number of ways. Firstly, it reinforces the view that the logic of school effectiveness, the factors identified and correlations measured, are correct and provide us with a right and best way of educating. This assertion, as we have demonstrated, is clearly problematic and contestable. Secondly, school effectiveness is represented as the only game in town. It is on center stage and other approaches are pushed to the margins. This is particularly the case for approaches which try to take into account the complexities of the social context of schooling and its influence on students, teachers, schools and communities. The result is that attempts to grapple with the more difficult aspects of the educational experience, particularly for students who are not succeeding in the current system, are displaced by the concentration on only those things that can be directly observed and measured. But those things are a very limited subset of the whole. Thirdly, and this is the point we particularly want to emphasize in this chapter, concepts of school effectiveness are typical of the current neo-liberal education policy framework in countries like Australia, UK and USA, which for the past two decades has been an overwhelmingly conservative and restrictive framework. Technical questions are on the agenda but not social or political ones. Referring to the situation in England and Wales, for example, Willmott (1999) maintains that:

> The intimate connection between school effectiveness research and past Right-wing and present Labour education policy is transparent. The marketisation of the education system and the concomitant idealised drive for efficiency ('value for money') have been aided by the factorial prescriptions designed to ameliorate 'average' or 'failing' schools that have emanated from the school effectiveness research. Many critics have convincingly demonstrated that such research is being used to lend a spurious support to right-wing policy because it advocates an approach in which it is assumed that 'educational problems' can be fixed by technical means and that inequality is an intra-school affair—to be managed within classrooms—and can be easily remedied as long as teachers and pupils alike adhere to the common-sense truisms proffered by school effectiveness researchers. (p. 254)

In all of these ways, as we continue to emphasize, it can be said that school effectiveness is archetypical of prevailing policy rationality in education, not just in Victoria and Australia but, it would seem from the rapidly accumulating evidence, globally—particularly in Western, English-speaking countries. The school effectiveness discourse is consistent with the prevailing policy language of performativity and managerialism. Indeed, both school effectiveness theory and management theory, as Ball (1995, p. 260) puts it, 'define human beings as objects to be managed'. Ball goes on to argue:

> Effectiveness research can be seen to have played a crucial role in laying the groundwork for the reconceptualisation of the school within which management discourse operates and has played its part in providing a technology of organisational measurement and surveillance. (Ball, 1995, p. 260)

School effectiveness rationality promotes particular, narrow types of teacher professional values and traditional, outdated characteristics of the work of teaching. It de-professionalizes teachers, in our view, by stripping them of their capacity to make professional judgments; yet, in a curious way, school effectiveness also re-professionalizes teachers in a particular, narrow sense in that they become 'deliverers' of instruction and 'managers' of learning. Within the logic and the discourse of school effectiveness, teachers are expected to be skilled exponents of 'what works'. But, as we will now go on to discuss, the question of 'what works' in education and school reform is a highly contested one. The school effectiveness version is extremely narrow; it lacks critique and self-reflection, and its predominance within education policy inhibits other discourses of teacher professionalism which, we will argue, provide much greater potential for authentic school reform that can be empowering and beneficial to all students.

The linear, rationalist logic of school effectiveness, to the extent that it has become 'normalized' in educational policy environments, sits comfortably not just with positivism but also with functionalist understandings of social control and values neutrality. The view of the world that is presented is simplistic and hopelessly idealized. For example, the literature seems to assume that schools and classrooms are more-or-less homogeneous. The taxonomy used within school effectiveness amounts to what Rassool and Morley (2000, p. 253) call 'a system of governmentality' within which . . .

> Quality can only be evaluated when like is compared with like. School effectiveness as part of the change agenda has, in effect, reduced heterogeneity in organizational forms. Instead of recognizing diversity and pluralism, there is an assumption that there is one best way of doing things and that this will work for all organizations, communities and individuals. (Morley and Rassool, 2000, p. 173)

Small wonder, then, that Morley and Rassool (2000) detect a 're-enchantment' with management and 'heroic' formulations of school leadership, which, like school effectiveness rationality, seem to have become 'relay devices' in generating the commitment of many educators to the broad modalities of linear control, management-driven policy and practice, and a misguided belief in the 'commonsense' necessity and reality of school effectiveness which, supposedly, 'works'. It is not that we are anti-management or anti-leadership, it is just that we are opposed to managerialist management and managerialist leadership. The consequence over the past two decades of managerialism has been the strengthening of top-down policy that is argued by policy-makers to be necessary in bringing about 'reform'. We argue below that all of this—all that is encapsulated in 'the school effectiveness movement' and its discourse—reflects the conservative power of power, and is anathema to genuine reform.

## SOCIAL CONTEXTS AND SOCIAL AGENTS IN EDUCATIONAL CHANGE

Within such a top-down, managerial policy environment as the one that is currently being encountered internationally in many educational jurisdictions, particularly in English-speaking countries, teachers and students are deemed to be people to whom policy is 'done' rather than as participants in the shaping, implementation and continual reformulation of education policy. The hierarchical, linear, paternalistic and functionalist logic of school effectiveness ignores the essential professionalism of education workers and the benefits of their organizational participation. Within the critical social science perspective that we have been arguing for, our approach draws upon a broad theoretical tradition that incorporates concepts such as 'the social construction of reality' and 'grounded theory' as well as our critique of positivism and managerialism. These concepts are particularly important in our work because, even within the limitations imposed upon alternative educational analysis and argument in the current educational environment that is dominated by school effectiveness rationality, they help us to explain the dogged persistence of reformers at all levels of the education system.

There is a clear assumption in school effectiveness research that schools and classrooms are generally homogeneous, and that teachers and students are much the same everywhere. There is a further assumption that we can generally agree on the particular outputs that are most important for schools. In terms of school effectiveness, these are generally high levels of achievement on universal standardized tests. The narrowness of such a concept of effectiveness needs to be emphasized. One might well ask: 'Effective' in terms of what? The answer would seem to be: 'school achievement, and student performance on narrowly defined standardized tests'. The fact that schools have an enormous multiplicity of outcomes, and need to be effective in a myriad of complex and messy ways, all of which are problematic, is ignored.

As we have indicated above, we have become increasingly concerned about the concentration in school effectiveness work on the immediate, school-level factors that can be identified within classrooms. Although some recent work, particularly that being conducted in England by people like Chapman (2006) and Harris and her colleagues (2006), has argued that advocates of school effectiveness need to become more aware of the varying contexts of schools, the narrow emphasis of the vast majority of the literature on school effectiveness excludes concerns about the multiple factors which derive from the socioeconomic context in which schools and their communities are located (Angus, 1993). Because of this narrow focus, as Power and Whitty (1999, p. 539) put it, the view arises 'that 'turning things around' is simply a matter of [teachers] having the right [school effectiveness] mind set. Such detachment of the school and its internal workings from its community and the world around it strikes us as being somewhat unreal and bereft of educational considerations. As Angus (1993) puts this point:

> Not only is context understood [in school effectiveness research] as something that exists outside or beyond schooling rather than in relation to it, but also it is something that is prior to schooling rather than being historically contiguous. Context has done its work by influencing input. Schools, then, are neutral and impartial institutions that do the best they can, given the 'quality' of their input, by implementing the best effectiveness practices. Power relationships are not seen to exist except in the form of legitimate management and teacher authority. (p. 341)

A growing number of critics of school effectiveness have become increasingly concerned about the blindness in education policy towards race and, particularly, social class. Some have referred, for instance to the 'death of class'. However, Teese (2004) maintains:

> How can we speak of the death of class when we are confronted by high levels of poverty amongst the working population, by the higher incidence of certain diseases in working-class families—cardiovascular disease, chronic bronchitis, stomach cancer, for example—by sub-standard housing, by long working hours at low rates, insecurity of employment, long-term unemployment of workers in the labour force, high indebtedness, poor access to human services, higher crime rates and incarceration, and high rates of family breakdown and violence? ... To believe that class is in all these things but not in education is merely to recycle the myth education makes of itself,

the promise to liberate all from class that it extends to all, but without the performance. (p. 19)

In this book we are on about changing schools and we do believe that schools can play a role, at least to some extent, in the liberation of people from some of the worst and most restrictive effects of class. But we maintain that current policy frameworks militate against this ideal. That is why we are interested in educational change, particularly in the ways in which schools can potentially relate better to students and their communities. We have argued that the school effectiveness movement represents schools as if they are solid, stable entities that are difficult if not impossible to change in any substantial way. We agree that schools often do look like this, but this appearance is the result of a variety of meanings, rules and structures of schooling having become entrenched and taken for granted over time. We believe that the school effectiveness logic reinforces this taken-for-grantedness. The entrenched, sedimented 'rules' legitimate existing arrangements, which may then appear very stable, natural and normal. But, unlike the school effectiveness advocates, we argue that schools are not naturally this way. And we would like to change them for the better.

Like all structures, schools have been constructed in their current fashion, and, in principle, could be reconstructed differently. This implies that, when it comes to investigating schools and society, it is not enough to merely measure and record existing arrangements, correlations and pre-specified outcomes (as school effectiveness researchers tend to do); instead, we must make all these things problematic and try to reveal what is taken for granted within them. That way we might get a sense of how to change them in ways that might contribute to more genuine school improvement. This is exactly what we are trying to do in this book.

As critical researchers, we are trying to make the familiar strange by problematizing it, questioning it, and generally critically 'reading' it. In this way we are following the advice of Henry Giroux (1984), who regards schools as social or cultural sites:

Schools must be seen as institutions marked by the same complex of contradictory cultures that characterize the dominant society. Schools are social sites constituted by a complex of dominant and subordinate cultures, each characterized by the power they have to define and legitimate a specific view of reality. Teachers and others interested in education must come to understand how the dominant culture functions at all levels of schooling to disconfirm the cultural experiences of the 'excluded majorities. (Giroux p. 37)

In other words, schools are important social institutions in which young people learn to live their lives, but in which they find that the interests of all children are not necessarily treated equally. We have tried to research organizational patterns and cultural struggles in schools and communities in ways that provide insight into broader patterns and possibilities of social and cultural as well as educational change. We try to do this by being fully conscious of the messy relationships between and among schools and the individuals, communities and society that surround and interact with them.

For the moment, let us briefly consider the small, immediate contexts and power relationships within schools. We take the perspective of researchers trying to investigate and to advocate possibilities for organizational change in the interests of less-advantaged students. One perspective that we find helpful for such analysis is offered by Ralf Dahrendorf (1979) in his influential book *Life Chances*. Dahrendorf regards human agency (our capacity to act independently and autonomously, and to make a difference) as being both facilitated and constrained by what he calls 'options' and 'ligatures'. We have attempted to summarize Dahrendorf's ideas diagrammatically in Figure 4.1. 'Options', Dahrendorf says, offer some possibilities for alternative action within social or organizational structures. That is, they offer opportunities for school participants to take initiatives and to exercise their fundamental human agency. On the other hand, 'ligatures' are the bonds or linkages that connect us to our established roles and positions, and to our conventional, learned ways of acting within social and organizational structures. According to Dahrendorf (1979, pp. 30–31), 'Ligatures create bonds and thus [are] the foundations of inaction; options require choices and are thus open for the future'. In other words, ligatures such as ingrained assumptions about schooling can be seen as reproductive forces that tend to bind us to the current structures and make it difficult for us to depart from the existing rules, while options provide us with moments of independence, resistance or transformation. But, for the latter to happen, we need to be able to conceive of alternative futures that incorporate alternative ways of 'doing' education.

*Table 4.1: Agency and structure in organizational dynamics*

| STRUCTURES | AGENCY |
|---|---|
| • ligatures/bonds/linkages<br>• represent institutionalized 'rules' that act as foundations of action<br>• are oriented to the past<br>• are reproductive | • options/alternative possibilities<br>• implies capacity for 'knowing' actions that require choices<br>• is future oriented and may or may not lead to the reproduction of existing structures<br>• are potentially transformative |

The combination of ligatures and options, agency and structure, results in strains and tensions between:
- continuity and change
- acceptance of past meanings and critical reflection

These tensions need to be understood in the context of both local and broad power and social relations which constrain and enable choices

*(Adapted from Dahrendorf, 1979)*

CHAPTER 4

Dahrendorf regards 'ligatures' or 'bonds' as the things, real or imaginary, that tie us to the social structure of schools as they currently exist (and to society as it currently exists). Such things might include traditions, accustomed practices, presumed expertise, hierarchy and bureaucratic rationality. These are 'structures' that shape what we do. They influence our choices when possible options emerge. The point Dahrendorf is making is broadly consistent with Giddens's essential argument that 'embodying a conception of action within social theory involves treating the human being as a knowledgeable and capable agent' (Giddens, 1982, p. 29) who can, with other people, potentially transform organizations like schools, and, ultimately, society.

Such understanding of the capacity of people to make changes in even restrictive environments, like schools, is essential to our approach and arguments in this book. We argue that it is possible to conceptualize and enact schools and schooling in vastly different ways to that envisaged in school effectiveness rationality. Indeed, we argue that to consider the social and organizational relationships in schools as simply organizational and structural realities, as school effectiveness researchers and advocates do, and 'to present them as if they were naturally occurring phenomena, historically neutral and obviously necessary, is to mystify people and to act to render them powerless. By helping people solely to adapt to 'what is', you help to maintain what is' (Simon, 1983, p. 238). We want to challenge, and ultimately to change, some of the accepted 'realities' about how schools work best.

We see organizational and social life, in Dahrendorf's terms, as a combination of options and ligatures, agency and structure. This view implies that people, including students and teachers, 'confront and react to organizational structures as a sequence of constrained choices which ... include past, present and future choices which have affected, are affecting or will affect human agency' (Watkins, 1985, p. 12). In such ways we are trying to grapple with one of the major theoretical issues that critical researchers have most trouble with—the dynamic relationship between agency and structure. We are also trying to present conceptions of an alternative educational future and more democratic and socially just ways of teaching and learning.

Our approach to thinking about alternative education futures is essentially 'dialectical', which means we consider schools from an organizational viewpoint that is articulated by Benson (1977, p. 12):

> Dialectical theory, because it is essentially a processual perspective, focuses on the dimensions currently missing in much organizational thought. It offers an explanation of the processes involved in the production, the reproduction, and the destruction of particular organizational forms. It opens analysis to the processes through which actors carve out and stabilize a sphere of rationality and those through which such rationalized spheres dissolve.

We accept that the mechanisms by which organizational forms (like conventional, established, and even stereotypical understandings about schools and how they work) are produced, reproduced and transformed by organizational actors (like teachers, parents, students and principals) must occur within an existing social structure that both constrains and enables human agency. There are both ligatures and options. Organizations such as schools must be seen as constituent parts of wider social arrangements, yet they necessarily retain partial autonomy from the broader society that may lead to tensions or 'contradictions' between the parts and the whole (Benson, 1977). As Bill Foster (1983), a researcher on educational leadership, points out in elaborating on Benson's dialectical approach:

> ... a social world, if indeed it is subjectively created, is created within the confines of an existing social structure which provides its own definitions and meanings. But it also allows for the critique of that structure so that people may transform it. A second dimension concerns the concept of totality: that one must see the organization as a unit in context, the context of the larger social system. (pp. 29–30)

This approach emphasizes the point that any substantial understanding of schools as organizations requires us to analyze not only the connections between issues of everyday activity in specific schools, but also the broader social, cultural and structural context that is related to such interaction. We argue, therefore, that investigations of schooling should attempt specifically to illuminate the processes and mechanisms by which the macro-forces of the society-wide education system are both reproduced and mediated through the everyday lived experiences and perceptions of human agents, at the level of specific schools and their communities. Such mediation, given the essential human agency of school participants, will never be simple. We do not accept, however, that there is ever an automatic reproduction of conventional school arrangements no matter how deeply such conventions are entrenched. We maintain that there can always be moments of contradiction that may signify new social or institutional forces, or 'options'—the beginnings of new organizational forms in education.

We are forced to recognize that any social and educational vision of democratic and participative school arrangements that will contribute to an equitable and socially just society has been dimmed by the neo-liberal regimes in many countries with their policy emphasis on market competition in education, managerialism, and the notion that education serves the private rather than public good. The voices of educationalists generally, and particularly of teachers, parent groups and members of communities, have become relatively marginalized in educational debates as the voices of business and industry, media, politicians and political appointees have been asserted. Educational activists may well feel that their position had been weakened in various countries because the 'educationalist' rhetoric of equity and democracy, which had been used to support progressive initiatives of the 1960s and 1970s, has been progressively devalued and marginalized during the 1990s and 2000s.

However, the expectations of educational reformers are likely to have been raised somewhat recently by the rhetoric of social justice and 'inclusion' that has been present to some extent in recent years in the education policy rhetoric of Labor governments, at least in the UK and in various States of Australia. More recently, from late 2007, the Australian Commonwealth Labor government has also incorporated a rhetoric of social inclusion in its social and educational policy discourse. Of course, we welcome the inclusion of notions of equity and social justice in education policy considerations. Our interpretation, however, is that the rhetoric of social justice and equity that is being employed, while it is contradictory to that of managerialism and school effectiveness, is currently being totally overwhelmed by the latter.

## IMAGINING ALTERNATIVE, REALLY EFFECTIVE, WAYS OF 'DOING' EDUCATION

In this section, after briefly examining participative and managerial conceptions of educational organization and the current education policy context with its climate of managerialism, performativity and control, we illustrate how developments in the literature of school management and educational leadership have unfortunately been compatible with the broadly neo-liberal framework of educational governance and school effectiveness that has been rampant over the past two decades. We believe that governments have endorsed such developments at the cost of equity, innovation and educational professionalism. We attempt to explain imagined alternatives to the current framework by first illustrating two opposed 'ideal' types (in the Weberian sense) of educational organization. We do this by discussing several aspects of practice which would be conceived of differently in the case of a school characterized by what we call a 'technical/managerial' form of organization compared with a 'participative/professional' one. This conceptualization, which involves a non-dualistic distinction between ways of thinking about organizational characteristics, was first employed by Angus (1994) in trying to advance a 'social and educational vision of democratic and participative school arrangements [that can contribute] to an equitable and socially just society' (p. 30). These broad conceptualizations are summarized in Figure 4.2.

Of course, we recognize that terms like 'technical' and 'managerial', or 'participative' and 'professional', have no universal, unproblematic meanings. The aim is not to establish any essential or actual binary, but merely to distinguish between two different, but easily recognizable, conceptualizations of the way in which schools might be organized and managed. These can then serve as heuristic devices for assisting us to think about a range of possible organizational forms that would be consistent with the promotion of particular practices and values. Although they do not use the same 'technical/managerial' and 'participative/ professional' terminology, Thrupp and Willmott (2003) similarly try to compare and contrast markedly different conceptualizations of the ways in which educational management is 'done' in their recent book titled *Education management in managerialist times: beyond the textual apologists*. They refer to the predominant, mainstream texts in educational leadership and management as embodying a 'managerialist' approach and they seek to explore alternative approaches. Thrupp explains that the first part of this book . . .

## TAKING A STAND AGAINST SCHOOL EFFECTIVENESS

*Table 4.2: 'Technical/managerial' and 'participative/professional' school organization*

| TECHNICAL/ MANAGERIAL | PARTICIPATIVE/ PROFESSIONAL |
|---|---|
| ***CHARACTERIZED BY*** | ***CHARACTERIZED BY*** |
| *implementation* mentality associated with top-down, external control and educational conformity | *reformulation* mentality associated with internal expertise and educational alternatives |
| *bureaucratic/hierarchical roles* specified by managerialist rationality | *social actors* in a specific context in which roles are open, at least in part, to negotiation and change |
| people at the school level are largely *objects* of organizational management/policy, which is *done* to them | people at the school level are largely *subjects* who participate in the creation/utilization of organizational policy and practices |
| *technical rationality* prevails with an emphasis on mandated requirements and top-down accountability for performance | *social/educational* concerns and issues prevail in which educational thinking has an emphasis on being answerable for community needs and to professional, educational values |
| school level participants *take* problems as defined by policy/ hierarchy: problems and solutions are identified in school effectiveness and/or managerial discourse to which 'best practice' and the incorporation of school effectiveness factors should apply | school level participants *make* problems as identified through the 'good practice' of local participants: issues are identified in relation to the local context and within a broad understanding of the relationship between educational and social responsibilities |
| emphasis is on *efficiency and effectiveness*: achieving pre-specified results and targets | emphasis is on *worthwhileness*: achieving educational and social gains that are empowering to local participants |
| *performativity*: student as 'client' and emphasis on narrowly defined student and teacher performance | *engagement*: students and community as 'members' and co-learners with education workers |
| ***RESULTS IN*** | ***RESULTS IN*** |
| linear outcomes / predicted results | uncertain effects / diverse consequences |

is an outline of what, it is argued, are well founded social, political and educational concerns about the kind of [managerialist] post-welfarist education reforms seen over the last decade or so, especially in England, since these market, managerial, performative and prescriptive policies clearly have many harmful effects . . . [D]rawing mostly on policy sociology literature it is argued that the main problems [of 'managerialist times' in education] include increasingly polarized schools and communities, a narrowed educational focus in schools and the loss of authenticity in the teaching and learning process, a reduction in the sociability of schools and communities, the commodification and marginalization of children, the distraction of existing teachers and school leaders from educational matters, the discouragement of potential teachers and school leaders and the undermining of more progressive policies. (Thrupp, 2003, p. 150)

This list of failings of managerialist management in managerialist times summarizes many of the concerns that we have already pointed to in relation to the current problems in education that are totally neglected in the school effectiveness literature. In the second part of the book, the authors go on to demonstrate how and why 'the education management literature generally fails to adequately reflect or respond to these concerns but rather, in subtle or more overt ways, acts to prop up recent managerialist reform' (Thrupp, 2003, p. 150). Thrupp explains that the book does this work 'through a fresh review of education management texts as well as through drawing on the arguments of writers like Lawrence Angus, Stephen Ball, Jill Blackmore and Gerald Grace' (Thrupp, 2003, p. 150). We, too, draw upon the arguments of such critical educationalists whom Thrupp and Willmott (2003) refer to as 'textual dissenters'. Such work is largely grounded in education policy sociology and critical educational scholarship, and it argues for more genuinely 'educational' and socially democratic ways of organizing and managing schools. In keeping with our focus on the relationship between schools, teachers, students and communities, we are trying to explore ways in which local, participative organizational forms can, in principle and actually, enhance both progressive opportunities for genuine partnerships between schools and communities and also foster collaborative forms of teacher professionalism that might promote social equality and commitment to the democratization of education.

This view recognizes that education serves social and cultural purposes as well as the economic purposes that are so strongly emphasized within current education policy and 'official' school leadership and management texts as well as within school effectiveness rationality. Our approach incorporates an understanding that school organization can be inclusive as well as exclusive. The 'dissenting' literature warns that it is the excessively managerial possibilities of current education policy, which emphasize performativity and control, rather than the inclusive and educative possibilities of professional educational leadership, that are currently in the ascendant. We see this as a huge problem. We are concerned that, in the current political climate, there is pressure on school leaders and managers to control and direct participants rather than, for instance, invite the diverse members of the school-level educational partnership to reflect upon and appraise the quality and effectiveness of the education afforded by schools in terms of its social, educative and democratic possibilities (Bottery, 1992; Bowe & Ball with Gold 1992).

As we have been emphasizing throughout this book, there has been a general dismissal, over at least the past two decades, of educational arguments in favor of economic arguments in the formulation of education policy. This seems in large part to have resulted from a perception that schooling has not sufficiently served the needs of the economy. The obvious problem with this perception is that it has resulted in a narrow emphasis in schools that ignores much of that which most educators would incorporate within their personal perspective of what counts as 'educational'. We have seen a rise in the general faith in managerialism in education, which has been socially constructed in industrial societies through the re-institutionalization of directive, rule-bound, top down practices that are consistent with bureaucracy and scientific management. These practices, now exemplified in the technical requirements of so-called 'school effectiveness', need to be recognized as more than neutral managerial devices but as significant contributors to patterns of unequal social relationships. The institutionalization of these technical and managerial practices as standard and proper ways of managing seems to have led to the largely taken for granted acceptance of the necessity of school efficiency and effectiveness, conceived of in a particularly narrow, managerial fashion.

One aspect of the technical/managerial approach that we want to emphasize is that it makes the exercise of creative human agency and autonomy at the school level more difficult. Indeed, it strips discretion from education professionals, both teachers and principals, at the school level and makes local knowledge and understanding, locally identified problems and solutions, and autonomous professional judgment virtually redundant. In short, technical/managerial approaches to school administration and organization have become largely accepted as orthodoxy and, as such, they legitimate particular technical/managerial concepts and forms of organization while constraining the conceptualization of alternatives. As we have shown, the managerialist logic that is associated with school effectiveness policy, and its resonance with other broadly neo-liberal positions including market competition and the presumed necessity of identifying underperforming schools, is a heavy weight for many schools to bear. Such weight militates against more progressive educational approaches. According to Angus (1994):

> Within the demands of the market in which schools must compete, schools themselves become more competitive places. Education may then be regarded as a commodity which gives its recipients a competitive advantage rather than as a social good of fundamental importance in its own right. The interests that are privileged seem to be those that are assumed to be consistent with the competitive interests of the nation, namely, the wealth producers, accumulators of capital, those who can contribute to a productive culture and high-tech future. To the extent that this is true, it follows that the interests of the socially and culturally marginalized, those not in tune with the new and competitive Australia, or simply those not organized into constituencies vying for a slice of the action, are less likely to be served or to be accommodated in curriculum which is not made relevant for distinctive communities and local cultures. Unless we are very careful the result is likely

to be increased polarization of schools and educational attainment along lines of social class and ethnicity. (p. 31)

In the broadly participative/professional conceptualization of school management that we are advocating in this book, the needs of students and their communities would be regarded as more important than the 'need' to be competitive within the educational marketplace. Leadership authority would not reside entirely with the occupants of management positions. From a participative/professional point of view, in which leadership would contribute to educational reform that goes beyond the reproduction of managerialism, it would be necessary to conceive of active participation in school governance as something that is not restricted to a top-down hierarchy. Participants such as students, teachers, and community members, as knowing and active human agents, would make connections between their everyday actions and the school practices which they attempt to influence. In such a participative/professional environment, various participants would be involved in the critical examination of, and would engage in dialogue about, educational issues and purposes so that they would be rendered problematic and subjected to scrutiny. Input would be sought and considered from all quarters in invited discourse, the aim of which would be to engage all education workers—teachers, parents, students and the community—in shaping educational and organizational processes. Through such engagement, the apparent permanence and stability of technical/ managerial structures and processes would be open to challenge and reconstruction through participative/professional means.

As has no doubt become obvious, one of the reasons that we are advancing the participative/professional perspective is that it is necessarily concerned with the social, cultural and political contexts within which the management of schools and education occurs. This is the main area that is dismissed within school effectiveness thinking. In technical and managerial approaches, as we have seen, context is regarded largely as a backdrop to school activity; it is just part of the environment beyond the boundary of the school. The young people who emerge from that context and enter the school are a source of inputs to which the school must respond through appropriate managerial action—like implementing school effectiveness processes more rigidly. In participative and professional approaches, however, schools and education are more likely to be seen as being in a state of constant interaction with multiple contexts as both causes and effects of social and educational concerns. This means that the definition of educational problems and solutions would be a very complex matter. They are likely to be seen as related to the interaction between education and society, and as issues to be addressed by the school community as a whole rather than simply by managerial means. The school would be regarded as a site of social, political and cultural interaction and negotiation. The orientation would be towards trying to understand the implicit social, educational and political causes and effects of educational success and failure. Management would not be seen as neutral in such processes, and neither would any other educational participants. All would be seen as social actors who are trying to make a difference.

We would argue that an important aspect of being an educational worker is to contribute to education debates. One of the most important debates at the moment concerns notions of teacher professionalism and the extent to which schools should take account of the social and cultural aspects of their contexts. We would argue that it is *only* by taking account of context that we can seriously try to engage with students and communities. From this perspective, teachers, students, administrators and school communities would exercise a critical scrutiny over decisions about education that would involve negotiated cultural and political choices. They would recognize that, as we have been arguing, most educational issues involve conflicts and contested questions of value rather than simply questions of efficiency and effectiveness.

Teachers would therefore have to see themselves not merely as instructional experts who deliver pre-specified knowledge for consumption, but as educational professionals whose role includes 'helping students to become creative, critical thinkers and active social participants, and to become capable of redefining the nature of their own lives in the society in which they live' (Gordon, 1985). Schools that were characterized by participative/professional concepts, then, would incorporate principles of professional judgment, reflective practice and critical scrutiny into the work of teachers. This would seem to be the essence of the kind of educational professionalism that is needed if education workers are to be capable of informed analysis of the educational possibilities of schooling in its social and political context.

## CONCLUDING REMARKS

Throughout this chapter we have been trying to make the point that the current technical/managerial policy orientation, which is exemplified by the school effectiveness movement, has brought about conservative changes in what is generally accepted as the nature of education and the role of teachers. We have argued that one of the most destructive aspects of school effectiveness is that it demarcates the roles of school managers and non-managers in a way that also demarcates educational management from education. We have pointed out that there is an overwhelming emphasis on the direct and indirect supervision of teachers through an obsession with the performance of students on standardized tests and other narrow performance indicators. At the same time, teachers' work on community relationships, if it occurs at all, has become more instrumental, impersonal and role-based. That is why we urge teachers and members of school communities to assert their professional judgment by refusing to be objects of education policy—people to whom the policy is done.

Like Ball and his colleagues (Bowe, et al., 1992; Ball, 1995), we regard education participants as active agents, or social actors, in the ongoing formulation and utilization of policy in ways that are appropriate in their arenas of practice. Also like Ball (1995), we wish to resist the renewed elevation of managerialism into an increasingly unchallengeable position. We also want to resist the reduction of important social, cultural and educational issues in schools to technical/

managerial concerns that can be rendered soluble by managerialist techniques, such as the top-down implementation of school effectiveness measures. So strongly has the technical/managerial policy discourse been asserted that we are concerned that many teachers and principals have been socialized into the prevailing bureaucratic, technical/managerial rationality against which we are taking a stand in this book.

Within the kind of participative/professional conceptualization of school organization that we are advocating, schools would be regarded as less certain and less predictable places than 'effective schools', in keeping with current technical/ managerial approaches to educational administration and policy, are supposed to be. Linear and instrumentally rational thinking would be rejected in favor of an acceptance of consequences that were somewhat uncertain, but which would result from participants' generation of their own meanings rather than their unproblematic acceptance of imposed meanings. There would be a rejection of the neutrality and bureaucratic rationality that is associated with managerialism and school effectiveness, which, we argue, can induce subordinates to surrender their professional responsibility to the mundane needs of narrow test results and the requirements of educational markets.

In the remainder of this book, therefore, we try to seek out and celebrate the essential human agency, creativity and obduracy of educators, community members and policy players at all levels who work within the constraints of social structures, community norms, embedded power relations and professional cultures in order to create a 'space for challenge' of the obstacles to achieving social justice in education. These are the kinds of educational activists that we want to recognize and encourage. They continue to work in ways that make a difference and which recognize the essential worth and dignity of those who are typically marginalized in education through no fault of their own. Such educationalists typically reject, at least to some extent, the policy linearity and limited perspective on the complexity of educational reality that is found in the stereotypes of school effectiveness and managerialism.

Our approach is to concentrate on the reformist work of such policy players and to try and learn from them. We try to contextualize these learnings within the theoretical perspectives we have outlined in this book, and to mutually interrogate the theory and the data. We are particularly concerned to uncover, as best we can, the embedded structural relations and power dynamics that such educational players come up against, and to understand the processes of disadvantaging which students, in particular, experience in their communities and schools. We want to recognize the reformist work being done in difficult educational circumstances and to work with activist educational reformers in bringing about our imagined educational futures. We do this in the following chapter by examining ways in which reformist teachers in the area of vocational education are, at least to some extent, able to challenge the neoconservative and neoliberal values associated both with managerialism and the linking of education with instrumental service to the economy. Such interruption to prevailing policy rationality, we assert, can provide practical resources, including resources of hope, to make the lives and futures of young people and their families more meaningful.

CHAPTER 5

# ENGAGING MEANINGFUL WORK

At the start they thought we were the stupid class until they saw what we can produce, now they don't think that we are so stupid. (Student)

Kids used to do more of a general education but employers understand certificates, competencies and skill identification not general knowledge. (Teacher)

Schools can train students to execute particular work skills and to survive economically; but schools can also engage students in the analysis of the relation between work and democracy and in the examination of the types of workplaces that are humane and desirable. (Kincheloe, 1995, pp. 27–28)

## INTRODUCTION

In the previous chapter we argued that the logic of school effectiveness, despite its serious intellectual and methodological flaws, has mesmerized politicians and educators alike because of its false appeals to 'science' and the pragmatism of 'what works'. One of our chief criticisms is the manner in which school effectiveness focuses on the culpability of individual students, schools, and teachers rather than redressing educational injustice and inequality. As a consequence, we see education policies and practices that are not only decontextualized and 'extraordinarily narrow' but which promote 'timid and conservative' approaches to teaching and learning. In this chapter we want to pursue this line of inquiry from a slightly different perspective, namely, the renewed emphasis on Vocational Education and Training (VET) in Schools in Australia with particular regard to disadvantaged schools and communities and the implications for education, social justice and democracy. Of particular interest is the ways in which neoconservative and neoliberal values are redefining educational commonsense around utilitarian and instrumental approaches to 'getting a job' and what this means for students from working-class backgrounds.

Typically, these vocational programs have a number of features including a niche profile e.g., horticulture, maritime studies, engineering, hospitality and tourism, community services and business studies; compliance with Australian Quality Framework (AQF) competency based requirements and certification; and school based apprenticeship schemes, involving a mix of school attendance, waged employment, and training with Registered Training Organizations (RTO's) such as Technical and Further Education (TAFE) Colleges. Our interest in these developments is the powerful cultural messages that vocationalization of the school curriculum sends to students, teachers and parents about what is deemed to be appropriate school knowledge for different classes of students. In this task, we borrow Kumashiro's (2004) notion of 'against commonsense' to provide a more 'troubling', 'disruptive', and 'discomforting' reading of the historical role of vocational education and training in the streaming (or tracking) of students from economically, socially and educationally disadvantaged circumstances. In pursuing this argument, we have structured the chapter around three main themes.

First, we want to challenge the commonsense assumption that more training will produce more jobs. In recent years, this article of faith has been seriously eroded by the profound changes unleashed by the techno-scientific revolution of modern day capitalism. Today, young people for the first time face the prospect of the 80/20 society—where 80% of the population will achieve the freedom, whether voluntary or not, of not having to work (Hinkson, 2006, p. 26). The evidence shows that jobs for young people are rapidly disappearing. Contrary to popular belief, most job openings in the future will not require high-tech skills or advanced levels of education. Official projections indicate that the largest expected job growth will be in the low-paying service sector where people will require less than an associate degree (Dwyer & Wyn, 2001, p. 61). Despite these 'shattering shifts in economic and cultural life' (Giroux, 1994, p. 286) numerous politicians, educators, parents and industry representatives continue to argue that young people today simply need more training to get a job.

Second, we want to argue that despite the numerous strengths and successes of VET in Schools programs, especially for disengaged and working-class students who typically drop out of school, these programs have historically failed to disrupt the strong correlation between social advantage, school achievement and the competitive academic curriculum (Teese & Polesel, 2003; Connell, 1993). Whilst the competitive academic curriculum continues to function as the gateway for university bound students from middle class backgrounds, VET in Schools programs will be confined to producing skilled and semi-skilled workers and a cadre of casualized and low-paid workers at the bottom end of a volatile youth labor market (McLaren & Farahmandpur, 2005, p. 44; Kincheloe, 1995; 1999; Kenway & Bullen, 2001).

Finally, we want to turn attention to the pedagogical question of what can be done. How might educators begin to think differently about the role of VET in Schools in producing a new generation of critically informed citizens and workers? This kind of project involves interrupting existing human capital approaches to education in order to reclaim the symbolic spaces for an alternative vision and practice based on the principles and values of economic and political democracy, meaningful work, critical inquiry, civic engagement and 'educated hope' (Giroux, 2001, p. 125). In this task, we are interested in exploring how teachers and students working collaboratively can begin to find 'new ways of knowing and producing knowledge that challenge the commonsense views of sociopolitical reality with which most individuals have grown so comfortable' (Kincheloe, 2001, p. 372). Freire (1998) alerts us to the political significance of this kind of analysis when he says 'To the degree that the historical past is not problematized so as to be critically understood, tomorrow becomes simply the perpetuation of today' (p. 102).

## CONFRONTING THE BIG LIE THAT TRAINING CREATES JOBS

Jim is a teacher in a large senior high school in Bountiful Bay, Australia and a strong advocate of workplace learning. For him, and many teachers, students and parents the primary purpose of schooling is about 'getting a job'. Jim argues that students are far more motivated, engaged and employable because of the industry knowledge, skills and values they acquire through vocational education and training programs. Jim argues that it's about giving his students whatever advantage he can in a volatile youth labor market. On the surface, the benefits are attractive to all concerned—students getting out of 'boring' classrooms; teachers planning relevant and meaningful activities; employers having a say in curriculum design; and parents anticipating that their kids will 'get a job'. What remains problematic, however, is the extent to which students actually do get a full-time job once they leave school and whether it provides them with meaningful work, fair wages and conditions and possibilities for alternative life choices. Furthermore, there are questions about the kind of education that students experience. For example, to what extent is the curriculum driven by business needs? How relevant is a narrow technical education in a rapidly changing economy? What knowledge and skills are marginalized in the curriculum? What knowledge is denied? What images of 'good' workers are created? Who creates these images? In whose interests? Who benefits? Where do students learn critical literacy skills?

Attempting to interrupt official discourses about the nexus between schooling, the economy and jobs is no easy matter. History illustrates the power of commonsense in constructing particular 'truths' and ways of 'talking and reasoning in schools' (Popkewitz, 1997, pp. 138–140). Over time the arguments for state involvement in secondary education have consistently referred to the themes of international survival, national efficiency and the need for a trained workforce (Down, 2000). There can be no doubt that secondary schooling remains largely an instrument of economic and political ends. After the Second World War in Australia, human capital theories underpinned a range of educational reports to realign the education system with the emerging requirements of the new international division of labor (Gallagher, 1979, p. 7). According to Crittenden (1988) the evidence indicates that the initial faith placed in human capital theory was wrong. He argued that there was no evidence that productivity and wealth in the economy increased by extending general education beyond basic schooling. On the contrary, Crittenden (1988) claimed that increased expenditure on education was 'an effect rather than a cause of economic prosperity' (p. 301). Nonetheless, human capital theorists contend that more schooling and better training would provide better paid jobs and social mobility for all. The evidence, however, indicates otherwise. What mattered most in determining who got what jobs, if any, were a person's class, gender and race and not the length of schooling or training (Fitzgerald, 1976; Greig, Lewins & White, 2003; Peel, 2003).

CHAPTER 5

Similar arguments for a closer correspondence between schooling and the needs of the global economy were mounted again in Australia in the mid 1970s. With the economic crisis of the 1970s deepening and youth unemployment on the rise, the neoliberal assault on the social welfare state created a conservative backlash in the 1980s and 1990s. Education (Weiner, 2005; Apple, 2001), like all aspects of peoples' lives was now subject to the seemingly 'inevitable' (Saul, 2005) and 'self-evident' (Bourdieu, 1998) forces of neoliberalism. At the national level, *Australia Reconstructed* (1987) was influential in shaping the inherent logic of the school and economy relationship:

> Evidence suggests that Australia is not producing the right skills as well as not producing enough skilled people ... Australia has a relatively low proportion of the population with degrees or qualifications in science, engineering or technology-related disciplines ... Australia's performance has improved in recent years but its competitors are not standing still. It must strive to improve the base skills and knowledge on which our future competitive position in world trade depends. (cited in Smyth, 1991, p. 33)

*Australia Reconstructed* (1987), was followed by a plethora of federal and state government educational reports which served to reinforce the dominant view that the solution to Australia's economic problems whether unemployment, lack of international competitiveness or skill shortages required an education system that was more attuned to the needs of the new economic realities (Down, 2000). According to Smyth and Dow (1997):

> ... the focus is on how to best control education by making it do its economic work through greater emphasis on vocationalism, as well as by changing the ideology and the discourse of schooling (where students = customers; teachers = producers; and learning = outcomes) and through a restoration of the primacy of notions of human capital theory. Coupled with this is a worldwide move towards re-centralizing control over education through national curricula, testing, appraisal, policy formulation, profiling, auditing, and the like, while giving the impression of decentralization and handing control down locally. (p. 2)

In all of these debates there seems to be one key question that is not being asked. What is happening to the paid labor market to which the neoliberals want to attach the education system? Without going into detail, it is suffice to say that over the past three decades the forces of global capitalism (McLaren & Farahmandpur, 2005) have radically transformed the nature of work. By way of summary, the following broad features and characteristics are evident:

> A reduction in the size of core full-time jobs and a growing number of people working in part-time, casualized, low-paying, and repetitive jobs in the retail, trade and service sectors (Hinkson, 2006, p. 26; Apple, 1998, p. 345; Anyon, 2005, p. 20; Furlong & Cartmel, 1997, p. 30; Wynhausen, 2007, p. 22).

It is projected that the majority of all new positions will be created in the service sector including food preparation and service, fast-food restaurants, waiters and waitresses, cashiers, retail salespersons, laborers, truck drivers, clerical services, and health aides (Apple, 1998, p. 345; Anyon, 2005, pp. 21-23; Berliner & Biddle, 1995, pp. 100–102).

In Australia, the proportion of professional workers has risen from 11% to 28% since the 1960s. Over the same period, the proportion of semiskilled and manual workers and laborers combined has declined from almost a third of the workforce to 19% (Greig, Lewins & White, 2005, p. 101).

The fragmentation of jobs to the degree that even technologically sophisticated processes now normally require a training period of only a few weeks (Kincheloe, 1995. p. 10; Agger, 2004, p. 75; Braverman, 1974; Grubb & Lazerson, 1975).

The replacement of the traditional craft labor system with a multi-level stratification system, which not only introduces craft-less 'utility workers', but management dominated evaluation schemes measuring both skills and attitude (Blum, 2000, p. 120).

From the late 1960s to the present, the proportion of male workers aged 15 to 19 in full-time work in Australia has fallen from 59% to 18 % (Greig, Lewins & White, 2005, p. 101).

Australia's workforce is increasingly divided between the overworked and the out-of-work; between the well paid and the poorly paid; between career and fringe jobs (Long, 2000, cited in Greig, Lewins & White, 2005, p. 100).

Despite the lowest official levels of unemployment in thirty years, Australia has the highest rate of underemployment in the OCED. Underemployment has increased from approximately 2% of the labor force in 1978 to almost 7% in 2006 (Campbell, cited in Wynhausen, 2007, p. 22).

The destabilization of labor market structures associated with labor hire firms and a common pattern of unstable, short-term employment or 'churning' interspersed with unemployment resulting from involuntary loss of jobs (Underhill, 2006, pp. 301–303).

The de-institutionalization of wages and conditions through the use of individualizing workplace contracts between employers and employees—The [Australian] WorkChoices Bill, 2005 (Peetz, 2006).

The emergence of the 'Wal-Mart factor' whereby large transnational companies shop around for the cheapest global wage rates, thus further deindustrializing national economies in search of profits (Hinkson, 2006, p. 26).

A growing sense of insecurity and uncertainty about work (Greig, Lewins & White, 2005, p. 3; Peel, 2003, p. 4).

CHAPTER 5

> A growing mismatch between the types of jobs available, the rhetoric of the highly skilled workforce and the future aspirations of young people (Dwyer & Wyn, 2001, p. 17).

With regard to the youth labor market, the Dusseldorp Skills Forum (2004) report *How Young People Are Fairing* identified a number of worrying trends:

> In 2004 15.5% of teenagers were not in full-time education or full-time employment; 27% of school leavers were not in study and were either working part-time, unemployed, or not in the labor force; and 47% of early leavers were not in study or full-time work (p. 4).

> Prospects of work and further education for early school leavers have changed very little in recent years despite the improving economic conditions—43% of early school leavers and 19% of school completers still experienced a troubled transition in 2003.

> In 2003, 50% of students in Years 11 and 12 were enrolled in a VET in Schools program (p. 4).

> The proportion of teenage apprenticeship commencements in traditional apprenticeships declined from 40% in March 1997 to 33 % in March 2003; and in the year after completing their qualification, 25% of TAFE graduates were not in full-time work or study (p. 4).

> More than two-thirds of young people start their working lives as casuals and growing numbers may never work any other way (Wynhausen, 2007, p. 22).

Agger (2004) confirms that what we are now witnessing is a proliferation of service sector jobs or 'McJobs' referring to their fast-food-franchise-like nature, including low wages. By assigning McJobs predominately to young people, he argues that 'we short-circuit their educations and don't challenge them intellectually' (p. 75). Agger (2004) goes on to explain that the fast-food industry requires 'virtually no training, or literacy to operate ovens, grills, and dishwashing machines. Zero work, the mantra of post industrialists, has been replaced by zero training as the goal of service-sector managers' (p. 75). Apple (1998) makes the point that this emerging reality is quite different from 'the overly romantic picture painted by the neoliberals who urge us to trust the market and to more closely connect schools to the 'world of work'' (p. 345).

The evidence tells us a lot about the neoliberal agenda for workers. Giroux (2004) argues that corporate ideology with 'its dubious appeals to universal laws, neutrality, and selective scientific research' (p. xix) has effectively obliterated those discourses that are central 'to the language of public commitment, democratically charged politics, and the common good' (p. xvi). Instead, market values, ruthless competitive individualism and corporate interests allow 'a handful of private interests to control as much of social life as possible in order to maximize their personal profit' (p. xvi). Underpinning this position is the vision of students as human capital or future workers who must be given the prerequisite skills, knowledge and values to compete in an increasingly hostile labor market (Apple, 1998, p. 342). Apple (1998) rightly argues, that any discussion of vocational education and training will 'have to deal not only with the place of vocational education itself, but also with its connections to an entire and interlocking ideological assemblage' (p. 348).

The irony in all of this is that Australian employers have been amongst the worst in the world in supporting skills training. The findings of a report prepared for the Dusseldorp Skills Forum are 'unambiguous': (i) according to OECD data Australian employers have been amongst the worst in the world in creating high skilled white collar jobs; (ii) while there are some differences between industries, employers' contribution to training and education funding has been falling; and (iii) the training provided to non-standard workers is limited at best and at worst non-existent (Hall, Buchanan & Considine, 2002, p. 1). Furthermore, the often repeated argument that the individualization of wages and conditions is necessary to improve productivity and create more jobs is not substantiated by the evidence. In evaluating the claims of the Business Council of Australia (BCA), Peetz (2006) concludes that 'even the modicum of evidence was erratic, selective and misleading, suggesting such industry-based claims had little or no value' (p. 66). He argues that the WorkChoices Act (2005) has 'delivered lower productivity growth than a period when centralized arbitration set wages, union membership was double what it is now, tariffs and quotas protected local industry from competition, some key enterprises were government-owned and the computer revolution was the stuff of science fiction' (pp. 63–64).

In this context, Blaug's (1985) argument that the primary function of state schooling has more to do with socializing students to 'co-operate in carrying out the tasks of the employing enterprise' than producing a high-skilled work force is persuasive (p. 55). According to Blaug (1985), schools serve the function of socializing, screening and segmenting the labor force in the interests of capitalist social relations (p. 8; Bowles & Gintis, 1976). In his view, screening through educational qualifications is 'economically efficient not because 'good' students are always 'good' workers but because educational credentialism avoids the inherent conflict of interests between workers and employers' (p. 5). As a consequence, education faces the contradictory function of reproducing the social relations of capitalism and at the same time, satisfying the democratic demands for equality of opportunity (Carnoy & Levin, 1985; Shapiro, 1982; Offe, 1981). On the one hand, schools are responsible for developing workers with appropriate cognitive skills for existing jobs; inculcating appropriate behaviors, habits and values; socializing and certifying children according to class, gender and race; and promoting an ideology that portrays capitalism as the embodiment of individual liberty and democracy. On the other hand, schools are responsible for producing citizens who know and care about democratic rights and equality of opportunity (Carnoy & Levin, 1985, p. 146).

There is no question that education has a role to play in equipping students with the capabilities to survive in a complex technological society and finding meaningful work. However, the often repeated argument that secondary schools are to blame for the present economic and social crisis because they do not teach the appropriate skills to enable students to 'get a job' is misleading. The simple fact is that the process of re-structuring and de-skilling of the labor force results in more not less unskilled, repetitive, boring and poorly paid jobs (Carlson, 1999, p. 17). Efforts by employers and governments to promote students' work skills and preparedness for the world of work may simply raise expectations and/or credentials, especially for the 15-20% who are most disadvantaged. Commenting on the British experience, Furlong and Cartmel (2001) argue that the government's heavy reliance on the rhetoric of the knowledge economy and skill training programs simply serves to 'perpetuate a false assumption about a one-on-one relationship between being qualified and being employed' (p. 69).

Kincheloe (1999) summarizes well the problems arising from a narrowly conceived human capital approach to VET in Schools when he argues:

> ... no one has produced convincing evidence of where skilled jobs in the twenty-first century are going to be found. Contrary to the corporate implication that a better educated workforce will keep employers from exporting jobs, factories will continue to be lost. When these factors are combined with increasing job loss from automation, the skilled-job future grows even more dismal. Government officials and vocational educators do not want to deal with this problem. How do we tell the workers of the future that they are being misled? (p. 362)

## DECONSTRUCTING JOB HIERARCHIES

Jack, another highly effective and engaging teacher in Bountiful Bay, shared with his colleagues a view that his students were not academically inclined and therefore, required a more practical and job orientated education. Typically, this involved students in work related experiences and the early selection of career pathways and specializations in their areas of interest. As one Deputy Principal explained to us, 'we only have a small cohort of TEE [Tertiary Entrance Examination] students—20 out of 86 year 12s'. She indicated that many 'bright students chose other pathways, partly because of the workload stress of TEE, but also because failure in TEE could leave students with few career choices'. For many of these students, according to one Deputy Principal, 'TAFE [Technical and Further Education] is seen as a viable option but university is too far away'. Another Deputy Principal spoke about the culture of the district and home background of kids not being conducive to tertiary aspirations. In the main, 'kids want a job and parents look to school to prepare them for work—hence the emphasis on VET courses'. It was not surprising to hear one industry representative argue that schools must 'adjust their programs to the demands of industry'. In her view, TEE students 'are at a disadvantage when it comes to apprenticeships because they have not had the workplace experience'. This seemed to be a strong motivating factor for many students and their parents as they searched for an advantage in a competitive job market. From the point of view of students, the possibility of spending one day in industry, one at TAFE and 3 days at school was far better than full-time school. For them, school was clearly at the bottom of the pecking order in regards to their learning. In the words of one student, 'The maths course could be improved—it's too easy and needs to be more relevant to the workplace. They throw you a book but they don't go through it with you'. This student wanted to engage in a rigorous and relevant curriculum but only in the context of his work. Unfortunately, only a few students were deemed capable of doing academic work while the rest seemed destined to focus on the manual skills relevant to the job at hand.

Despite the overwhelming press for VET in Schools programs, many students, teachers and principals expressed concern about maintaining a balance between the academic and vocational curriculum. One principal noted that while he had a 'very strong VET in Schools program, in some ways that works as a disadvantage—the parents see this as not providing for university entrance'. Many teachers commented on the impact of the drift of academic students away from public schools to private schools or as one teacher put it 'private schools cream off the 'smart kids''. At a staff meeting, another teacher suggested 'that perhaps the long term goal of the school is to put a spanner in the hands rather than to offer TEE … we have to do something for the better kids'. Another teacher indicated that 'We have had to limit the number of TEE subjects … more of our resources now go into non-TEE courses. This is far more equitable'. In these schools, academic TEE pathways were no longer perceived to be the core business of the school and as a result, struggled for survival. One explanation offered was that students tend to overestimate their ability and as a consequence do not cope with the TEE as illustrated by one teacher who said 'we've all seen students who think they are going to university—don't get in—and then don't have a backup plan—and then they can't get into TAFE either'.

These stories provide some important insights into the dilemmas and contradictions facing schools, teachers, parents and students with regard to the hierarchy of school knowledge and its relationship to the job market. Clearly there is something going on here in terms of 'advantaging and disadvantaging' different classes of students and their families (Angus, 2006, p. 61; Gillborn & Youdell, 2000; Ball, 2006d; Anyon, 2005). Almost thirty years ago, Apple (1979) attempted to explain these larger cultural processes:

> I want to argue that the problem of educational knowledge, of what is taught in schools, has to be considered as a form of the larger distribution of goods and services in a society. It is not merely an analytic problem (what shall be construed as knowledge?) nor simply a technical one (how do we organize and store knowledge so that children may have access to it and 'master' it?), nor, finally, is it a purely psychological problem (how do we get students to learn?). Rather, the study of educational knowledge is a study in ideology, the investigation of what is considered legitimate knowledge … by specific social groups and classes, in specific institutions, at specific historical moments. (p. 45)

## CHAPTER 5

Historically, schooling in Australia has served different classes of students in different ways. Prior to the Second World War, secondary schooling was the right of the wealthy and a few selected and deserving children from the working class. The private church schools established a market in educating the sons and daughters of the Australian colonies elite. Then, with the rapid expansion of secondary schooling in the first two decades of the twentieth century, the Roman Catholic Church opened schools for the poorer and humbler classes. However, it wasn't long before they too, established select and superior fee-paying schools for the wealthier and upwardly mobile Catholics (Ely, 1978, pp. 43–45). It was only after the Second World War that comprehensive state high schools were introduced to cater for all students irrespective of their backgrounds. With the rapid expansion of universal state secondary schooling in the 1950s and 1960s, McCallum (1990) argues that 'selection by differentiation replaced selection by exclusion' (p. 98). As more students entered secondary schooling, it was necessary to find other mechanisms of social selection and differentiation, this time under the guise of intelligence, mental testing and meritocracy (Down, 2001).

With the psychological capture of education, individual merit and ability soon became the basis for allocating children into different school classes and courses of study (McCallum, 1990, p. 74). Intelligence testing became a way of life for all children transferring from primary into secondary school. The emergence of the vocational guidance movement assumed that a hierarchy of natural ability determined who got what jobs, if any. The assumption was that only a limited number of students were capable of doing a limited number of well-paid jobs (Miller, 1986, p. 5). School Guidance Officers with their barrage of intelligence tests, personality inventories and aptitude tests were able to convince children and their parents that it was nature and not the economic system that determined their future work and class location. The result of all this scientific effort was to reinforce some strongly entrenched views of educational inequality. In other words, children of the rich were probably brighter than working class children and definitely smarter than Indigenous and migrant children (Down, 2001, p. 17). The power of the vocational guidance movement was not so much its capacity to impose a particular world view on the individual but to establish consent to these social arrangements from within (Gramsci, 1971).

In this context, Furlong and Cartmel (2001) argue that as individuals are made more accountable for their 'labor market fates' (p. 28) young people from advantaged backgrounds have been 'relatively successful in protecting privileged access to the most desirable routes' (p. 34). This means that 'middle-class children … are increasingly placed in schools with a 'name', while working-class children are left in schools with inferior resources which rapidly become ghettoized' (p. 19). Likewise, Lipman (2004) argues that 'School accountability policies that discipline, sort, and teach students they are responsible for their own failure serve as a powerful form of ideological preparation for integration into a stratified and compliant workforce' (p. 136). In her view, 'We should not underestimate the centrality of education policy to labor discipline in a global economy that demands an uninterrupted flow of low-wage labor' (p. 137).

As Ball (2006e) explains, there has been a 'collapse of the social and economic fields of education into a single, over-riding emphasis on policy-making for economic competitiveness' (p. 131). According to Brown and Lauder (1997) this market approach to schooling fosters the mentality of the 'survival of the fittest', based on parental choice and competition (p. 176). Underpinning this world view is the assumption that choice, competition and accountability will raise standards and consumers (students and parents) will pick schools, subjects and courses where there is demand for labor, thus addressing the problem of skill shortages (p. 177). Bourdieu (1998) views this as a new kind of neo-Darwinism where it is 'the 'brightest and best' who come out on top' and this can be explained by a 'philosophy of competence according to which it is the most competent who govern and have jobs, which implies that those who do not have jobs are not competent. There are 'winners' and 'losers'' (p. 42).

Of particular concern, is the way in which public high schools in disadvantaged communities are being constructed 'as a residual place of last resort for those unable to exercise choice or flight to private schooling' (Smyth, 2005, p. 225; Hiatt, 2007, p. 1). As one teacher explained to us, 'other schools have taken all our kids—with Howard's [The former Prime Minister of Australia] push it has done enormous damage—we'll end up a residual school—you'll only go to a government school when you can't afford anything else'. In short, schooling has become 'inextricably mired in the capitalist relations of the market economy and capitalist labor market' (Willis, 2004, p. 193). This leads to a narrowing of the curriculum in terms of knowledge and skills (competencies) relevant to the work place, greater curriculum differentiation, course specialization, and ultimately, a highly stratified education system that is geared to the short term interests of a hierarchical labor market (Teese, 2000; Teese & Polesel, 2003; Lipman, 2004). Evidence is now mounting that these kinds of narrowly conceived and instrumentalist policy responses are producing significant 'collateral damage' (Nichols & Berliner, 2007) not only to the way young people are (mis)treated (Grossberg, 2005) but (mis)educated (Meier, 2002).

As Giroux (2001) observes, young people today are increasingly 'being framed as a generation of suspects' (p. 31). By pathologizing and individualizing issues of academic performance and student behavior the focus shifts from the broader sociological aspects of society, in particular the 'predatory culture' that contributes to the problems confronting young people (McLaren, 1995). As a consequence, students and their families are constrained within the 'parameters of political possibility and acceptability' (Ball, 2006f, p. 39). The challenge ahead is to understand how 'schooling creates and perpetuates images of children in ways that are destructive, in ways that predispose some children to be successful, confident, and engaged, and others to become lower achievers, timid, or aggressive, reluctant, and disengaged' (Shields, Bishop & Mazawi, 2005, p. 1). Hudak (2001) believes that the labeling of students becomes 'toxic' when it demonstrates 'a moment of exploitation where one's ontological vocation—being fully human—is hindered' (p. 14).

CHAPTER 5

For this reason, Brantlinger (2003) argues that the practice of segregating children from poor and working-class backgrounds from the mainstream and referring to them in 'disparaging epithets' (p. 11) inflicts 'symbolic violence (humiliation, alienation, and rejection) on those labeled and educated in the lower echelons of stratified schools' (p. 12). Kincheloe (1995) adds that 'young people no longer look to the school or to work as venues in which the creative spirit can be developed' (p. 124). In his view, there is a crisis of motivation as evidenced by a malaise—low quality work, absenteeism, sullen hostility, waste, alcohol and drug abuse (p. 124) and cognitive illness created by a loss of meaning and purpose in education (p. 125). According to Shor (1992), 'playing dumb' and 'getting by' are two acts of student resistance to a school culture 'that ignores their language, interest, conditions, and participation' and 'makes their subjectivity invisible' (p. 138).

The problem, according to Bernstein (1996), is that because there is 'an unequal distribution of images, knowledges, possibilities and resources' in schools, there will be a corresponding affect on 'the rights of participation, inclusion and individual enhancement of groups of students' (p .xxii). Bernstein (1996) provides some insights into these cultural processes:

> A school metaphorically holds up a mirror in which an image is reflected. There may be several images, positive and negative. A school's ideology may be seen as a construction in a mirror through which images are reflected. The question is: who recognizes themselves as of value? What other images are excluded by the dominant image of value so that some students are unable to recognize themselves? In the same way, we can ask about the acoustic of the school? Whose voice is heard? Who is speaking? Who is hailed by this voice? For whom is it familiar? (p. xxi)

Vocational guidance has played a key role in shaping students' identities by helping them to choose the 'right' subjects to match their abilities, interests and backgrounds (Wexler, 1992). The emphasis is on getting to know students in order to better manage their expectations. As one teacher explained, this kind of career guidance involves 'a lot more tracking of kids' performances ... the school is looking for hard data'. On this basis, schools are seen as places that reward individual abilities, interests and effort rather than a person's social position, despite evidence to the contrary (Brantlinger, 2003; Devine, 2004). Harris (1982) elaborates on how this notion of meritocracy works in schools:

> In more fleshed-out form, it claims that children differ in general mental ability or intellectual merit, that the relevant differences can be measured by standardized tests or cognitive or mental ability, and that the demands of school work increase in direct proportion to this particular merit such that the more able one is the longer one can stay on at school mastering increasingly difficult and more demanding content. It is then taken to follow that this intellectual merit is a reliable indicator of a person's productive value, and that schooling thus fairly and properly selects the more able people for the

more intellectually demanding jobs: jobs which in turn bring with them high social status, economic and other privileges, and increased life chance along many dimensions. The end result of this merit, as measured by school performance, tends to become indicative of personal merit in a far wider sense, such that a large range of opportunities open up for those who have demonstrated particular capabilities at school. (p. 106)

Such views fail to acknowledge that social hierarchies are already structured into society. Therefore, schools must be seen to be fair, impartial and independent of external power relations between competing social groups (Brantlinger, 2003, p. 2). The only way that schools can legitimately justify school failure is through 'inborn facilities both cognitive and affective or to cultural deficits relayed by the family' (Bernstein, 1996, p. xxiv). This is where Bourdieu's (1971) understanding of cultural capital helps us to explain:

... the unequal scholastic achievement of children originating from the different social classes by relating academic success, i.e., the specific profits which children from the different classes and class fractions can obtain in the academic market, to the distribution of cultural capital between the classes and class fractions. This starting point implies a break with the presuppositions inherent both in the commonsense view, which sees academic success or failure as an effect of natural aptitudes, and in human capital theories. (p. 47)

In the case of vocational education and training, Welch (1996) argues that the options for students are limited to: (i) blame the student which leads to a focus on improving attitudes towards work, and a narrow vocationalism; (ii) educate for unemployment whereby young people must accept, or learn to cope with it; (iii) adjust content so that work related skills are enhanced, and pupils find out more about career prospects; and (iv) terminal programs for the lower streamed pupils, labeled as of poor academic ability (p. 65). Once identified, Kincheloe (1999) argues that students 'are initiated into the sixth circle of educational hell—the realm of the low achiever' (p. 258). Anyon's (1981) research on social class and its relation to curriculum and instruction demonstrates that working-class students are domesticated into the world of blue-collar labor, where passivity, conformity and following instructions are a part of the hidden curriculum. On the other hand, students from more affluent schools learn sophisticated analytical skills and develop personality traits of self-reliance, problem-solving, flexibility and leadership (Finn, 1999).

On these counts, Kincheloe (1999) summarizes some of the main criticisms of vocational education and training:

It has segregated poor and minority youth into a curriculum that reduces their access to high-skill, high-status, high-pay careers. Such segregation creates the impression that vocational education is a dumping ground for 'children other than mine';

CHAPTER 5

It teaches skills that are obsolete in a rapidly changing economy. By the time vocational education students get to the job market, the specific work skills they have learned are out of date;

Its instruction is narrow—so narrow that students who graduate are often unequipped for existing jobs. Vocational students do not have access to a curriculum that teachers them how to think;

It has failed to offer students an alternative to dropping out of school. At the same time, it has not enhanced the employability of a large segment of the youth population, especially the poor and nonwhite;

Its image revolves around a picture of students working with their hands but *not* their minds. The popular prejudice against manual jobs and the persistent reduction of such jobs to repetitive, deskilled labor has rubbed off on vocational education, making it a place where incompetent students can seek shelter;

It leads too often to nonprestigious jobs—bad work. (pp. 138–139)

These shortcomings run counter to the seductive rhetoric of the neoliberal promise of a high-tech and high-skilled future. In a climate where Australia's booming resource sector is driving unprecedented corporate profits, exorbitant salaries for Chief Executive Officers, and the lowest official unemployment figures in thirty years, the growing divide between 'winners' and 'losers' appear beside the point (Greig, Lewins & White, 2003; Vinson, 2007). Nationally, evidence consistently shows that working-class students have different educational experiences to their more affluent counterparts: only 59.2% of boys from unskilled or working class families complete Year 12, compared with 88.6% from professional backgrounds (Ainley, 1998, p. 55); for girls the figures are 69% and 95% respectively (p. 55); the proportion of young people from rural areas who complete Year 12 is 51% (p. 56); and 60.6% of Aboriginal and Torres Strait Islanders leave school before the age of 16 and fail to complete a secondary education (Smyth & Down, 2004, p. 57). Our contention is that the renewed emphasis on VET in Schools cannot be divorced from the dynamics of the broader shifts in the global economy as well as the cultural processes of advantaging and disadvantaging based on pre-existing social hierarchies of class, gender and race.

## RECLAIMING SYMBOLIC SPACES FOR MEANINGFUL WORK

Potential early school leavers, Mick and Johnny, were involved in designing and constructing a courtyard project under the direction of their teacher who has a special interest in horticulture and science. Both students talked about the transformation in their attitude to schooling when they were engaged in a community-based project that encouraged them to take greater responsibility for their own learning and enabled them to work as part of a team. Not only did they appreciate the hands-on approach to learning but they soon discovered the contextualized nature of their learning gave them a deeper understanding of mathematical concepts than their peers in the so-called smarter classes. The kind of learning promoted by their teacher gave them a reason for staying on at school and brightened their aspirations for the future. Johnny indicated that he felt more comfortable in the horticulture program. In his words, 'It's just not student and teacher it's like you have friends. You get a chance to work in groups and it's not as hard. You learn to communicate with other people whether you like them or not. We listen a lot of the time and input a lot of information into our heads'. Mick wanted to work 'In a trade—or some other type of job ... but I'm not sure at the moment ... I'm still thinking ... maybe an electrician or mechanic or something'. Asked about the perceptions of other students towards the project, Johnny commented 'At the start they thought we were the stupid class until they saw what we can produce now they don't think that we are so stupid'. Mick explained that he valued the opportunity to do something worthwhile 'The difference is in other classes you just get heaps and heaps of assignments but we get to do big projects. Maybe the teacher gets something out of me doing an assignment but I don't get anything out of it. When you have finished a project you are proud of it'.

Mick and Johnny are typical of many vocational education and training students in Bountiful Bay. They wanted to be involved in meaningful work and learning. Like Dewey (1916/1944) these students understood the importance of searching for meaning based on their own experience, knowledge, passions and interests. Dewey himself warned, that 'failure to bear in mind the difference in subject matter from the respective standpoint of teacher and student is responsible for most of the mistakes made in the use of texts and other expressions of pre-existent knowledge' (pp. 182–183). To do otherwise, Dewey (1916/1944) argued, 'is simply to abdicate the education function' (p. 73).

This story helps us to understand that education is not something 'done to students' (Shor, 1992, p. 20). Education should provide learning experiences that will: (i) challenge and extend students interests; (ii) emphasize group work rather than individualized learning; (iii) respect student knowledge and experience; (iv) engage students in learning that is socially worthwhile; (iv) provide opportunities to publicly demonstrate competence; and (v) prepare students for a life of meaningful work. According to Shor (1992), this is the only way 'to shake students out of their learned withdrawal from intellectual and civic life' (p. 20). In this task, Freire (1970/2000) offers some timely advice when he reminds us that the purpose of education is to affirm men and women 'as beings in the process of *becoming*— as unfinished, uncompleted beings in and with a likewise unfinished reality' (p. 78). For him, education is an ongoing process of personal and social transformation whereby people transcend themselves, move forward and look ahead, and 'for whom immobility represents a fatal threat, for whom looking at the past must only be a means of understanding more clearly what and who they are so that they can more wisely build the future' (p. 79). In short, education is about 'making kids powerful' (Smyth & Fasoli, 2007; Smyth & McInerney, 2007, p. 205).

This kind of empowering education confronts head on the current obsession with impoverished market driven approaches to education such as paper and pencil testing, standardization, rote memorization, vocationalization, streaming and 'back to basics' reforms advocated by neoconservative commentators (Donnelly, 2004). As Pinar (1995) argues 'We are what we know.' We are, however, also what we do not know' (p. 23). On this count, McMurtry (1998) warns about the dangers of closed value systems such as the global market because they 'are blind in principle to the harm they cause' (p. 23). Worse, he argues, the market value system 'cannot see past its own demands for ever more market activities of society, what is good for the market's expansion and control of civil life is assumed to be good for society' (p. 22). McMurtry (1998) elaborates:

> When we approach a value structure as global and as universally practiced as 'the market value system,' with an immense edifice of technical experts, government ministries, national and international banks, transnational corporations, and international trade regimes all promulgating and implementing its prescriptions, we are faced by an especially difficult value program to investigate and question. Still it is important to make the effort to do this investigation, this questioning. If a value system is simply presupposed and obeyed as the given structure of the world that all are made to accept and serve, it can become systematically destructive without our knowing there is a moral choice involved. (p. 10)

In the final section of this chapter, we attempt to address this shortcoming by mapping some alternative 'ways of seeing' (Tyack, 1976) the field of vocational education and training. For us, this means reclaiming the symbolic spaces for a more egalitarian and democratic society. Like Giroux (2004), we believe that educators must move beyond the 'limited story' of 'market fundamentalism' (p. xxii) in order to 'imagine otherwise' (p. 143). Central to this larger democratic project, is an attempt to form alliances in and across national boundaries 'in which matters of global justice, community, and solidarity provide a common symbolic space and multiple public spheres where norms are created, debated, and engaged as part of an attempt to develop a new political language, culture, and set of relations' (p. xxvi). In a similar vein, McMurtry (1998) adopts the notion of 'civil commons' or 'what people ensure together as a society to protect and further life, as distinct from money aggregates' (p. 24). He goes on to explain how a commitment to the ideal of the civil commons 'guarantees access of all to the goods required to safeguard and advance life-capacities' (p. 24).

Drawing on these broader democratic aspirations, we want to now pursue the implications for re-imagining a more activist and socially critical approach to vocational education and training in schools. In the space available, we will briefly allude to three sets of ideas that might assist teachers in framing a more democratically inspired vision and practice: (i) developing an understanding of good versus bad work; (ii) breaking down the artificial division between academic and manual education; and (iii) fostering a commitment to the values of critical citizenship, democracy and social justice.

## DEVELOPING AN UNDERSTANDING OF GOOD VERSUS BAD WORK

In schools today, you will hear little discussion about the changing nature of work. The assumption in most vocational education and training programs is that students must simply be prepared for jobs, no matter what kind, if any, or how rewarding. If we are going to create a truly democratic society where students are able to construct their individual and collective identities as future workers and future citizens then there is an urgent need to critically examine the changing nature of work, in particular what it means to be engaged in meaningful work. In light of the current neoliberal assault on workers' rights, wages and conditions as outlined earlier, this task becomes even more urgent (Peetz, 2006).

Here we draw on Kincheloe's (1995; 1999) well articulated vision of a critical democratic approach to vocational education and training in schools. At the heart of his writing is a desire to connect democracy, work and education in ways that will produce socially just futures for all citizens. For Kincheloe (1999), this involves building an 'ethical basis on which social, educational, and, contrary to the prevailing sentiments, economic institutions are constructed' (p. 64). In contrast to narrowly conceived skills training approaches, he urges teachers and students to become critically aware of the complexities of the modern workplace, in particular an understanding of good versus bad work.

This approach engages students in the task of separating 'the concept of work from the notion of a job in that a job is simply a way of making a living while work involves a sense of completion and fulfillment' (Kincheloe, 1999, p. 66). From this perspective, students and teachers together set out to investigate questions such as: What constitutes good work? Socially beneficial work? Just work? Fulfilling work? Democratic work? (p. 64). These questions we believe can provide a foundation for building an ethical and socially just alternative to vocational education and training. In mapping this broader democratic vision of vocational education and training, Kincheloe (1999, pp. 64–75) identifies a number of characteristics of good versus bad work. By way of summary:

In comprehending the nature of good work, Kincheloe (1999) advocates the benefits of critical constructivism (Kincheloe, 1995). Underpinning this approach to vocational education and training is the constructivist learning theories of educational writers such as John Dewey, Jermone Bruner, and Lev Vygotsky. For them, knowledge is socially constructed and developed by individuals in context. Put simply, constructivist learning theories assert that learners must actively construct or generate knowledge and meaning from experience. Rather than treating students as depositories for storing content which is often divorced from reality (Freire, 1970/2000), teachers and students begin to explore their own worlds, produce knowledge, generate meaning and engage in social action. Such views challenge traditional conceptions of the curriculum about what students need to know, what they might want to know, how they might learn from their own experience, and what benefits their learning might bring. Significantly though, what makes this kind of pedagogy critical, according to Kincheloe (1995), is the emphasis on helping students to develop a critical consciousness, that is:

# CHAPTER 5

*Table 5.1: Good Work Versus Bad Work*

| Good Work | Bad Work |
| --- | --- |
| The principle of self-direction: good work as a labor of risk. | Social Darwinism: workers must operate under the law of the jungle. Those who succeed at work are the fittest. |
| The principle of the job as place of learning: work as a research laboratory. | Nature as enemy: One of the most basic of human struggles involves man versus nature. |
| The principle of work variety: freedom from repetitive boredom. | Science as fact provider: Positivism covertly shapes the nature of the workplace. |
| The principle of workplace cooperation: overcoming the fractured social relations of the workplace. | Efficiency as maximum productivity: worshipping the bottom line. |
| The principle of individual work as a contribution to social welfare. | The supremacy of systems-efficiency and cost-benefit analysis models, or the effectiveness of standardized inputs in the quest for agreed-upon outputs. |
| The principle of work as expression of self: workers as more than a sum of their behaviors. | People-proof jobs: designing work so that no matter how dumb a worker might be, the job can still be done. |
| The principle of work as a democratic expression: freedom from the tyranny of authoritarian power. | Short-term goals; the absence of ethical vision. |
| The principle of workers as participants in the operation of an enterprise: until workers are participants, talk of workplace cooperation rings hollow. | The contingency of human happiness and human motivation on the acquisition of better consumer items: the first commandment of modernism is Thou Shalt Consume. |
| The principle that play is a virtue that must be incorporated into work: play principles as path to freedom and fairness. | |
| The principle of better pay for workers in relation to the growing disparity between managers and workers. | |

... an ability to step back from the world as we are accustomed to perceiving it and to see the ways our perception is constructed through linguistic codes, cultural signs, and embedded power. Such an ability constitutes a giant step in learning to think, in gaining deeper levels of understanding. Critical constructivism is a theoretically grounded form of world making. We ask penetrating questions. How did that which has come to be, come to be? Whose interests do particular institutional arrangements serve? How did the status hierarchy in the world of work develop? (pp. 183–184)

## INTEGRATING THE VOCATIONAL AND ACADEMIC CURRICULUM

We argued earlier that current approaches to vocational education and training are premised on the assumption that schools should develop a practical and job orientated curriculum for 'non academic' students because of their perceived intellectual inferiority. Throughout this book we have attempted to distance ourselves from these kinds of deficit and pathologizing views of students, families and communities (Shields, Bishop & Mazawi, 2005). Instead, we acknowledge like Bessant (1989) that the vocationally orientated curriculum has been historically used to restrict the numbers of students climbing the educational ladder previously preserved for the wealthier classes, on the grounds that 'the masses would 'lower standards', threaten 'excellence' and impede the progress of the academic elite' (p. 70). As Blackmore (1992) contends, vocational education and training in schools is really about who is taught what curriculum, how and by whom.

We believe the integration of academic and vocational education provides an important first step in dismantling social hierarchies of class, knowledge and power (Lawton, 1997; Apple, 1998). We share Kincheloe's (1995) view that the current divide between academic and non-academic students serves no useful purpose other than perpetuating social divisions based on class, race and gender. Furthermore, it damages the majority of students who no longer look to the school or work as venues in which the creative spirit can be developed (p. 124). Kincheloe (1995) goes on to argue that integration can create situations where students can learn to use material and conceptual tools in authentic activities. In this way, students and teachers come to 'appreciate the use of academic skill in real life context; at the same time, they understand the vocational activity at a level that activates their creativity' (p. 254).

Kincheloe (1995) believes that vocational education approached in this manner is not only more respectful of the intellectual and creative potential of all learners but recognizes that crafts and trades involve higher orders of intellect. Importantly, he states that such an approach refuses 'to validate the common assumption within the culture of formal education that the theoretical ways of knowing of the academic disciplines are innately superior to the practical ways of knowing of the vocations' (p. 270). Thinking about the integration of vocational education and training and academic learning opens up possibilities for building a new democratic vision and practice. This kind of orientation becomes interested in the following kinds of questions: What knowledge is of most worth? How is it organized and for what reason? What are the assumptions about students abilities and capacities? How did it get this way? Who benefits? Who loses? What are the obstacles to integration? How might integration work? What kinds of conditions need to be created? How should workplace experience and expertise be incorporated?

We shall briefly allude to one example in America where teachers have grappled with the separation of the academic and vocational divide successfully. Rosenstock and Steinberg (2007), respectively Director and Academic Coordinator of the Rindge School of Technical Arts in Cambridge, Massachusetts, describe how they attempted to move beyond the traditional dualism of vocational and academic studies. At the center of their efforts was the CityWorks program whereby students work on individual and group projects, bringing aspects of their community into the classroom by creating numerous artifacts of Cambridge: maps, photographs, tapes, oral histories, and three-dimensional models. (p. 111). Rosenstock and Steinberg (2007) outline the main features that make this program unusual:

> CityWorks combines key characteristics of vocational programs—a project approach, apprentice-master relationships, and real clients—with the broader content and essential skills of academic education;
>
> CityWorks is taught in a space—studio—designed for collaborative project work. Students have the flexibility to group, team up, or borrow tools and materials as the project requires; and
>
> Community representatives are invited to help create a context for student's efforts. Staff members from city agencies and programs identify unmet community needs that students could address and also serve as an authentic audience for students' finished products and presentations. (pp. 111–112)

Rosenstock and Steinberg (2007) go on to explain the importance of seeing teachers as 'thinkers as well as doers' when undertaking this kind of innovation (p. 115). In fostering a professional learning culture they adopted a number of strategies such as: common planning time; including 'outsiders'; and creating genuine independence (pp. 116–117). Furthermore, there was a focus on democratizing relations between teachers and students, doing away with streaming and insisting on a high expectation for all students. The intent of City Works was 'to counter the reduction of education to job training ... and to broaden the creative intellectual work for all students' (p. 123).

Rosenstock adopted these same principles in establishing High Tech High, in San Diego, California. In this new school the first emphasis was to 'engage students in work worth doing, and then to 'reverse engineer' that work back into standards, SAT requirements, and those elements expected by the world outside of the school' (Rosenstock & Steinberg, 2007, p. 125). This approach fundamentally inverts the traditional high school model in order to develop a student centered, relevant and rigorous curriculum. Rosenstock and Steinberg (2007) argue that High Tech High and similar schools are now at the forefront of the small schools movement across America (Meier, 2002).

## FOSTERING CRITICAL CITIZENSHIP, DEMOCRACY AND SOCIAL JUSTICE

Helen and Elizabeth are two teachers who work as a team with a group of year 11 students enrolled in a Community Services program in Bountiful Bay. Helen says that 'the girls have made a choice to do the course and they want to come to classes. We make things relevant and develop skills that people can use in their lives. The work is hands-on and varied. Within negotiated limits, kids can work at their own pace'. 'We teach differently in here', she exclaims. 'We have considerable flexibility with the timetable and can use the time as we see fit. Most students will complete a TAFE accredited Certificate 3 course (taught by the school) by the end of year 12. Students voted with their feet and we now have a strong presence in the middle school. Topics for study are quite broad, e.g. Who am I?, which looks at their identity and place in the world. Students are involved in family research and have done some investigative work in the genealogical record'.

Helen and Elizabeth explain the extensive nature of community links in this course. Students have an ongoing association with a nearby special school where students work with severely disabled children, and a local aged care home where they were involved in a garden make-over. They have also spent time getting to understand the nature of the work in a day care center and a youth refuge which some girls have actually used themselves. Some girls work in a local primary school supporting student's literacy and getting to know more about teaching methods, curriculum and reporting.

Students talked openly about positive aspects of the Community Services course and their relationships with their teachers. One girl stated 'I like this course because you get a certificate out of it—for jobs this is important. The teachers keep you motivated and they push you along. I've worked in respite care and a hospital for disabled children. I feel a sense of pride in what I've accomplished at school. My mother is very proud of me. My parents have high expectations. They were a bit shocked about me working with disabled kids but I've learned a lot about autism, Down Syndrome and other disabilities from the year 4 kids at the special school'.

Another student commented 'I'm enjoying this course a lot. I've had work experience in a hospital and a nursing home. I think I'd like to be a nurse. You can do that through TAFE or university. My friends out of school keep me motivated with my studies. They tell me to stay on at school and complete my courses … not to leave early like some of them did. My teachers help me a lot and give me a lot of one-on-one counseling'.

The Community Services program is a good example of how teachers can effectively combine the role of schools in 'developing forms of critical citizenship, while at the same time, helping students gain the knowledge and skills needed to participate in the social relations of the economy' (Simon, Dippo & Schenke, 1991, p. 6). Helen and Elizabeth's approach incorporates the student's personal experience of work in the community to not only deepen their own self-awareness and sense of civic mindedness but to appreciate the nature of meaningful work.

Significantly, the Community Services program highlights how a more democratic approach to education can open up a range of alternative questions to guide curriculum planning e.g., How might schools use community assets and resources? What kinds of community partnerships and networks are desirable? How is the curriculum negotiated with students? How are students' lives and experiences acknowledged? What resources are required? How might students demonstrate their learning?

Simon, Dippo and Schenke (1991) argue that work education programs like this one should encourage students to: (i) question taken-for-granted assumptions about work; (ii) comprehend workplaces as sites where identities are produced; (iii) see this production as a struggle over competing claims to truth and to correctness; and (iv) envisage ways in which the quality of their working lives can be improved (p. 15). For Shor (1992), this means inviting students 'to make their education, to examine critically their experience and social conditions, and to consider acting in society from the knowledge they gain' (p. 188). Classroom practitioners such as Bigelow, et al., (2006) argue that this more empowering education is grounded in: the lives of our students; critical; multicultural; anti-racist; pro-justice; participatory; experiential; hopeful, visionary; activist; academically rigorous; and culturally and linguistically sensitive (p. 2).

Specifically, this kind of empowering education seeks to make sense of the changing nature of work, structural unemployment, trade unions, power relations, health and safety, child labor, industrial legislation, and wages and conditions (Simon, Dippo & Schenke, 1991). Aronowitz (cited in Brosio, 1994, p. 240) argues that these issues are typically marginalized in the school curriculum because of the effectiveness of capital and mass culture in colonizing the public and social spaces available to ordinary citizens for purposes of reading, talking, analysis and exchange (p. 240). Under a sustained period of neoliberalism there has been a 'manufacture of consent' (Chomsky, 1999, p. 10) leading to a depoliticized citizenry marked by apathy and cynicism or what Macedo (1995) describes as 'literacy for stupidification' (p. 81).

Teachers like Helen and Elizabeth demonstrate how it is possible to break down some of the institutional barriers between students and schools by creating a homely and relaxed learning environment where students can speak honestly and openly about their lives and aspirations. Their course takes students into the community where they develop a great deal of knowledge and understanding about social structures, programs and primary care organizations such as schools, day care centers and hospitals. Obviously there is a strong vocational orientation to this learning but it does extend well beyond the acquisition of community service employment skills. Not only do these teachers feel a strong responsibility to hang in with these students but they have developed pedagogically engaging strategies that motivate students and encourage them to persist with their schooling. Individual counseling, explicit teaching, negotiated assessment deadlines, community-based learning and courses adapted to the school context all seem to play a role in keeping students switched on.

Ultimately, the purpose of a critical democratic vocational education and training is to enable students and teachers to not only better understand the world of work but to actively participate in creating alternative conceptions of their individual and collective futures. It means restoring 'schools as democratic public spheres' (Giroux 1997, p. 218) with its 'emphasis on social justice, respect for others, critical inquiry, equality, freedom, civic courage, and concern for the collective good' (Giroux, 2004, p. 102).

## CONCLUSION

With the demise of the social welfare state in the 1970s and the current dominance of the neoliberal agenda, schools are being refashioned around the narrowly conceived imperatives of global capitalism. The official rhetoric focuses on producing students with the knowledge and skills (competencies) relevant to the workplace, curriculum differentiation, specialization, standardization, high stakes paper and pencil testing, school choice, league tables, and accountability. In this chapter, we have argued that the renewed emphasis on VET in Schools cannot be divorced from the wider shifts in the global economy and the changing nature of the youth labor market, in particular the escalation of part-time, casualized, and marginal jobs in the service sector of the economy. As McMurtry (1998) explains, the global market is a 'monstrous system of value' because 'it subjugates and sacrifices ever more life to its demands—if not by destruction and consumption, then by instrumentalization or starvation of what does not serve it' (p. 390).

In this brave new world increasing numbers of young people in public schools are being streamed into vocational education and training programs based on deficit logics that serve to perpetuate their relative disadvantage compared to their middle class counterparts. We have attempted to provide a more 'troubling' perspective on these practices with a view not only to interrupting the dominant human capital discourses but mapping an alternative vision and practice founded on the principles and values of economic and political democracy, critical inquiry, civic engagement and 'educated hope' (Giroux, 2001, p. 125). In the words of Kincheloe (1995), 'Critical work educators want to turn out workers who appreciate the dynamics of the relationship between technological development and ecological concern, between economic growth and the basic material and spiritual needs of all citizens, between technological progress and the demand for knowledgeable citizens in a democratic society' (pp. 309–310). In short, a critical vocational education and training would have broad social meaning, take students experiences seriously, help them to give meaning to their lives, and enable them to envisage alternative conceptions of their individual and collective futures. We shall now turn to the final chapter where we will reassemble the emergent themes and ideas of this book around a heuristic of intersecting 'storylines', comprising—policy, pedagogy and research.

CHAPTER 6

# NEW STORYLINES ON SCHOOL/COMMUNITY RENEWAL

INTRODUCTION

A principal aim of this book has been to develop an activist and socially critical view of school/community renewal which privileges the voices, experiences, lives and aspirations of the people most affected. Our intent has been to open up spaces where those individuals and social groups most marginalized by official discourses and institutional practices can begin to assert their own 'self-direction and group solidarity by using the productive ability of power' (Kincheloe, 2007, p. 32). With a particular focus on disadvantaged communities in Australia, we have consciously set out to provide a more 'discomforting' and 'disruptive' (Kumashiro, 2004) interpretation of the 'profoundly destructive' (Fielding, 1999, p. 284) and anti-educative effects of the 'metallic language of the market' (p. 287) in order to create what Maxine Greene (1995) calls a new 'social imagination'. In her words, this involves 'a vision of what should be and what might be in our deficient society, on the streets where we live, in our schools' (p. 5). In pursuing this counter-hegemonic work we have attempted to bring issues of school reform and community renewal in disadvantaged settings into conversation with one another. We believe this approach offers a more sophisticated and powerful set of ideas and tactics to help guide the work of educational and community activists committed to creating a fairer and more just world. Accordingly, in the preceding chapters we have drawn attention to:
- how schools, young people and teachers transcend deficit narratives of disadvantage;
- how communities resist social construction and assumptions of subordination made for them by others and instead create more hopeful visions for themselves;
- how politically engaged educators contest the most damaging aspects of the school accountability movement in developing curriculum that is oriented to the needs and aspirations of students and local communities; and
- how as researchers we pursued an activist 'inquiry of discomfort' (Wolgemuth & Donohue, 2006) that assisted participants in dismantling the 'prisons of received identities and discourses of exclusion' (Best & Kellner, 1991, p. 57).

Our account has involved a critique of contemporary education policies and practices, especially those associated with neoliberal forms of governance which we believe have seriously eroded the democratic ideals of public schooling and led to greater inequalities in the educational landscape. We have also taken a critical look at schools and their complicity in reproducing socially unjust practices.

## CHAPTER 6

However, we have not been overly preoccupied with the kind of 'school pathology' (Wood 1992, xxii) that generates so many 'texts of despair' (Fine & Weis, 1998) on school reform. In the spirit of optimistic critical inquiry, we have focused on two Australian communities, Wirra Wagga and Bountiful Bay, where there is emerging evidence of democratic, community-oriented and socially-just forms of schooling that offer a greater sense of hope and possibility for those young people who have been placed at risk by an unjust economy and market-driven approaches to schooling.

Because the processes of education are inseparable from the day-to-day struggles of people's lives, schooling must necessarily engage in an overtly political manner with issues of oppression and social injustice if it is to make a difference for young people. We conclude our account with a synthesis of key ideas and insights emerging from our study in the realms of policy, pedagogy and research and by tracing what Mishler (1999) calls 'storylines'—that is to say, the way people reinvent themselves through school and community renewal by 'speak[ing] their identities' (p. 19) in activist and socially critical ways. In what follows we attempt to bring these evolving understandings together in a profile of an activist and socially critical view of school/community renewal as illustrated in Figure 6.1.

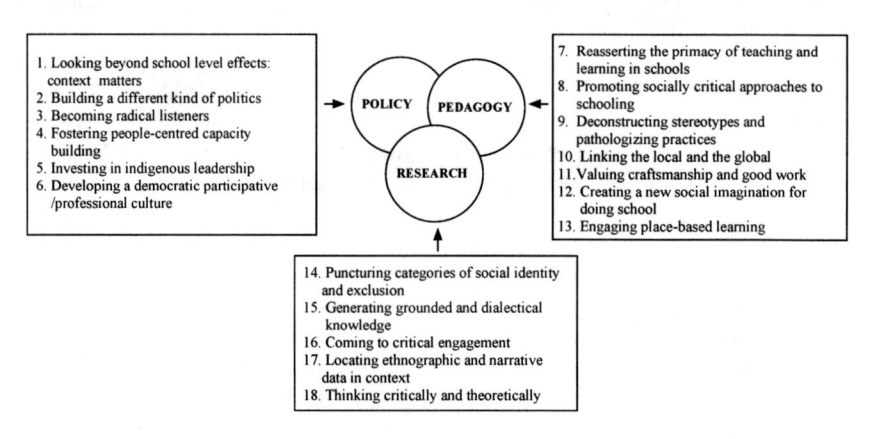

```
┌─────────────────────────────────┐                    ┌─────────────────────────────────────┐
│ 1. Looking beyond school level  │                    │ 7. Reasserting the primacy of       │
│    effects: context matters     │                    │    teaching and learning in schools │
│ 2. Building a different kind of │   ┌──────┐┌──────┐ │ 8. Promoting socially critical      │
│    politics                     │──▶│POLICY││PEDAGOGY│◀─│    approaches to schooling       │
│ 3. Becoming radical listeners   │   └──────┘└──────┘ │ 9. Deconstructing stereotypes and   │
│ 4. Fostering people-centred     │      ┌────────┐    │    pathologizing practices          │
│    capacity building            │      │RESEARCH│    │ 10. Linking the local and the global│
│ 5. Investing in indigenous      │      └────────┘    │ 11. Valuing craftsmanship and       │
│    leadership                   │                    │     good work                       │
│ 6. Developing a democratic      │                    │ 12. Creating a new social           │
│    participative /professional  │                    │     imagination for doing school    │
│    culture                      │                    │ 13. Engaging place-based learning   │
└─────────────────────────────────┘                    └─────────────────────────────────────┘
                                           ▲
                        ┌──────────────────┴──────────────────┐
                        │ 14. Puncturing categories of social │
                        │     identity and exclusion          │
                        │ 15. Generating grounded and         │
                        │     dialectical knowledge           │
                        │ 16. Coming to critical engagement   │
                        │ 17. Locating ethnographic and       │
                        │     narrative data in context       │
                        │ 18. Thinking critically and         │
                        │     theoretically                   │
                        └─────────────────────────────────────┘
```

*Figure 6.1: Activist and socially critical school/community renewal*

### RECLAIMING EDUCATIONAL POLICY: PURSUING A PEDAGOGY OF HOPE

One of the tasks we have undertaken in this book is to counter the myths, misconceptions and downright lies of the 'conservative assault' and 'new authoritarianism' (Giroux, 2005) on schooling. It is abundantly clear from research in Australia and elsewhere that neoliberal solutions to the so-called 'crisis in education' have failed spectacularly in their efforts to lift education standards, improve school retention and participation rates, ameliorate educational disadvantage, and improve the quality of teaching in schools. Reductions in government funding for public schools, together with the introduction of high stakes testing regimes, the widespread adoption of managerialist practices, and marketized approaches to schooling, have had a devastating impact on disadvantaged schools. As the principle of parental choice has taken hold in policy circles, we have witnessed the residualization of public education and a widening of the achievement gap between children from middle class and working class backgrounds.

We have been especially critical of the dominance of economic goals in formal schooling which have led to a much greater emphasis on vocational education and training at the expense of a more liberal education, especially in disadvantaged schools. This shift has not only failed to deliver on the promise of ensuring more rewarding jobs for young people but, as Wyn (2007) explains, it has reinforced the level of disadvantage experienced by students in low socioeconomic communities by narrowing their curriculum options, thereby restricting career and further education pathways. We have taken a strong stand against the school effectiveness movement arguing that a lack of a sociological perspective has led to a 'politics of blame' with much of the responsibility for school failure being attributed to individual, family and cultural deficits, and to deficiencies in schools. We roundly reject the arguments that the key to improving educational attainment can be reduced solely to a set of generic school-based, technical solutions.

There is little evidence that current policies have empowered local communities. Indeed, teachers, students, parents and community members—those with the greatest interest and involvement in schooling—have been largely sidelined from policy making that has staked so much of its credibility on the need for accountability. However, the authenticity of accountability in mandated reforms and high stakes testing is highly questionable. Discussing the situation in the United States, Wood (1992) highlights the folly of coercive and prescriptive solutions in the following words:

> How can we believe that a teacher who is told how to teach, what to teach, how long to teach it, and how to test it can be held genuinely accountable for the outcome? It's like telling a physician how to diagnose, what treatment must be given, when it is to be given, and then holding him/her responsible if the patient dies. (p. 252)

What we have proposed as an alternative to this impoverished view of education is a relational politics of school and community activism that places a premium on trust, respect and high regard for the knowledge and wisdom of teachers and community members. We are under no illusion as to the difficulty of contesting the prevailing paradigm of school improvement in the current political environment. However, as shown in our case studies, there are hospitable spaces within schools and communities where teachers, in concert with local residents, can modify, exploit or refashion centrally-determined policies to create more socially-just curriculum (McInerney, 2004). Affirming human agency is a vital dimension to our study. As Freire (1998, p. 72) points out so evocatively, 'the world is not finished

[but] is always in the process of becoming'; hence there always exists the possibility that social arrangements can be changed to serve more emancipatory ideals. Although schools have shown great resilience as institutions in the wake of 'business-minded prescriptions' (Cuban, 2004, p. 60), we believe that they are capable of transformation. Evidence of the 'multiple faces of agency' (Rodriguez, 2008) and social activism were revealed in the efforts of progressive education administrators and community leaders seeking to re-align schooling for disengaged youth in the Wirra Wagga neighborhood. It was apparent amongst those Bountiful Bay teachers who engaged young people in learning that promoted cooperation, civic responsibility and commitment to the welfare of the community. It emerged too in the socially-engaged learning initiated by students and the drive for more community-oriented schooling by parents.

Because of the multidimensional nature of disadvantage, we have argued most strongly that school reform and neighborhood renewal must proceed in tandem if we are to achieve significant improvements in the education of young people in low socioeconomic communities. The neoliberal state has failed these communities to such a degree that only a major investment in economic infrastructure and human services can reverse the damage wrought by the barbarism of global capitalism. However, we reject the idea that outside leverage is needed to lift these communities out of their despair, or that we need to implement a welfare model of reconstruction underpinned by notions of charity and paternalism. A new kind of politics is required that draws its inspiration from a capacity-building approach that affirms working class identity, acknowledges and builds on the social networks and funds of knowledge in communities, and creates a climate of opportunity for all citizens to contribute to community renewal.

Drawing on the experiences of Wirra Wagga and Bountiful Bay, we want to now briefly elaborate on six key elements of an activist and socially critical policy response to school/community renewal as indicated in Figure 6.1.

*1. Looking beyond 'school level effects': Context matters*

There is a continual focusing on the broader economic, social and political ideologies impacting on school life. Teachers and community activists are skeptical about the claims of 'school level effects' to resolve complex matters of educational disadvantage, social inequality and student performance. As Shor and Freire (1987, p. 94) point out, 'our economic system creates some human damage that cannot be repaired with our present resources, including the resources of liberating education'. Accordingly, there is a conscious effort to move beyond the 'black box' of the classroom to investigate 'the messy relationships between and among schools and the individuals, communities and society that surround and interact with them' (Warren, 2005, p. 167). In short, there is a preparedness and willingness to acknowledge that the problems of schooling for low-income communities are 'the result of unequal power relationships in our society' (p. 167).

## 2. Building 'a different kind of politics'

There is a strong commitment to building 'a different kind of politics' (Boyte with Gust, 2003) based on relational power and trust with a range of groups in schools and their communities around a common vision of how schooling can work for all, including those most marginalized and excluded. Instead of imposing authoritarian or paternalistic solutions on communities, the policy focus is on community organizing, solidarity and social action in the interests of the least advantaged (Alinsky, 1989a). In this 'new paradigm', school and community activists, rather than politicians or educational experts, 'own this trickle-up revolution' (Kincheloe, Slattery & Steinberg, 2000, p. 251). The emphasis is on 'building schools into the fabric of communities' (Schlechty, 2008, p. 553) and working with local residents for the betterment of the community.

## 3. Becoming 'radical listeners'

Outside agencies and experts acknowledge and work against their own ascribed and inscribed 'expert' status by continually challenging and working against their training and upbringing. Invoking Fiumara's (1990) notion of 'radical listeners', Giles (2001, p. 132) says being a radical listener involves outsiders becoming 'aware of the undertow dragging [them] towards benumbment' (Fiumara, 1990, p. 86). Radical listeners are people who cultivate a sense of how 'language enters [their] thinking through names, labels and scripts' as they develop reflective ways of seeing these as 'the enemy' 'drowning out and suffocating ... the words of others' (p. 133). Put another way, radical listeners are outsiders who work with the community, rather than speaking for the community or owning the community renewal process.

## 4. Fostering people-centered 'capacity building'

Efforts are made to foster three interrelated conditions of people-centered 'capacity building' (Eade, 1997): (i) a respect for the knowledge, language, class location, culture and experiences of communities of disadvantage; (ii) an understanding that 'awareness, learning, self esteem and the capacity for political action are mutually reinforcing' (Eade, 1997, p. 11); and (iii) a realization that people who are placed at disadvantage have the right and, more importantly, the capacity to challenge authoritative 'solutions' to their problems and supplant them with better alternatives. The task of re-making schools can only proceed by 'drawing on strengths and capacities in communities, rather than focusing obsessively on deficiencies and difficulties' (Ayers, 2004, p. 21). Importantly, says Ayers (2004) 'the people with the problems are also essential to creating the solutions' (p. 21).

CHAPTER 6

*5. Investing in indigenous leadership*

Allowing and enabling local people to own and develop leadership is pivotal to an activist school/community renewal approach. There is a strong commitment 'to engage and train leaders to take public action for the improvement of their communities' (Warren, 2005, p. 159)—where leadership training is taken to have a loose and generative rather than prescriptive meaning. What this means practically speaking is regarding community members as 'change agents' rather than 'clients'. The emphasis shifts from seeing children, families and their communities as problems to be fixed, towards an appreciation of their potential strengths and contributions.

*6. Developing a democratic participative/professional culture*

The development of a democratic participative/professional culture is given priority. Here, the needs of teachers, students and parents are seen as more important than the 'need' to be competitive within the educational marketplace or the demands of the technical/managerial elite. Professional judgment, reflective practice and critical scrutiny around social and educational issues, are encouraged with an emphasis on being answerable for community needs and to professional, educational values. A feature of these schools is that they 'create educational forums for members of the community in which the purposes and processes of education can be discussed, debated and deliberated' (Eisner, 2002, p. 583). Policy is developed through community consultation and only after a careful consideration of local context and research data.

REINVENTING PEDAGOGY: TOWARDS A CRITICAL PEDAGOGY OF SCHOOL/COMMUNITY ENGAGEMENT

In *Pedagogy of Freedom*, Freire (1998) claims that many educators have succumbed to the 'fatalistic philosophy of neoliberal politics' (p. 93), which brazenly asserts that we have no choice but to adapt to the new global market and prepare students to take their place in the corporate order. The concept of education as training is now so dominant that the liberal ideals of schooling in the United States have largely been evacuated from the curriculum (Freire, 1998). In many quarters, we are witnessing a return to a transmission model of teaching with an emphasis on instrumental learning and 'teaching to the test' as educators seek to meet the objectives of externally prescribed curricula that has little connection to the lives of young people. However, from our research in Wirra Wagga and Bountiful Bay we believe that there are teachers who have not surrendered their sense of agency and ideals to the tyranny of neoliberal reforms. There is a basis of hope for a humanizing education that is grounded in democratic ideals, respectful of the lives and aspirations of young people, and committed to working with communities to achieve a greater measure of socially just schooling.

Making education work for the powerless demands a critical pedagogy of school/community engagement that moves beyond the frontiers of the officially endorsed curriculum to encompass far more inclusive, community-oriented and socially relevant learning for young people. Many students experience schooling as something that is done to them, rather than something that is done for them. This is especially so for working class students who are on the receiving end of testing regimes, curriculum frameworks, behavior management codes and school policies that seem more intent on regulating their lives than expanding their educational horizons. All too often, the officially sanctioned curriculum lacks a sense of connection to their families, cultures and communities, and is indifferent to the inequalities confronting young people.

The pedagogy that we advocate begins with a questioning of the taken-for-granted assumptions about traditional schooling (Eisner, 2003, pp. 650–656), such as the merits of age grading, competitive assessment practices, reliance on test scores for determining what students have accomplished, sorting and streaming students into perceived ability groups, the division of knowledge into subject disciplines, and the idea that students learn only what they are taught in schools. It challenges the artificial distinctions between school and community, between adult learners and young people, between teaching and learning, between academic and non-academic studies. It raises crucial questions about the distribution of power and resources in schools, the abuse of authority and the values and beliefs that are legitimized in the school curriculum. A critical pedagogy rejects the idea of a 'one size fits' all approach to education and stresses the importance of teachers being open to the worlds of students (Freire, 1998) as the basis for dialogic learning and curriculum development. The educator's role in a critically engaged classroom is to arouse students' curiosity about their world, to introduce them to multiple perspectives and to encourage critically reflective practices. Problem-posing is valued over problem-solving. Importantly, education is linked to social change through the agency of local communities. The vision of a critical pedagogy of school/community engagement highlighted in Figure 6.1 includes the following features.

## 7. Reasserting the primacy of teaching and learning in schools

There is a strongly held conviction that issues of student engagement and educational disadvantage can only be addressed in a meaningful way by reclaiming and reasserting the primacy of teaching and learning in schools (Smyth, 2001). This accords special 'recognition of the important role of indigenous, traditional and culturally-based knowledges in schooling [as] a valuable resource for the learner' (Dei, 2003, p. 253). Rather than relying exclusively on standardized testing information, schools have their own methods of evaluating achievement for various cohorts of students and for satisfying their own quality assurance requirements. School leaders see themselves first and foremost as curriculum leaders, rather than managers, and they actively promote a culture of research and debate about teaching and learning within the school community. Leadership is more broadly distributed across the school and matters of equity and social justice are placed at the forefront of curriculum.

*8. Promoting socially critical approaches to schooling*

The school promotes the principles and values of critical pedagogy including problem-posing, situated, participatory, dialogic, multicultural and activist approaches to name a few (Shor, 1992, p. 17). This kind of education is committed to providing students, teachers and community activists with 'a new language of analysis—through which they can assume a critical distance from their familiar subject positions in order to engage in a cultural praxis better designed to further the project of social transformation' (McLaren, 1997, p. 37). These 'critical counter-cultural communities of practice' are interested in developing 'a critical and engaged citizenry with a democratic sensibility that critiques and acts against all forms of inequality' (Duncan-Andrade & Morrell, 2008, p. 11). A critical perspective encourages students to question the established order and work for the common good rather than self-interest. Viewed through a critical/transformative lens:

> the purpose of education is not so much preparatory ... but to take up, examine and work on the world as it presents itself to students (and teachers) here and now. A critical lens commits educators to take seriously a number of concerns: the democratic purposes of schooling; the inevitability of the political dimensions of education and teaching; the importance of dealing explicitly with issues of race, class, gender, and all embodiments of social difference as a concern for social justice ... From a critical perspective, engagement in learning and school life is a form of engagement with the world at large. (Vibert & Shields, 2003, p. 228)

*9. Deconstructing stereotypes and pathologizing practices*

The school and community are actively engaged in deconstructing stereotypes about the perceived deficits of children, families and communities from working class backgrounds. There is a deliberate effort to build a counter-narrative to the process of 'othering' by which a group or individual is marked as fundamentally different from what is perceived to be the normal or mainstream' (Dimitriadis, 2008, p. 1). Resisting images of the 'diminished self' (Ecclestone (2007), such as those contained in the notion of students at risk, involves 'shifting the paradigm' (Swadener, 1995, p. 33) and 'viewing all children as facing great challenges and yet 'at promise', and doing the hard curricular, structural, personal, and relational work required' to succeed in school (p. 42). It also involves a deliberate effort on the part of educators to value and utilize the multiple (yet often hidden) literacies that students bring to school, especially those associated with the home environment, the local community and popular culture. (Perry, 2006)

## 10. Linking the local and the global

Critically engaged communities assist students to develop an awareness of themselves as social agents, capable of acting upon and changing the world. According to Kincheloe and Steinberg (1998, p. 7), 'this ... requires that teachers and students contextualize what happens in the classroom in relation to power and social justice as well as in relation to real life experiences'. For example, a study of nuclear fission should involve students in a consideration of the risks associated with the use of nuclear energy and the environmental and human consequences of atomic warfare; or when students investigate the operations of the water cycle they should be encouraged to explore the ways in which human intervention can dramatically affect rainfall patterns and run-off. Just as importantly, as Bigelow and Peterson (2002) point out, students' own experiences of oppression, exploitation and injustice can become a point of entry into discussions about global issues, such as poverty, child labor, environmental threats and mass consumption.

## 11. Valuing craftsmanship and good work

The school moves beyond narrowly conceived and instrumentalist approaches to skills training and job readiness (Rosenstock & Steinberg, 2007). It consciously develops a curriculum that is not only more respectful of the intellectual and creative potential of all learners but recognizes that crafts and trades involve higher orders of intellect (Kincheloe, 1995). Pursuing the idea of craftsmanship, according to Sennett (2006), involves 'doing something well for its own sake. Self discipline and self-criticism adhere in all domains of craftsmanship; standards matter and the pursuit of quality ideally becomes an end in itself' (p. 104). To this end, a socially critical approach to vocational education and training seeks to help students understand the nature of good work, integrate practical and theoretical ways of knowing, and foster a spirit of critical citizenship, democracy and social justice.

## 12. Creating a new 'social imagination' for doing school

Rather than 'seeing schooling small', that is, a preoccupation with test scores, time on task, management procedures and accountability measures, the emphasis is on 'actual living persons' (Greene, 1995, p. 11). Schools and communities begin to articulate a new 'social imagination' based on an 'ethic of care and connecting to students' lives' (p. 12). This approach 'speaks to the existential heart of life—one that draws attention to our passions, attitudes, connections, concerns, and experienced responsibilities' (Noddings, 2005, p. 47; see Spring, 2007).

## 13. Engaging place-based learning

Place-based education 'aims to enlist teachers and students in the firsthand experience of local life and in the political process of understanding and shaping what happens there' (Gruenewald, 2003b, p. 620). '[P]laces teach us about how the world works and how our lives fit into the spaces we occupy. Further places make us: As occupants of particular places with particular attributes, our identity and our possibilities are shaped' (p. 621). The emphasis is on revitalizing face-to-face local communities, building relationships and restoring a spirit of 'public good' (Hutchinson, 2004). As Theobold (1997) says, 'commitment, allegiance and obligation must reenter conversations concerning the fate of places' (p. 120).

## REINVIGORATING RESEARCH: ADVANCING AN ACTIVIST AND SOCIALLY CRITICAL RESEARCH AGENDA AROUND SCHOOL/COMMUNITY RENEWAL

Within the positivist tradition of value-free objectivist science, a good deal of what currently passes as educational research is principally concerned with questions of efficiency, 'best practice' and 'what works' in schools and communities. Underpinning this 're-emergent scientism' is the preferred methodology of 'classical experimentalism' with its emphasis on causal models using independent and dependent variables ... in the context of randomized controlled experiments' (Denzin, Lincoln & Giardina, 2006, p. 772). Moreover, 'conservative regimes are enforcing evidence—or scientifically based, biomedical models of research ... born out of methodological fundamentalism' (p. 770). Denzin et al (2006) claim that these approaches are based on an incorrect assumption that they are 'more transparent and more objective' (p. 772). Critics such as Gordon, Smyth and Diehl (2008) put it bluntly when they say that the 'apparent "science" ... is not simple positivistic and reductionist, it is often nonexistent' (p. 23) and 'nothing short of a complete sham' (p. 42). We need to look no further than the abuse of evidence-based research under the Bush Administration. According to Denzin, et al (2006) 'a fact or piece of evidence is true if it meets three criteria: (a) it has the appearance of being factual; (b) it is patriotic; and (c) it supports a political action that advances the White House's far-right neoconservative agenda' (p. 775). They (2006) go on to provide a scathing assessment of positivist science because:

> It ignores the contexts of experience. It turns subjects into numbers. It turns social inquiry into the handmaiden of a technocratic, globalizing managerialism. It gives research a dirty name. And it offers false hopes for practitioners'. (p. 772)

What is largely missing from the 'scientific evidence-based' approach that characterizes so much of the school effectiveness movement is any rigorous analysis of the broader social, political and economic context of schooling, and the complex factors that contribute to educational disadvantage. Preoccupied as it is with narrow educational outcomes and psychologistic explanations of school failure, this kind of research takes little heed of the influences of the classed, gendered and radicalized experiences of young people on school participation and scholastic achievement. In response, we have pursued an activist and socially critical approach to research which is openly ideological in its commitment to exposing unequal power relations and in siding with the most oppressed groups and communities. In doing so, we draw on Freire's (2004) advice that in the process of 'speaking about reality as it is and denouncing it, also announces a better world' (p. 105). Putting it another way, as critical researchers we are not only interested in critiquing the fallout from neoliberalism but creating 'the power for positive, ethical, communitarian change' (Denzin, Lincoln & Giardina, 2006, p. 779).

Affirming the power of social activism, we align ourselves with a school of critical researchers seeking to reclaim human agency from the depths of misery that characterized the deterministic accounts of the early reproductionist theorists. Investigating the cultural politics of schools and communities has allowed us to expose the spaces and opportunities for resistance to the prevailing orthodoxies of school reform. It has led us places where there is a sense of optimism about the transformative possibilities of schooling. We are very mindful that this kind of critical intellectual work in the current neoconservative political and ideological climate is not without risk. Kincheloe and McLaren (2005) provide us with a timely reminder of why critical, interpretative qualitative research of the kind we advocate is so problematic in official policy and research circles:

> Operating in this way, an evolving criticality is always vulnerable to exclusion from the domain of approved modes of research. The forms of social change it supports always positions it in some places as an outsider, an awkward detective always interested in uncovering social structures, discourses, ideologies, and epistemologies that prop up both the status quo and a variety of forms of privilege. (p. 307)

So what kind of research do we do? Returning to Figure 6.1 we will briefly elaborate on five key elements that comprise a more 'politically and socially engaged' research agenda around school/community renewal (Ladson-Billings & Donnor, 2005, p. 292):

## *14. Puncturing categories of social identity and exclusion*

As critical researchers, we advocate an activist 'inquiry of discomfort' (Wolgemuth & Donohue, 2006) to assist participants in dismantling the 'prisons of received identities and discourses of exclusion' (Best & Kellner, 1991, p. 57). Like Fine and Weis (2005), we 'take very seriously the notion that categories [class, race, ethnicity, gender] become "real" inside institutional life, yielding dire political and economic consequences' (p. 67). As a counter, we have attempted to illuminate 'how individuals make sense of, resist, embrace and embody social categories, and, just as dramatically, how they situate "others", ... in relation to themselves' (p. 67). In short, an activist and socially critical approach to research is interested in puncturing the deficit and pathologizing constructions associated with class, race and gender, with a view to 'fighting for institutional reforms' (Foley & Valenzuela, 2005, p. 222).

CHAPTER 6

*15. Generating grounded and dialectical knowledge*

Drawing on Willis' (2004) call for research approaches with an 'ethnographic and theoretical sensibility' (Willis, 2004, p. 168), this study seeks to advance the importance of 'lived culture', 'worldly experiences' and 'practical sense making' (Willis & Trondman, 2000, p. 5). This research approach amounts to a process in which fieldwork data and theoretical aspects are in continual conversation with each other as they are 'conjoined to produce a concrete sense of the social as internally sprung and dialectically produced' (p. 6). The process of dialectic theory-building (Lather, 1986) 'is a heuristic device through which data constructed in context is used to clarify and reconstruct existing theory' (Smyth & Hattam, 2004, pp. 27–28). The aim is to gain a more 'intimate understanding of the views of the participants in order to better inform theoretical constructs' (p. 28).

*16. Coming to critical engagement*

In opposition to a 're-emergent scientism' with its positivist and so-called evidence-based epistemology and objectivity (Denzin, Lincoln & Giardina, 2006, p. 771), we advance the idea of 'coming to critical engagement' (Fear, Rosaen, Bawden & Foster-Fishman, 2006) as a way of breaking the debilitating cycle of socioeconomic disadvantage. Fear, et al., (2006) elaborate on how they came to understand critical engagement 'as opportunities to share our knowledge and learn with those who struggle for social justice; and to collaborate with them respectfully and responsibly for the purpose of improving life' (p. xiii). This kind of 'moral and ethical activist' (Ladson-Billings & Donnor, 2005, p. 292) research is 'imbued with social purpose and grounded in grassroots, popular organizing movements' (p. 296; see Horton & Freire, 1990; Smyth, 2009). Like Denzin, Lincoln & Giardina (2006) we are committed to building 'a collaborative, reciprocal, trusting, mutually accountable relationship with those studied' so that we might 'positively contribute to a politics of resistance, hope and freedom' (p. 776).

*17. Locating ethnographic and narrative data in context*

In the tradition of critical ethnography we acknowledge that 'analyses of public and private institutions, groups and lives, are lodged in relation to key social and economic structures' (Fine & Weis, 2005, p. 65). Researchers within the positivist tradition often go to great lengths to prevent their methodologies from being contaminated by the social ugliness of poverty, racism and sexism. They do so by appealing to the so-called apolitical, objective and value-free nature of their research. However, as Macedo in the Foreword to *Pedagogy of Indignation* points out, 'an empirical study will produce conclusions without truths if is disarticulated from the sociocultural reality within which the subjects of the study are situated' (Freire, 2004, p. xxii). How can we understand the reasons behind the poor performances of children in urban ghettos if we do not take account of the squalid conditions under which they live their lives? How can we make sense of the persistent gulf in educational achievements of indigenous and non-indigenous Australian students without an understanding of the history of exploitation, dispossession and violence that has caused so much damage to the culture and identity of Aboriginal peoples?

*18. Thinking critically and theoretically*

Following Ball's argument (2006a), we contend that social theory is important in the making of good research (p. 1). As he put it, 'social theory rather than being an indulgence or irrelevance to research [as proponents of evidence-based research suggest], plays a key role in forming and reforming key research questions, invigorating the interpretation of research, and ensuring reflexivity in relation to research practice and the social production of research' (p. 1). In pursuing this work, we draw on Kincheloe and McLaren's (2005) notion of 'evolving criticality' to help us search out 'new and interconnected ways of understanding power and oppression and the ways they shape everyday life and human experience' (p. 306). In their words, such approaches 'are always evolving, always encountering new ways to irritate dominant forms of power, to provide more evocative and compelling insights' (p. 306).

## WHAT CAN BE DONE?

Bringing about changes in disadvantaged school communities, where participation rates are historically low, requires a shift in the dominant policy paradigm beyond the notion of school effectiveness to one of school/community engagement. As Nixon, Walker and Baron (2002, p. 348) point out, the effectiveness of schools ultimately depends on the effectiveness of families, neighborhoods and civil society as a whole. Because the roots of educational inequality lie within the deeply ingrained injustices of the political economy and the cultural and political marginalization experienced by particular groups in society (Lipman, 2008), an expanded education paradigm (Anyon, 2005) is needed to bring about more enduring and substantial improvements in schooling for the most disadvantaged young people. If we really want to do something worthwhile for young adolescents, 'we should work to overcome the poverty and prejudice that relentlessly work against those students' chances of success inside school and for a decent life outside' (Beane & Lipka, 2006, p. 30).

Based on research into mixed-income policies in Chicago, Lipman (2008) claims that neoliberal solutions to the problems of affordable housing, education, and social services, are unlikely to reduce inequalities in poor urban communities because they are framed within a discourse of individual choice in the marketplace that fails to address the fundamental cause of poverty and unequal opportunities to learn. Building on Nancy Fraser's (1997) model of social justice, Lipman proposes a framework for just housing and education policy centered on economic redistribution, cultural recognition and parity of political representation. We suggest that these three areas for social action are essential components in an activist and socially critical agenda for school/community renewal.

*1. Redistribution*

An unjust economy and the policies through which it is attained create enormous barriers to educational success for many young people (Anyon, 2005). A politics of redistribution is therefore necessary to ensure that all people have access to decent housing, health and social services as a basic human entitlement. This can only be achieved by reforming public policy to generate sustainable employment opportunities, guarantee fair wage conditions and improve the physical and social infrastructure of urban communities (Anyon, 2005).

*2. Recognition*

The sources of injustice are not confined to the political economy. A politics of recognition is also needed to address the cultural oppression experienced by indigenous people, women, ethnic minorities, gay and lesbian people and those with disabilities. We have suggested that school can make a contribution to this goal through the provision of culturally relevant curricula and policies to ensure that all students are treated with respect and dignity.

*3. Political representation*

A socially-just approach to reconstructing schools and communities 'requires the full participation of those affected—public housing residents, families, community members and committed teachers' (Lipman, 2008, p. 130). We have given some insights into the ways in which greater parity of political representation was achieved in the Wirra Wagga neighborhood through an asset-based approach to community renewal, an investment in local leadership, building local skills to increase public participation, resident ownership of decision-making processes and a major emphasis on relationship building.

Education has a tradition of social justice activism that can be a powerful source for social change, especially when linked to broader movements for progressive change. Anyon (2005) makes the point that:

> education policy cannot remain closeted in school classrooms and educational bureaucracies. It must join the world of communities, families and students; it must advocate for them and emerge from their urgent realities. (Anyon, 2005, p. 199)

It is our hope that in sharing these storylines we have revealed some of the transformative possibilities, as well as the dilemmas and limitations, of pursuing an activist and socially critical response to school/community renewal in exploitive times.

# REFERENCES

Abbs, P. (2003). *Against the flow*. Routledge Falmer.
Adorno, T. (1994 [1974]). *Minima Moralia: Reflections from damaged life*. London: Verso.
Agger, B. (2004). *Speeding up fast capitalism: Internet culture, work, families, food, bodies*. Boulder, CO: Paradigm Publishers.
Ainley, J. (1998). School participation, retention and outcomes. In Dusseldorp Skills Forum (Ed.), *Australia's youth: Reality and risk* (pp. 51–65). Sydney: Dusseldorp Skills Forum.
Alexander, C., Ishikawa, S., & Silverstein, M., with Jacobson, M., Fiksdahl-King, I., & Angel, S. (1977). *Pattern language*. New York: Oxford University Press.
Alinsky, S. (1989a). *Reville for radicals* (Rev. ed.). New York: Vintage Books.
Alinsky, S. (1989b). *Rules for radicals: A pragmatic primer for realistic radicals*. New York: Vintage.
Anderson, G., & Herr, K. (Eds.). (2007). *Encyclopedia of activism and social justice*. Thousand Oaks, CA: SAGE Publishers.
Angus, L. (1986). Research traditions, ideology and critical ethnography. *Discourse, 7*(1), 61–77.
Angus, L. (1993). The sociology of school effectiveness. *British Journal of Sociology of Education, 14*(3), 333–345.
Angus, L. (1994). Educational organisation: Technical/managerial and participative/professional. *Discourse: The Australian Journal of Educational Studies, 14*(2), 30–44.
Angus, L. (2006). Transcending educational inequalities across multiple divides: Schools and communities building equitable literate futures. *Learning Communities: International Journal of Learning in Social Contexts, 3*, 40–64.
Angus, L. (2008). The politics of community renewal and educational reform: School improvement in areas of social disadvantage. In E. Samier (Ed.), *Political approaches to educational administration and leadership* (pp. 204–219). London & New York: Routledge.
Angus, L., Snyder, I., & Sutherland-Smith, W. (2004). ICT and educational (dis)advantage: Families, computers and contemporary social and educational inequalities. *British Journal of Sociology of Education, 25*(1), 3–18.
Anyon, J. (1981). Social class and school knowledge. *Curriculum Inquiry, 11*(1), 3–43.
Anyon, J. (1997). *Ghetto schooling: A political economy of urban educational reform*. New York: Teachers College Press.
Anyon, J. (2005). *Radical possibilities: Public policy, urban education and a new social movement*. New York: Routledge.
Appadurai, A. (2004). The capacity to aspire: Culture and the terms of recognition. In V. Rao & M. Walton (Eds.), *Culture and public action* (pp. 59–84). Stanford, CA: Stanford University Press with the World Bank.
Apple, M. (1979). *Ideology and curriculum*. Boston: Routledge & Kegan Paul.
Apple, M. (1996). Remembering capital: On the connections between french fries and education. *Journal of Curriculum Theorising, 11*(1), 113–128.
Apple, M. (1998). Work, power and curriculum reform: A response to Theodore Lewis's "vocational education as general education". *Curriculum Inquiry, 28*(3), 339–360.
Apple, M. (2001). *Educating the 'right' way: Markets, standards, god and inequality*. New York & London: RoutledgeFalmer.
Avila, M. (2006). *Transforming society by transforming academic culture*. Unpublished manuscript, Occidental College, Los Angeles, CA.
Avila, M. (2008). *How community organizing can build reciprocal academic civic engagement: Stories and voices from an evolving model at Occidental College*. Paper presented at the Conference Name|. Retrieved Access Date|. from URL|.

# REFERENCES

Avramidis, E., Bayliss, P., & Burden, R. (2002). Inclusion in action: An in-depth case study of an effective inclusive secondary school in the South-West of England. *International Journal of Inclusive Education, 6*(2), 143–163.

Ayers, W. (2004). *Teaching the personal and the political: Essays on hope and justice*. New York: Teachers College Press.

Bacchi, C. (2000). Policy as discourse: What does it mean? Where does it get us? *Discourse: Studies in the Cultural Politics of Education, 21*(1), 45–57.

Ball, S. (1995). Intellectuals or technicians? The urgent role of theory in educational studies. *British Journal of Educational Studies, 43*(3), 255–271.

Ball, S. (2006a). Symposium "educational research and the necessity of theory": Introduction. *Discourse: Studies in the Cultural Politics of Education, 27*(1), 1–2.

Ball, S. (2006b). The necessity and violence of theory. *Discourse: Studies in the Cultural Politics of Education, 27*(1), 3–10.

Ball, S. (2006c). Policy sociology and critical social research: A personal review of recent policy and policy research. In S. Ball (Ed.), *Education policy and social class: The selected works of Stephen J. Ball* (pp. 1–25). London: Routledge.

Ball, S. (2006d). *Education policy and social class: The selected works of Stephen J. Ball*. London: Routledge.

Ball, S. (2006e). Standards in education: Privatization, profit and values. In S. Ball (Ed.), *Education policy and social class: The selected works of Stephen J. Ball* (pp. 130–142). London: Routledge.

Ball, S. (2006f). Discipline and chaos: The new right and discourses of derision. In S. Ball (Ed.), *Education policy and social class: The selected works of Stephen J. Ball* (pp. 26–42). London: Routledge.

Bardsley, D. (2007). Education for all in a global era? The social justice of Australian secondary school education in a risk society. *Journal of Education Policy, 22*(5), 493–508.

Beane, J., & Lipka, R. (2006). Guess again: Will changing the grades save middle level education. *Educational Leadership, 63*(7), 26–30.

Belfield, C., & Levin, H. (Eds.). (2007). *The price we pay: Economic and social consequences of inadequate education*. Washington, DC: Brookings Institution Press.

Benson, J. (1977). Organizations: A dialectical view. *Administrative Science Quarterly, 22*(1), 1–21.

Berliner, D. (2006). Our impoverished view of educational research. *Teachers College Record, 108*(6), 949–995.

Berliner, D., & Biddle, B. (1995). *The manufactured crisis: Myths, fraud, and the attack on America's public schools*. Reading, MA: Addison-Wesley Publishing.

Bernstein, B. (1970). Education cannot compensate for society. *New Society, 26*(February), 344–347.

Bernstein, B. (1971). *Class, codes and control, volume 1: Theoretical studies towards a sociology of language*. London: Routledge and Kegan Paul.

Bernstein, B. (1996). *Pedagogy symbolic control and identity: Theory, research, critique*. Bristol, PA: Taylor & Francis.

Bernstein, R. (1978). *The restructuring of social and political theory*. Philadelphia: University of Pennsylvania Press.

Berry, K. (1998). Nurturing the imagination of resistance: Young adults as creators of knowledge. In J. Kincheloe & S. Steinberg (Eds.), *Unauthorized methods: Strategies for critical teaching* (pp. 43–55). New York & London: Routledge.

Bessant, J. (1989–1990). An historical perspective on the standards debate of the 1970s and 1980s. *Melbourne Studies in Education*, 63–70.

Best, S., & Kellner, D. (1991). *Postmodern theory: Critical interrogations*. London: Macmillan.

Bigelow, B. (2006). Getting to the heart of quality teaching. *Rethinking Schools, 20*(2), 6–8.

Bigelow, B., & Peterson, B. (2002). *Rethinking globalization: Teaching for social justice in an unjust world*. Milwaukee, WI: Rethinking Schools Press.

Bingham, C., & Sidorkin, M. (Eds.). (2004). *No education without relation*. New York: Peter Lang Publishing.

# REFERENCES

Blackmore, J. (1992). The gendering of skill and vocationalism in twentieth-century Australian education. *Journal of Education Policy, 7*(4), 351–377.

Blaug, M. (1985). Where are we now in the economics of education? *Economics of Education Review, 4*(1), 17–28.

Blum, J. (2000). Degradation without deskilling: Twenty-five years in the San Francisco shipyards. In M. Burawoy et al. (Eds.), *Global ethnography: Forces, connections, and imaginations in a postmodern world* (pp. 106–136). Berkeley: University of California Press.

Blumin, S. (1989). *The emergence of the middle class: Social experience in the American city*. Cambridge, UK: Cambridge University Press.

Bottery, M. (1992). *The ethics of educational management*. London: Cassell.

Bourdieu, P. (1971). Cultural reproduction and social reproduction. In J. Karabel & A. Halsey (Eds.), *Power and ideology in education* (pp. 487–511). New York: Oxford University Press.

Bourdieu, P. (1998). *Acts of resistance: Against the new myths of our time*. Oxford: Polity Press.

Bourdieu, P., & Passeron, J. (1977). *Reproduction in education, society and culture*. London: Sage Publications.

Bowe, R., Ball, S., & with Gold, A. (1992). *Reforming education and changing schools: Case studies in policy sociology*. London & New York: Routledge.

Bowles, S., & Gintis, H. (1976). *Schooling in capitalist America: Educational reform and the contradictions of economic life*. New York: Basic Books.

Boyte, H. (1984). *Community is possible: Repairing America's roots*. New York: Harper & Row.

Boyte, H. (2002, November 1). *A different kind of politics: John Dewey and the meaning of citizenship in the 21st century*. Paper presented at the Conference Name|. Retrieved Access Date|. from URL|.

Boyte, H. (2004). *Everyday politics: Reconnecting citizens and public life*. Philadelphia, PA: University of Pennsylvania Press.

Boyte, H., & with Gust, S. (2003). A different kind of politics. Interview with Susan Gust. Retrieved April 24, 2008, from www.publicwork.org

Brantlinger, E. (2003). *Dividing classes: How the middle class negotiates and rationalizes school advantage*. New York and London: Routledge Falmer.

Braverman, H. (1974). *Labor and monopoly capital: The degradation of work in the twentieth century*. New York: Monthly Review Press.

Broadhurst, K., Paton, H., & May-Chahal, C. (2005). Children missing from school systems: Exploring divergent patterns of disengagement in the narrative accounts of parents, carers, children and young people. *British Journal of Sociology of Education, 26*(1), 105–119.

Brookover, W., Beady, C., Flood, R., Schweitzer, J., & Wisenbaker, J. (1979). *School social systems and student achievement: Schools can make a difference*. New York: Praeger.

Brosio, R. (1994). *A radical democratic critique of capitalist education*. New York: Peter Lang.

Brown, P., & Lauder, H. (1997). Education, globalization and economic development. In A. Halsey, H. Lauder, P. Brown, & A. Wells (Eds.), *Education: Culture, economy and society* (pp. 172–192). Oxford & New York: Oxford University Press.

Carlson, D. (1999). The rules of the game: detracking and retracking the urban high school. In F. Yeo & B. Kanpol (Eds.), *From nihilism to possibility: Democratic transformations for the inner city* (pp. 15–35). New Jersey: Hampton Press.

Carnoy, M., & Levin, H. (1985). *Schooling and work in the democratic state*. Stanford, CA: Stanford University Press.

Cass, B., & Brennan, D. (2002). Communities of support or communities of surveillance and enforcement in welfare reform debates. *Australian Journal of Social Issues, 37*(3), 247–262.

Chambers, E., & Cowan, M. (2004). *Roots for radicals: Organizing for power, action and justice*. New York: Continuum.

Chapman, C. (2006). *Improving schools through external intervention*. London: Continuum.

Chetkovich, C., & Kunreuther, F. (2006). *From the ground up: Grassroots organizations making social change*. Ithaca: Cornell University Press.

# REFERENCES

Chomsky, N. (1999). *Profit over people: Neoliberalism and global order.* New York: Seven Stories Press.
Christensen, L., & Karp, S. (Eds.). (2003). *Rethinking school reform: Views from the classroom.* Milwaukee, WI: Rethinking Schools Press.
Cochran-Smith, M., & Lytle, S. (2006). Troubling images of teaching in No Child Left Behind. *Harvard Educational Review, 76*(4), 668–697.
Coffield, F. (2008). *Just suppose teaching and learning became the first priority.* London: Learning and Skills Network.
Coleman, J., Campbell, E., Hobson, C., McPartland, J., Mood, A., Weinfeld, F., et al. (1966). *Equality of educational opportunity.* Washington, DC: U.S. Government Printing Office.
Collin, R., & Apple, M. (2007). Schooling, literacies and biopolitics in the global age. *Discourse: Studies in the Cultural Politics of Education, 28*(4), 433–454.
Collins, R. (1981). *Sociology since mid-century.* New York: Basic Books.
Commission of Inquiry into Poverty. (1976). *Poverty and education in Australia. (The Fitzgerald Report).* Canberra: Australian Government Publishing Service.
Commonwealth of Australia. (1997). *Bringing them home: National inquiry into the separation of aboriginal and Torres Strait islander children from their families.* Sydney: Human Rights and Equal Opportunity Commission.
Compton-Lilly, C. (2004). *Confronting racism, poverty and power; Classroom strategies to change the world.* Portsmouth, NH: Heinemann.
Connell, B. (1993). *Schools and social justice.* Toronto: Our Schools/Our Selves Education Foundation.
Corson, D. (1998). *Changing education for diversity.* Buckingham: Open University Press.
Cortes, E. (1993). Reweaving the fabric: The iron rule and the IAF strategy for power and politics. In H. Cisneros (Ed.), *Interwoven destinies: Cities and the nation* (pp. 294–319). New York: W.W. Norton.
Cortes, E. (1995). Making the public the leaders in education reform. *Education Week, 15*(12), 34.
Cortes, E. (1997). Reweaving the social fabric. *Families in Society, 78*(2), 196–200.
Cox, E. (1995). *A truly civil society.* Sydney: Australian Broadcasting Corporation Books.
Crang, M., & Thrift, N. (Eds.). (2000). *Thinking space.* New York: Routledge.
Crittenden, B. (1988). Policy directions for Australian secondary schools: A critique of some prevalent assumptions. *Australian Journal of Education, 32*(3), 287–310.
Cuban, L. (2004). *The blackboard and the bottom line: Why schools can't be businesses.* Cambridge, MA: Harvard University Press.
Dahrendorf, R. (1979). *Life chances: Approaches to social and political theory.* Chicago: University of Chicago Press.
Darling-Hammond, L. (2007). The flat earth of education: How America's commitment to equity will determine our future. *Educational Researcher, 36*(6), 318–334.
Day, D. (2008). Disappeared. *The Monthly,* April, 70–72.
de los Reyes, E., & Gozemba, P. (Eds.). (2002). *Pockets of hope: How students and teachers change the world.* Westport, CT: Bergin & Garvey.
Dei, G. (2003). Schooling and the dilemma of youth disengagement. *McGill Journal of Education, 38*(2), 241–256.
Denzin, N., Lincoln, Y., & Giardina, M. (2006). Disciplining qualitative research. *International Journal of Qualitative Studies in Education, 19*(6), 769–782.
Devine, F. (2004). *Class practices: How parents help their children get good jobs.* Cambridge: Cambridge University Press.
Dewey, J. (1916). *Democracy and education.* New York: Macmillan.
Dimitriadis, G. (2008). *Studying urban youth culture primer.* New York: Peter Lang Publishing.
Dobozy, E. (2007). Effective learning of civic skills: Democratic schools succeed in nurturing the critical capacities of students. *Educational Studies, 33*(2), 115–128.
Donnelly, K. (2004). *Why our schools are failing?* Retrieved February 5, 2005, from http://www.mrcltd.org.au/

# REFERENCES

Down, B. (2000). State secondary schooling for all. *Education Research and Perspectives, 27*(1), 57–80.

Down, B. (2001). Educational science, mental testing, and the ideology of intelligence. *Melbourne Studies in Education, 42*(1), 1–23.

Duncan-Andrade, J., & Morrell, E. (2008). *The art of critical pedagogy*. New York: Peter Lang Publishing.

Dusseldorp Skills Forum. (2004). *How are young people faring 2004*. Sydney: Dusseldorp Skills Forum.

Dwyer, P., & Wyn, J. (2001). *Youth, education and risk: Facing the future*. London: RoutledgeFalmer.

Dyson, A., & Raffo, C. (2007). Education and disadvantage: The role of community-oriented schools. *Oxford Review of Education, 33*(3), 297–314.

Eade, D. (1997). *Capacity-building: An approach to people-centerd development*. Oxford: Oxfam.

Ecclestone, K. (2007). Resisting images of the 'diminished self': The implications of emotional well-being and emotional engagement in education policy. *Journal of Education Policy, 22*(4), 455–470.

Eisner, E. (2002). The kind of schools we need. *Phi Delta Kappan, 83*(8), 576–583.

Eisner, E. (2003). Questionable assumptions about schooling. *Phi Delta Kappan, 84*(9), 648–657.

Eisner, E. (2005). *Reimagining schooling: The selected works of Elliot W. Eisner*. London: Routledge.

Ely, J. (1978). *Reality and rhetoric: An alternative history of Australian education*. Sydney, NSW: Alternative Publishing Co-operative.

Evans, S., & Boyte, H. (1986). *Free spaces: The sources of democratic change in America*. Chicago & London: University of Chicago Press.

Fay, B. (1975). *Social theory and political practice*. London: Allen & Unwin.

Fear, F., Rosaen, C., Bawden, R., & Foster-Fishman, D. (2006). *Coming to critical engagement: An autoethnographic exploration*. Lanham, MD: University Press of America.

Feinstein, L., Duckworth, K., & Sabates, R. (2004). *A model for the inter-generational transmission of educational success* (Wider Benefits of Learning Research Report No. 10). London: Center for Research on the Wider Benefits of Learning.

Fielding, M. (1999). Target setting, policy pathology and student perspectives: Learning to labour in new times. *Cambridge Journal of Education, 29*(2), 277–287.

Fielding, M. (2006). Leadership, personalisation and high performance schooling: Naming the new totalitarianism. *School Leadership and Management, 26*(4), 347–369.

Fine, M. (1989). Silencing and nurturing voice in an improbable context: Urban adolescents in public school. In H. Giroux & P. McLaren (Eds.), *Critical pedagogy, the state and cultural struggle* (pp. 152–173). Albany, NY: State University of New York Press.

Fine, M., & Weis, L. (1998). Writing the 'wrongs' of fieldwork: Confronting our own research/writing dilemmas in urban ethnographies. In G. Shacklock & J. Smyth (Eds.), *Being reflexive in critical educational and social research* (pp. 13–35). London: Falmer Press.

Fine, M., & Weis, L. (2005). Compositional studies in two parts: Critical theorizing and analysis on social (in) justice. In N. Denzin & Y. Lincoln (Eds.), *The SAGE handbook of qualitative research* (3rd ed., pp. 65–84). Thousand Oaks, CA: SAGE.

Finn, P. (1999). *Literacy with an attitude: Educating working-class children in their own self-interests*. Albany, NY: SUNY Press.

Fitzgerald, T. (1976). *Poverty and education in Australia: Commission of inquiry into poverty, 5th Main Report*. Canberra: Australian Government Publishing Service.

Fiumara, G. (1990). *The other side of listening: A philosophy of listening*. London: Routledge.

Foley, D., & Valenzuela, A. (2005). Critical ethnography: The politics of collaboration. In N. Denzin & Y. Lincoln (Eds.), *The SAGE handbook of qualitative research* (pp. 217–234). Thousand Oaks, CA: SAGE.

Foster, W. (1983). *Loose coupling revisited: A critical review of Weick's contribution to educational administration*. Geelong: Deakin University Press.

Foucault, M. (1980). *Power/knowledge: Selected interviews and other writings 1972–1977*. New York: Pantheon.

# REFERENCES

Fraser, D., & Petch, J. (2007). *School improvement: A theory of action*. Melbourne: Office of School Education, Department of Education, Victoria.

Fraser, N. (1997). *Justice interruptus: Critical reflections on the "postsocialist" condition*. New York & London: Routledge.

Fraser, N., & Naples, N. (2004). To interpret the world and to change it: An interview with Nancy Fraser. *Signs: Journal of Women in Culture and Society, 29*, 1103–1124.

Freire, P. (1970). *Pedagogy of the oppressed*. Harmondsworth: Penguin.

Freire, P. (1998). *Pedagogy of freedom: Ethics, democracy, and civic courage*. Lanham, MD: Rowman & Littlefield.

Freire, P. (2004). *Pedagogy of indignation*. Boulder, CO: Paradigm Press.

Furlong, A., & Cartmel, F. (1997). *Young people and social change: Individualization and risk in late modernity*. Buckingham & Philadelphia: Open University Press.

Gale, T., & Densmore, K. (2003). *Engaging teachers: Towards a radical democratic agenda for schooling*. Maidenhead, UK: Open University Press.

Gallagher, M. (1979). The restructuring of the education system in Australia: Its relationship to the new international division of labor. *The Australian TAFE Teacher, 11*(3), 5–9.

Gecan, M. (2004). *Going public: An organizer's guide to citizen action*. New York: Anchor Books.

Giddens, A. (1982). Power, the dialectic of control and class structuration. In A. Giddens & G. McKenzie (Eds.), *Social class and the division of labor: Essays in honour of Ilya Neustadt*. London: Macmillan.

Giles, H. (2001). A word in hand: The scripted labeling of parents by schools. In G. Hudak & P. Kihn (Eds.), *Labeling: Pedagogy and politics* (pp. 127–146). London: RoutledgeFalmer.

Gillborn, D. (2006). Critical race theory and education: Racism and anti-racism in education theory and praxis. *Discourse: Studies in the culture politics of education, 27*(1), 11–32.

Gillborn, D., & Youdell, D. (2000). *Rationing education: Policy, practice, reform and equity*. Buckingham & Philadelphia: Open University Press.

Giroux, H. (1984). Rethinking the language of schooling. *Language Arts, 61*(1), 33–40.

Giroux, H. (1994). Doing cultural studies: Youth and the challenge of pedagogy. *Harvard Educational Review, 64*(3), 278–308.

Giroux, H. (1997). *Pedagogy and the politics of hope: Theory, culture and schooling*. Boulder, CO: Westview Press.

Giroux, H. (2001). *Public spaces, private lives: Beyond the culture of cynicism*. Lanham, MD: Rowman & Littlefield.

Giroux, H. (2004). *The terror of neoliberalism: Authoritarianism and the eclipse of democracy*. Boulder, CO: Paradigm Press.

Giroux, H. (2005). The conservative assault on America: Cultural politics, education and the new authoritarianism. *Cultural Politics, 1*(2), 139–164.

Goodman, J. (1992). *Elementary schooling for critical democracy*. Albany, NY: State University of New York Press.

Goodman, J., & Kuzmic, J. (1997). Bringing a progressive pedagogy to conventional schools: Theoretical and practical implications from harmony. *Theory into Practice, 36*(2), 79–86.

Gordon, L. (1985). Towards emancipation in citizenship education: The case of Afro-American cultural knowledge. *Theory and Research in Social Education, 12*(4), 1–23.

Gordon, S., Smyth, J., & Diehl, J. (2008). The Iraq war, "sound science" and "science-based" educational reform: How the Bush administration uses deception, manipulation and subterfuge to advance its chosen ideology. *Journal for Critical Education Policy Studies, 6*(1).

Gorski, P. (2008). Peddling poverty for a profit: Elements of oppression in Ruby Payne's framework. *Equity and Excellence in Education, 41*(1), 130–148.

Gramsci, A. (1971). *Selection from the prison notebooks*. New York: International Publishers.

Green, P. (2002). *Slices of life: Qualitative research snapshots*. Melbourne: RMIT University Press Publishing.

# REFERENCES

Greene, M. (1995). *Releasing the imagination: Essays on education, the arts, and social change.* San Francisco: Jossey-Bass.

Greig, A., Lewins, F., & White, K. (2003). *Inequality in Australia.* Port Melbourne, Victoria: Cambridge University Press.

Grossberg, L. (2005). *Caught in the crossfire: Kids, politics and America's future.* Boulder, CO: Paradigm Publishers.

Grubb, W., & Lazerson, M. (1975). Rally 'round the workplace: Continuities and fallacies in career education. *Harvard Education Review, 45*(4), 451–474.

Gruenewald, D. (2003a). The best of both worlds: a critical pedagogy of place. *Educational Researcher, 32*(4), 3–12.

Gruenewald, D. (2003b). Foundations of place: A multidisciplinary framework for place-conscious education. *American Educational Research Journal, 40*(3), 619–654.

Gulson, K. (2005). Renovating educational identities: Policy, space and urban renewal. *Journal of Education Policy, 20*(2), 141–158.

Gulson, K. (2008). Urban accommodations: Policy, education and a politics of place. *Journal of Education Policy, 23*(2), 153–163.

Haberman, M. (1991). The pedagogy of poverty versus good teaching. *Phi Delta Kappan, 73*(4), 290–294.

Hall, R., Buchanan, J., & Considine, G. (2002). *"You value what you pay for": Enhancing employers contributions to skill formation and use.* Unpublished manuscript, Dusseldorp Skills Forum, Sydney.

Hansard. (2008). *Kevin Rudd's apology to the stolen generation.* House of representatives Votes and Proceedings, Wednesday 13th February 2008. Canberra: Commonwealth of Australia.

Harris, A., James, S., Gunraj, J., & Clarke, P. (2006). *Improving schools in exceptionally challenging circumstances.* London: Continuum.

Harris, K. (1982). *Teachers and classes: A marxist analysis.* London: Routledge Kegan & Paul.

Hayes, D., & Chodkiewicz, A. (2005). Beyond the school fence: Supporting learning in the middle years. *Education Links, 69,* 11–16.

Hebson, G., Earnshaw, T., & Marchington, L. (2007). Too emotional to be capable? The changing nature of emotion work in definitions of 'capable teaching'. *Journal of Education Policy, 22*(6), 675–694.

Hiatt, B. (2007, August 18). State schools 'left only for the poor'. *The West Australian,* 1.

Hinchey, P. (2004). *Becoming a critical educator: Defining a classroom identity, designing a critical pedagogy.* New York: Peter Lang Publishing.

Hinkson, J. (2006). The sum of all fears. *Arena Magazine, 82*(April-May), 25–28.

Holdsworth, R. (2005). The tussle of community: Learning through community action. *Education Links, 69,* 6–11.

hooks, b. (1994). *Teaching to transgress: Education as the practice of freedom.* New York & London: Routledge.

Horton, M., & Freire, P. (1990). *We make the road by walking: Conversations on education and social change.* Philadelphia: Temple University Press.

Horwitt, S. (1989). *Let them call me a rebel: Saul Alinsky, his life and legacy.* New York: Knopf.

Hudak, G. (2001). On what is labelled 'playing': Locating the 'true' in education. In G. Hudak & P. Kihn (Eds.), *Labelling: Pedagogy and politics* (pp. 9–26). London: RoutledgeFalmer.

Hursh, D. (2007). Assessing No Child Left Behind and the rise of neoliberal education policies. *American Educational Research Journal, 44*(3), 493–518.

Hutchinson, J. (2004). Democracy needs strangers, and we are them. In C. Bingham & A. Sidorkin (Eds.), *No education without relation* (pp. 73–89). New York: Peter Lang Publishing.

Jencks, C., Smith, M., Ackland, H., Bane, M., Cohen, D., Grintlis, H., et al. (1972). *Inequality.* New York: Basic Books.

Kenway, J., & Bullen, E. (2001). *Consuming children: Education, entertainment, advertising.* Buckingham & Philadelphia: Open University Press.

# REFERENCES

Kincheloe, J. (1995). *Toil and trouble: Good work, smart workers, and the integration of academic and vocational education.* New York: Peter Lang Publishing.

Kincheloe, J. (1999). *How do we tell the workers: The socioeconomic foundations of work and vocational education.* Boulder, CO: Westview Press.

Kincheloe, J. (2001). *Getting beyond the facts: Teaching social studies/social sciences in the twenty-first century* (2nd ed.). New York: Peter Lang Publishing.

Kincheloe, J. (2003). *Teachers as researchers: Qualitative inquiry as a path to empowerment.* London & New York: RoutledgeFalmer.

Kincheloe, J. (2007). Critical pedagogy in the twenty-first century: Evolution for survival. In P. McLaren & J. Kincheloe (Eds.), *Critical pedagogy: Where are we now?* (pp. 9–42). New York: Peter Lang Publishing.

Kincheloe, J., & McLaren, P. (2005). Rethinking critical theory and qualitative research. In N. Denzin & Y. Lincoln (Eds.), *The SAGE handbook of qualitative research* (3rd ed., pp. 303–342). Thousand Oaks, CA: SAGE.

Kincheloe, J., Slattery, P., & Steinberg, S. (2000). *Contextualizing teaching: Introduction to education and educational foundations.* New York: Longman.

Kincheloe, J., & Steinberg, S. (Eds.). (1998). *Unauthorized methods: Strategies for critical teaching.* New York & London: Routledge.

Knights, D., & McCabe, D. (2000). 'Ain't misbehavin'? Opportunities for resistance under new forms of 'quality' management. *Sociology, 34*(3), 421–436.

Kozol, J. (1992). *Savage inequalities: Children in America's schools.* New York: Harper Perennial.

Kumashiro, K. (2004). *Against common sense: Teaching and learning toward social justice.* New York & London: Routlege/Falmer.

Ladson-Billings, G., & Donnor, J. (2005). The moral activist role of critical race theory scholarship. In N. Denzin & Y. Lincoln (Eds.), *The sage handbook of qualitative research* (3rd ed., pp. 279–301). Thousand Oaks, CA: Sage Publications.

Lareau, A. (2000). *Home advantage: Social class ad parental intervention in elementary education.* Lanham, MD: Rowman & Littlefield.

Lareau, A. (2003). *Unequal childhoods: Class, race and family life.* Berkeley, CA: University of California Press.

Lather, P. (1986). Research as praxis. *Harvard Educational Review, 56*(3), 257–277.

Lauder, H., Jamieson, I., & Wikeley, F. (1998). Models of effective schools: Limits and capabilities. In R. Slee, G. Weiner, & S. Tomlinson (Eds.), *School effectiveness for whom? Challenges to the school effectiveness and school improvement movements* (pp. 51–69). London: Falmer Press.

Law, J. (2003). *Making a mess with method.*

Law, J. (2004). *After method: Mess in social science research.* London: Routledge.

Lawrence-Lightfoot, S. (2003). *The essential conversation: What parents and teachers can learn from each other.* New York: Random House.

Lawton, D. (1997). What is worth learning? In R. Pring & G. Walford (Eds.), *Affirming the comprehensive ideal* (pp. 99–108). London: Routledge Falmer.

Lipman, P. (2004). *High stakes education: Inequality, globalization, and urban school reform.* New York: Routledge.

Lipman, P. (2008). Mixed income schools and housing: Advancing the neoliberal agenda. *Journal of Education Policy, 23*(2), 119–134.

Lipsky, M. (1980). *Street-level bureaucracy: Dilemmas of the individual in public service.* New York: Russell Sage foundation.

Lister, R. (2004). *Poverty.* Cambridge: Polity Press.

Lukacs, G. (1971). *History of class consciousness.* London: Merlin.

Macedo, D. (1995). Literacy for stupidification: The pedagogy of big lies. In C. Sleeter & P. McLaren (Eds.), *Multicultural education, critical pedagogy and the politics of difference* (pp. 71–104). Albany, NY: State University of New York Press.

Mackay, H. (2007). *Advance Australia where?* Sydney: Hachette Australia.

# REFERENCES

Mahony, P., Menter, I., & Hextall, I. (2004). The emotional impact of performance-related pay on teachers in England. *British Educational Research Journal, 30*(3), 435–456.

Martin, J. (1992). Critical thinking for a humane world. In S. Norris (Ed.), *The generalizability of critical thinking: Multiple perspectives on an educational ideal* (pp. 163–180). New York: Teachers College Press.

McCallum, D. (1990). *The social production of merit: Education, psychology and politics in Australia 1900–1950.* London & Philadelphia.

McDermott, K. (2007). "Expanding the moral community" or "blaming the victim"? The politics of state education accountability policy. *American Educational Research Journal, 44*(1), 77–111.

McInerney, P. (2004). *Making hope practical: School reform for social justice.* Flaxton, Queensland: Post Pressed.

McLaren, P. (1995). *Critical pedagogy and predatory culture: Oppositional politics in a postmodern era.* London & New York: Routledge.

McLaren, P. (1997). *Revolutionary multiculturalism: Pedagogies of dissent for the new millennium.* Boulder, CO: Westview Press.

McLaren, P., & Farahmandpur. (2005). *Teaching against global capitalism and the new imperialism: A critical pedagogy.* Lanham, MD: Rowman & Littlefield.

McMahon, B., & Portelli, J. (2004). Engagement for what? Beyond popular discourses of student engagement. *Leadership and Policy in Schools, 3*(1), 59–76.

McMurtry, J. (1998). *Unequal freedoms: The global market as an ethical system.* Toronto: Garamond Press.

McPeck, J. (1981). *Critical thinking and education.* New York: St. Martin's Press.

Meier, D. (2002). *In schools we trust: Creating communities of learning in an era of testing and standardization.* Boston: Beacon Press.

Melaville, A., Berg, A., & Blank, M. (2006). *Community-based learning: Engaging students for success and citizenship.* Washington, DC: Coalition for Community Schools.

Miller, P. (1986). *Long division: State schooling in South Australian society.* Adelaide: Wakefield Press.

Mills, C. (1970[1959]). *The sociological imagination.* Harmondsworth: Penguin.

Mills, D., Gibb, R., & with Willis, P. (2004). "Center" and periphery - An interview with Paul Willis. In N. Dolby & G. Dimitriadis, with P. Willis (Eds.), *Learning to labor in new times* (pp. 197–226). New York & London: Routledge Falmer.

Mishler, E. (1999). *Storylines: Craftartists' narratives of identity.* Cambridge, MA: Harvard University Press.

Morley, L., & Rassool, N. (2000). School effectiveness: New managerialism, quality and the Japanization of education. *Journal of Education Policy, 15*(2), 169–183.

Mortimore, P., Sammons, P., Stoll, L., Lewis, D., & Ecob, R. (1988). *School matters: The junior years.* Wells, Somerset: Open Books.

Muijs, D., Harris, A., Chapman, C., Stoll, L., & Russ, J. (2004). Improving schools in socio-economically disadvantaged areas—A review of research evidence. *School Effectiveness and School Improvement, 15*(2), 149–176.

Murphy, J. (1990). Review of David J. Smith and Sally Tomlinson, the school effect: A study of multi-racial comprehensives. *School Effectiveness and School Improvement, 1*(1), 81–86.

Nader, C. (2008, May 24). In search of a way to involve all. *The Age,* 6.

Nichols, S., & Berliner, D. (2007). *Collateral damage: How high stakes-testing corrupts America's schools.* Cambridge, MA: Harvard University Press.

Nixon, J., Walker, M., & Baron, S. (2002). The cultural mediation of state policy: The democratic potential of new community schooling in Scotland. *Journal of Education Policy, 17*(4), 407–421.

Noddings, N. (1996). On community. *Educational Theory, 46*(3), 245–267.

Noddings, N. (2005). *The challenge to care in schools: An alternative approach to education* (2nd ed.). New York: Teachers College Press.

# REFERENCES

O'Connor, A. (2001). *Poverty knowledge: Social science, social policy and the poor in twentieth century U.S. history*. Princeton, NJ: Princeton University Press.

Oakes, J., Rogers, J., & with Lipton, M. (2006). *Learning power: Organizing for education and justice*. New York: Teachers College Press.

Offe, C. (1981). Some contradictions of the modern welfare state. *Praxis International, 1*(3), 219–229.

Ohanian, S., & Kovacs, P. (2007). Make room at the table for teachers. *Phi Delta Kappan, 89*(4), 270–274.

Osterman, P. (2002). *Gathering power: The future of progressive politics in America*. Boston: Beacon Press.

Payne, R. (1998 [2005]). *Framework for understanding poverty*. Highlands, TX: Aha Process Inc.

Payne, R. (2002). *Hidden rules of class and work*. Highlands, TX: Aha Process Inc.

Peel, M. (2003). *The lowest rung: Voice of Australian poverty*. Melbourne: Cambridge University Press.

Peetz, D. (2006). *Brave new workplace: How individual contracts are changing our jobs*. Sydney: Allen & Unwin.

Perry, T. (2006). Multiple literacies and middle school students. *Theory into Practice, 45*(4), 328–336.

Pinar, W. (1995). The curriculum: What are the basics and are we teaching them?. In J. Kincheloe & S. Steinberg (Eds.), *Thirteen questions: Reframing education's conversations* (pp. 23–30). New York: Peter Lang Publishing.

Popkewitz, T. (1997). The production of reason and power: Curriculum history and intellectual traditions. *Journal of Curriculum Studies, 29*(2), 131–164.

Portelli, J., & McMahon, B. (2004). Why critical democratic engagement? *Journal of Maltese Education Research, 2*(2), 39–45.

Power, S., & Whitty, G. (1999). New labour's education policy: First, second or third way? *Journal of Education Policy, 14*(5), 535–546.

Rassool, N., & Morley, L. (2000). School effectiveness and the displacement of equity discourses in education. *Race, Ethnicity and Education, 3*(3), 237–258.

Reynolds, D., & Teddlie, C. (2001). Reflections on the critics, and beyond them. *School Effectiveness and School Improvement, 12*(1), 99–114.

Rodriguez, A. (Ed.). (2008). *The multiple faces of agency: Innovative strategies for effecting change in urban school contexts*. Rotterdam, The Netherlands: Sense Publishers.

Rosenstock, L., & Steinberg, A. (2007). Beyond the shop: Reinventing vocational education. In M. Apple & J. Beane (Eds.), *Democratic schools: Lessons in powerful education* (pp. 107–129). Portsmouth, NH: Heinemann.

Saltman, K. (2007). *Capitalizing on disaster: Taking and breaking schools*. Boulder, CO: Paradigm Press.

Sammons, P., Hillman, J., & Mortimore, P. (1995). *Key characteristics of effective schools: A review of school effectiveness research*. London: Office for Standards in Education.

Sanders, M. (1970). *The professional radical: Conversations with Saul Alinsky*. New York: Harper and Row.

Saul, R. (2005). *The collapse of globalism and the reinvention of the world*. Camberwell, Victoria: Penguin.

Schlechty, P. (2008). No community left behind. *Phi Delta Kappan, 89*(8), 552–559.

Schultz, J., & Oyler, C. (2006). We make this road as we walk together: Sharing teacher authority in a social action curriculum project. *Curriculum Inquiry, 36*(4), 423–451.

Schutz, A. (2008). Social class and social action: The middle-class bias of democratic theory in education. *Teachers College Record, 110*(2), 405–442.

Sennett, R. (2006). *The culture of the new capitalism*. New Haven, CT: Yale University Press.

Shapiro, H. (1982). Education in capitalist society: Toward a reconsideration of the state in educational policy. *Teachers College Record, 83*(4), 515–527.

Shields, C., Bishop, R., & Mazawi, A. (2005). *Pathologizing practices: The impact of deficit thinking on education*. New York: Peter Lang Publishing.

# REFERENCES

Shirley, D. (1997). *Community organizing for urban school reform.* Austin, TX: University of Texas Press.

Shirley, D. (2002). *Valley interfaith and school reform.* Austin, TX: University of Texas Press.

Shor, I. (1992). *Empowering education: Critical teaching for social change.* Chicago: University of Chicago Press.

Shor, I., & Freire, P. (1987). *Pedagogy for liberation: Dialogues on transforming education.* Westport, CT: Bergin and Garvey.

Shweder, R. (1986, September 21). Storytelling among anthropologists. *New York Times Book Review,* 1 & 38.

Sibley, D. (1995). *Geographies of exclusion: Society and difference in the west.* London & New York: Routledge.

Sidorkin, A. (2002). *Learning relations.* New York: Peter Lang.

Simon, R. (1983). But who will let you do it? Counter hegemonic possibilities for work education. *Journal of Education, 165*(3), 235–256.

Simon, R., Dippo, D., & Schenke, A. (1991). *Learning work: A critical pedagogy of work education.* New York: Bergin & Garvey.

Smith, G. (2002). Place-based education: Learning to be where we are. *Phi Delta Kappan, 83*(8), 584–595.

Smyth, J. (1991). *Higher educational policy reform in Australia in the context of the 'client state'.* Paper presented at the Annual Meeting of the Comparative and International Education Society, Pittsburgh, 14–17 March.

Smyth, J. (2001). *Critical politics of teachers' work: An Australian perspective.* New York: Peter Lang Publishing.

Smyth, J. (2005). Modernizing the Australian education workplace: A case of failure to deliver for teachers of young disadvantaged adolescents. *Educational Review, 57*(2), 221–233.

Smyth, J. (2006). Schools and communities put at a disadvantage: Relational power, resistance, boundary work and capacity building in educational identity formation. *Journal of Learning Communities: International Journal of Learning in Social Contexts, 3,* 7–39.

Smyth, J. (2007a). Teacher development against the policy reform grain: An argument for recapturing relationships in teaching and learning. *Teacher Development: An International Journal of Teachers' Professional Development, 11*(2), 221–236.

Smyth, J. (2007b). Toward the pedagogically engaged school: Listening to student voice as a positive response to disengagement and 'dropping out'. In D. Thiessen & A. Cook-Sather (Eds.), *International handbook of student experience of elementary and secondary school* (pp. 635–658). Dordrecht, The Netherlands: Springer Science Publishers.

Smyth, J. (2008). Listening to student voice in the democratisation of schooling. In E. Samier, & with G. Stanley (Eds.), *Political approaches to educational administration and leadership* (pp. 240–251). London & New York: Routledge.

Smyth, J. (2009). Critically engaged community capacity building and the 'community organizing' approach in disadvantaged contexts. *Critical Studies in Education, 50*(in press).

Smyth, J., & Angus, L. (2006). *Individual, institutional and community 'capacity building' in a cluster of disadvantaged schools and their community.* Canberra: Funded project proposal to the Australian Research Council, Discovery Grant Scheme.

Smyth, J., Angus, L., Down, B., & McInerney, P. (2006). Critical ethnography for school and community renewal around social class differences affecting learning. *Journal of Learning Communities: International Journal of Learning in Social Contexts, 3,* 121–152. Retrieved from http://www.cdu.edu.au/ehs/lrg/journal.html

Smyth, J., Angus, L., Down, B., & McInerney, P. (2008). *Critically engaged learning: Connecting to young lives.* New York: Peter Lang Publishing.

Smyth, J., & Dow, A. (1997). *What's wrong with outcomes? Spotter planes, action plans, and targeted groups at the margins of the educational landscape.* Occasional Paper, No. 11. Flinders Institute for the Study of Teaching, Flinders University, Adelaide.

# REFERENCES

Smyth, J., & Down, B. (2004). Beyond the divide: Individual, institutional and community capacity building in a western Australian regional context. *Education in Rural Australia, 14*(2), 54–68.

Smyth, J., & Down, B. (2005). *Enhancing school retention: School and community linkages in regional/rural Western Australia.* Canberra: Funded project proposal to the Australian Research Council, Linkage Grant Scheme.

Smyth, J., Down, B., & McInerney, P. (forthcoming). *'Hanging in with kids': Promoting student engagement in secondary schooling.*

Smyth, J., & Fasoli, L. (2007). Climbing over the rocks in the road to student engagement and learning in a challenging high school in Australia. *Educational Research, 49*(3), 273–295.

Smyth, J., Hattam, R., Cannon, J., Edwards, J., Wilson, N., & Wurst, S. (2000). *Listen to me, I'm leaving: Early school leaving in South Australian secondary schools.* Adelaide: Flinders Institute for the Study of Teaching; Department of Employment, Education and Training; and Senior Secondary Assessment Board of South Australia.

Smyth, J., Hattam, R., with Cannon, J., Edwards, J., Wilson, N., & Wurst, S. (2004). *'Dropping out', drifting off, being excluded: Becoming somebody without school.* New York: Peter Lang Publishing.

Smyth, J., & McInerney, P. (2007). *Teachers in the middle: Reclaiming the wasteland of the adolescent years of schooling.* New York: Peter Lang Publishing.

Sobel, D. (1996). *Beyond ecophobia: Reclaiming the heart in nature education.* Barrington, MA: The Orion Society and the Myrin Institute.

Speer, P., & Hughey, J. (1995). Community organizing: An ecological route to empowerment and power. *American Journal of Community Psychology, 23*(5), 729–748.

Speer, P., Ontkush, M., Schmitt, B., Raman, P., Jackson, C., Rengert, K., et al. (2003). The intentional exercise of power: Community organizing in Camden, New Jersey. *Journal of Community and Applied Social Psychology, 13*(5), 399–408.

Spring, J. (2007). *A new paradigm for global school systems.* Mahwah, NJ: Lawrence Erlbaum & Associates.

St Pierre, D. (2004). Refusing alternatives: A science of contestation. *Qualitative Inquiry, 10*(1), 130–139.

Stronach, I., & Piper, H. (2008). Can liberal education make a comeback? The case of 'relational touch' at Summerhill School. *American Educational Research Journal, 45*(1), 6–37.

Swadener, B. (1995). Children and families 'at promise': Deconstructing the discourse of risk. In B. Swadener & S. Lubeck (Eds.), *Children and families "at promise": Deconstructing the discourse of risk* (pp. 17–49). Albany: State University of New York Press.

Teddlie, C., & Reynolds, D. (2001). Countering the critics: Responses to recent criticisms of school effectiveness research. *School Effectiveness and School Improvement, 12*(1), 41–82.

Teddlie, C., Reynolds, D., & Sammons, P. (2000). The methodology and scientific properties of school effectiveness research. In C. Teddlie & D. Reynolds (Eds.), *International handbook of school effectiveness research* (pp. 55–133). London: Falmer Press.

Teese, R. (2000). *Academic success and social power: Examinations and inequality.* Melbourne: Melbourne University Press.

Teese, R. (2004). *Class war and the war on class: The two faces of neo-conservative research in the Australian media.* Paper presented at the Conference Name|. Retrieved Access Date|. from URL|.

Teese, R., & Polesel, J. (2003). *Undemocratic schooling: Equity and quality in mass secondary education in Australia.* Melbourne: Melbourne University Press.

Theobold, P. (1997). *Teaching the commons: Place, pride and the renewal of community.* Boulder, CO: Westview Press.

Thomson, P. (2002). *Schooling the rustbelt kids: Making the difference in changing times.* Crowsnest, NSW: Allen & Unwin.

Thomson, P. (2005). Who's afraid of Saul Alinsky? Radical traditions in community organizing. *Forum, 47*(1 & 2), 199–206.

Thomson, P. (2006). Miners, diggers, ferals and show-men: School-community projects that affirm and unsettle identities and place? *British Journal of Sociology of Education, 27*(1), 81–96.

# REFERENCES

Thrupp, M. (1998). Exploring the politics of blame: School inspection and its contestation in New Zealand and England. *Comparative Education, 34*(2), 195–209.

Thrupp, M. (1999). *Schools making a difference: Let's be realistic ! school mix, school effectiveness and the social limits of reform.* Buckingham: Open University Press.

Thrupp, M. (2003). The school leadership literature in managerialist times: Exploring the problem of textual apologism. *School Leadership & Management, 23*(2), 149–172.

Thrupp, M., & Willmott, R. (2003). *Educational management in managerialist times: Beyond the textual apologists.* Buckingham: Open University Press.

Tyack, D. (1976). Ways of seeing: An essay on the history of compulsory schooling. *Harvard Educational Review, 46*(3), 355–389.

Underhill, E. (2006). The role of employment agencies in structuring and regulating labor markets. In C. Arup, P. Graham, R. Howe, R. Johnstone, R. Mitchell, & A. O'Donnell (Eds.), *Labor law and labor market regulation* (pp. 282–304). Sydney: The Federation Press.

Valli, L., & Buese, D. (2007). The changing role of teachers in an era of high-stakes testing. *American Educational Research Journal, 44*(3), 519–558.

Vaughan, M., Brighouse, T., Neill, A. S., Readhead, Z., & Stronach, I. (2006). *Summerhill and A S Neill.* Maidenhead: Open University Press.

Vibert, A., & Shields, C. (2003). Approaches to student engagement; Does ideology matter? *McGill Journal of Education, 38*(2), 221–240.

Vinson, T. (2007). *Dropping off the edge: The distribution of disadvantage in Australia.* Richmond, VIC: Jesuit Social Services & Catholic Social Services Australia.

Wacquant, L. (1999). Urban marginality in the coming millennium. *Urban Studies, 36*(10), 1639–1647.

Warr, D. (2007). 'The stigma that goes with living here': Socio-spatial vulnerability in poor neighbourhoods. In J. McLeod & A. Allard (Eds.), *Learning from the margins: Young women, social exclusion and education* (pp. 6–19). London & New York: Routledge.

Warren, M. (2001). *Dry bones rattling: Community building to revitalize American democracy.* Princeton, NJ: Princeton University Press.

Warren, M. (2005). Communities and schools: A new view of urban school reform. *Harvard Educational Review, 75*(2), 133–173.

Warren, M., Thompson, J., & Saegert, S. (2001). The role of social capital in combating poverty. In S. Saegert, J. Thompson, & M. Warren (Eds.), *Social capital and poor communities* (pp. 1–28). New York: Russell Sage Foundation.

Warren, M., & Wood, R. (2001). *Faith-based community organizing: The state of the field.* Jericho, NY: Interfaith Funders.

Watkins, P. (1985). *Agency and structure: Dialectics in educational administration.* Geelong, Victoria: Deakin University Press.

Webb, P. (2005). The anatomy of accountability. *Journal of Educational Policy, 20*(2), 189–208.

Weiner, E. (2005). *Private learning, public needs: The neo-liberal assault on democratic education.* New York: Peter Lang Publishing.

Weis, L., & Fine, M. (2001). Extraordinary conversations in public schools. *International Journal of Qualitative Studies in Education, 14*(4), 497–523.

Welch, A. (1996). *Australian education: Reform or crisis.* St Leonards, NSW: Allen & Unwin.

Wexler, P. (1992). *Becoming somebody: Toward a social psychology of school.* London: Falmer Press.

Williams, M. (1989). *Neighborhood organizing for urban school reform.* New York: Teachers College Press.

Willis, P. (1977). *Learning to labor: How working class kids get working class jobs.* Westmead, England: Gower.

Willis, P. (2000). *The ethnographic imagination.* Cambridge: Polity Press.

Willis, P. (2004). Twenty-five years on: Old books, new times. In N. Dolby, G. Dimitriadis, & with P. Willis (Eds.), *Learning to labor in new times* (pp. 167–196). New York & London: RoutledgeFalmer.

Willis, P., & Trondman, M. (2000). Manifesto for ethnography. *Ethnography, 1*(1), 5–16.

# REFERENCES

Willmott, R. (1999). School effectiveness research: An ideological commitment? *Journal of Philosophy of Education, 33*(2), 253–268.

Wolgemuth, J., & Donohue, R. (2006). Toward an inquiry of discomfort: Guiding transformation in "emancipatory" narrative research. *Qualitative Inquiry, 12*(5), 1022–1039.

Wood, G. (1992). *Schools that work: America's most innovative public education programs.* New York: Dutton.

Worley, M. (2008, June 23). Student dropout rates top 50%. *The Mercury (Hobart)*.

Wrigley, T. (2004). 'School' effectiveness: The problem of reductionism. *British Educational Research Journal, 30*(2), 227–244.

Wyn, J. (2007). Learning to 'become somebody well': Challenges to educational policy. *Australian Educational Researcher, 34*(3), 35–52.

Wynhausen, E. (2007, June 9-10). Lives on hold in a casual affair. *The Australian*, 22.

Youdell, D. (2006). Diversity, inequality and a post-structural politics for education. *Discourse: Studies in the Cultural Politics of Education, 27*(1), 33–42.

# AUTHOR INDEX

## A

Abbs, P., 9
Adorno, T., 45
Agger, B., 107, 108
Ainley, J., 116
Alexander, C., 56
Alinsky, S., 14, 43, 53, 57–61, 73, 131
Anderson, G., 2, 3
Angus, L., 10, 11, 51, 67, 76, 78, 82, 86, 91, 96, 98, 99, 111
Anyon, J., 21, 40, 41, 78, 106, 107, 111, 139, 140
Appadurai, A., 1
Apple, M., 19, 22, 106–109, 111, 121
Aronowitz, S., 124
Avila, M., 59, 60
Avramidis, E., 86
Ayers, W., 131

## B

Bacchi, C., 47
Ball, S., 8, 9, 18, 88, 89, 98, 101, 111, 113, 139
Bardsley, D., 20
Baron, S., 139
Bawden, R., 138
Beane, J., 29, 139
Belfield, C., 1
Benson, J., 94, 95
Berg, A., 32
Berliner, D., 40, 107, 113
Bernstein, B., 77, 78, 114, 115
Bernstein, R., 87
Berry, K., 38
Bessant, J., 121
Best, S., 127, 137
Biddle, B., 107
Bigelow, B., 38, 124, 135
Bingham, C., 46
Bishop, R., 113, 121
Blackmore, J., 98, 121
Blank, M., 32
Blaug, M., 109
Blum, J., 107
Blumin, S., 48
Bottery, M., 98
Bourdieu, P., 78, 106, 113, 115
Bowe, R., 8, 98, 101

Bowles, S., 78, 109
Boyte, H., 14, 51, 52, 56–59, 62, 72, 73, 131
Brantlinger, E., 114, 115
Braverman, H., 107
Brennan, D., 4
Broadhurst, K., 20
Brookover, W., 76
Brosio, R., 124
Brown, P., 113
Bruner, J., 119
Buchanan, J., 109
Buese, D., 22
Bullen, E., 104

## C

Campbell, E., 107
Carlson, D., 110
Carnoy, M., 109
Cartmel, F., 106, 110, 112
Cass, B., 4
Chambers, E., 58
Chapman, C., 6, 91
Chetkovich, C., 56
Chodkiewicz, A., 25, 27
Chomsky, N., 124
Christensen, L., 26
Cochran-Smith, M., 79
Coffield, F., 14
Coleman, J., 76–78
Collin, R., 22
Collins, R., 78
Compton-Lilly, C., 25, 38
Connell, B., 104
Considine, G., 109
Corson, D., 25
Cortes, E., 58, 60
Cowan, M., 58
Cox, E., 39
Crang, M., 59
Crittenden, B., 105
Cuban, L., 130

## D

Dahrendorf, R., 93, 94
Darling-Hammond, L., 21, 22
Day, D., 45
Dei, G., 133

# AUTHOR INDEX

de los Reyes, E., 19, 20, 24, 26, 38, 41
Densmore, K., 24, 32
Denzin, N., 136–138
Devine, F., 114
Dewey, J., 51, 52, 117, 119
Diehl, J., 6, 136
Dimitriadis, G., 64, 134
Dippo, D., 123, 124
Dobozy, E., 38
Donnelly, K., 118
Donnor, J., 137, 138
Donohue, R., 127, 137
Down, B., 10, 11, 51, 67, 105, 106, 112, 116
Duncan-Andrade, J., 134
Dusseldorp Skills Forum 108, 109
Dwyer, P., 104, 108
Dyson, A., 39

## E

Eade, D., 6, 47, 131
Ecclestone, K., 24, 134
Eisner, E., 37, 132, 133
Ely, J., 112
Evans, S., 51

## F

Farahmandpur, 104, 106
Fasoli, L., 49, 117
Fay, B., 87
Fear, F., 138
Feinstein, L., 39
Fielding, M., 18, 20, 26, 127
Fine, M., 5, 128, 137, 138
Finn, P., 115
Fitzgerald, T., 105
Fiumara, G., 71, 131
Foley, D., 137
Foster, W., 95
Foster-Fishman, D., 138
Foucault, M., 80
Fraser, D., 82–84, 85
Fraser, N., 16, 139
Freire, P., 15, 19, 26, 42, 104, 117, 119, 129, 130, 132, 133, 136, 138
Furlong, A., 106, 110, 112

## G

Gale, T., 24, 32
Gallagher, M., 105
Gecan, M., 58
Giardina, M., 136–138
Gibb, R., 10
Giddens, A., 94

Giles, H., 71, 131
Gillborn, D., 9, 111
Gintis, H., 78, 109
Giroux, H., 26, 92, 104, 108, 113, 118, 125, 128
Gold, A., 8, 98
Goodman, J., 26, 36, 38
Gordon, L., 101
Gordon, S., 6, 136
Gorski, P., 66, 70
Gozemba, P., 19, 20, 24, 26, 38, 41, 42
Grace, G., 98
Gramsci, A., 112
Green, P., 11, 62
Greene, M., 127, 135
Greig, A., 105, 107, 116
Grossberg, L., 113
Grubb, W., 107
Gruenewald, D., 32, 36, 135
Gulson, K., 1, 10
Gust, S., 14, 51, 52, 56, 62, 73, 131

## H

Haberman, M., 22
Hall, R., 109
Hansard, 17, 18
Harris, A., 6, 91
Harris, K., 114
Hattam, R., 138
Hayes, D., 25, 27
Hebson, G., 85
Herr, K., 2, 3
Hiatt, B., 113
Hinchey, P., 83
Hinkson, J., 104, 106, 107
Holdsworth, R., 37
Hooks, B., 26
Horton, M., 41, 42, 138
Horwitt, S., 58, 59
Hudak, G., 113
Hughey, J., 47
Hursh, D., 21, 22, 37
Hutchinson, J., 136

## J

Jencks, C., 76–78

## K

Karp, S., 26
Kellner, D., 127, 137
Kenway, J., 104
Kincheloe, J., 23, 103, 104, 107, 110, 114, 115, 119, 121, 125, 127, 135, 137, 139
Knights, D., 9

# AUTHOR INDEX

Kovacs, P., 22
Kozol, J., 18
Kumashiro, K., 104, 127
Kunreuther, F., 56
Kuzmic, J., 36

## L

Ladson-Billings, G., 137, 138
Lareau, A., 48
Lather, P., 138
Lauder, H., 85, 113
Law, J., 7
Lawrence-Lightfoot, S., 7, 8
Lawton, D., 121
Lazerson, M., 107
Levin, H., 1, 109
Lewins, F., 105, 107, 116
Lincoln, Y., 136–138
Lipka, R., 29, 239
Lipman, P., 21, 22, 40, 112, 113, 139, 140
Lipsky, M., 70
Lister, R., 64
Long, 107
Lukacs, G., 87
Lytle, S., 79

## M

Macedo, D., 20, 124, 138
Mackay, H., 38
Mahony, P., 85
Martin, J., 73
Mazawi, A., 113, 121
McCabe, D., 9
McCallum, D., 112
McDermott, K., 21
McInerney, P., 10, 11, 21, 51, 67, 117, 129
McLaren, P., 104, 106, 113, 134, 137, 139
McMahon, B., 46, 73
McMurtry, J., 118, 125
McPeck, J., 73
Meier, D., 41, 113, 122
Melaville, A., 32
Miller, P., 112
Mills, C., 3–5
Mills, D., 10
Mishler, E., 128
Morley, L., 79, 81, 82, 86, 90
Morrell, E., 134
Mortimore, P., 76
Muijs, D., 6
Murphy, J., 78

## N

Nader, C., 1
Nichols, S., 113
Nixon, J., 139
Noddings, N., 135

## O

Oakes, J., 50, 51
O'Connor, A., 7, 67
Offe, C., 109
Ohanian, S., 22
Osterman, P., 59
Oyler, C., 38

## P

Passeron, J., 78
Payne, R., 66, 70
Peel, M., 67, 68, 105, 107
Peetz, D., 107, 109, 119
Perry, T., 134
Petch, J., 82–84, 85
Peterson, B., 38, 135
Pinar, W., 118
Piper, H., 49
Polesel, J., 83, 84, 104, 113
Popkewitz, T., 105
Portelli, J., 46, 73
Power, S., 91

## R

Raffo, C., 39
Rassool, N., 79, 81, 82, 86, 90
Reynolds, D., 76–78, 80, 84, 85
Rodriguez, A., 130
Rogers, J., 50, 51
Rosaen, C., 138
Rosenstock, L., 122, 135
Russ, J., 6

## S

Saegert, S., 47
Saltman, K., 45
Sammons, P., 78, 81–83
Sanders, M., 58
Saul, R., 106
Schenke, A., 123, 124
Schlechty, P., 131
Schultz, J., 38
Schutz, A., 48, 49, 72

# AUTHOR INDEX

Sennett, R., 135
Shapiro, H., 109
Shields, C., 113, 121, 134
Shirley, D., 57, 58
Shor, I., 26, 42, 114, 117, 124, 130, 134
Shweder, R., 70
Sibley, D., 28
Sidorkin, A., 46
Simon, R., 94, 123, 124
Slattery, P., 131
Smith, G., 32
Smyth, J., 2, 6, 10, 11, 21, 46, 49, 51, 52, 57, 59, 62, 67, 106, 113, 116, 117, 133, 136, 138
Sobel, D., 36
Speer, P., 47
Spring, J., 135
Steinberg, S., 122, 131, 135
Stoll, L., 6
St.Pierre, D., 6
Stronach, I., 49
Swadener, S., 134

## T

Teddlie, C., 76–78, 80, 84, 85
Teese, R., 20, 83, 84, 91, 104, 113
Theobold, P., 136
Thompson, J., 47
Thomson, P., 20, 24, 32, 59
Thrift, N., 59
Thrupp, M., 40, 78, 79, 96, 98
Trondman, M., 10, 138
Tyack, D., 118

## U

Underhill, E., 107

## V

Valenzuela, A., 137
Valli, L., 22
Vaughan, M., 49
Vibert, A., 134
Vinson, T., 116
Vygotsky, L., 119

## W

Wacquant, L., 63, 64
Walker, M., 139
Warr, D., 63, 64
Warren, M., 40, 47, 57, 59–62, 130, 132
Watkins, P., 94
Webb, P., 80
Weiner, E., 106
Weis, L., 5, 128, 137, 138
Welch, A., 115
Wexler, P., 114
White, K., 105, 107, 116
Whitty, G., 91
Williams, M., 58
Willis, P., 9, 10, 78, 113, 138
Willmott, R., 89, 96, 98
Wolgemuth, J., 127, 137
Wood, G., 128, 129
Wood, R., 59
Worley, M., 1
Wright-Mills, C., 3–5
Wrigley, T., 84, 85
Wyn, J., 104, 108, 129
Wynhausen, E., 106–108

## Y

Youdell, D., 9, 111

# SUBJECT INDEX

## A

Aboriginal peoples 17, 139
abstracted empiricism 85
academic success 20, 115
accountability 11, 13, 18–23, 41, 61, 79, 80, 88, 97, 112, 113, 127, 129
active creators of knowledge 38
active human agents 100
active partner 69
activism 1–3, 14, 26, 27, 38, 41, 46, 51–53, 129, 130, 137, 140
advantaging and disadvantaging 78, 111, 116
advocacy 10, 68
against the flow, 9
agency 4, 10, 25, 28, 36, 76, 93–95, 99, 102, 129, 130, 132, 133, 137
alien and totalizing discourses 73
Alinsky 14, 43, 47, 53, 57–61, 73, 131
alliances 19, 41, 57, 118
ameliorate disadvantage 39
anti-democratic 75
anti-educational 75
anti-harassment policies 36
apology 17, 18, 45
apprenticeship 103, 108, 110
assault on public schools 14
at risk 8, 24, 33, 34, 83, 128, 134
audits 19, 49, 79, 106
Australian Commonwealth Labor government 96
Australian context 11, 52, 57, 59, 69
Australian quality framework (AQF) 103
Australia reconstructed 106
authentic dialogue 42
authenticity of outsiders 64
authentic partnership 14, 62, 69–73
authentic school reform 84–89
authoritarian solutions 6, 43, 47, 131
authoritative discourses 47
autonomy 19, 37, 70, 79, 95, 99

## B

Back of the Yards 57
backward mapping 59
battlers 67
behavior management 133
being in community 15–16
belongingness 27, 36, 42
best practice 23, 83, 85, 97, 136
bigger picture 62
big issues 53, 55

big lie 15, 105
biography 3, 5
black box 85, 130
Blueprint for Government Schools 83
boardwalk project, 35
bonds 63, 81, 93, 94
borderlands, 7
boundaries of traditional subject disciplines 35
boundary crossing 3
boundary of the school 100
breakfast programs 33
brutalizing effects of globalization 15
bull shit detectors 72
bullying 36
bundles of dispositions 48
bundles of pathologies 47
bureaucratic insurgent 72
Business Council of Australia (BCA) 109

## C

capacity building 6, 19, 31, 47, 128, 130, 131
capitalism 15, 104, 109, 130
cardholders 72
casualized and low-paid work 104
celebration 54
Central Park East public school 41
change agents 61, 132
charity approach 54
Chicago School Reform Act 40
choice 4, 13, 19–21, 23, 46, 48, 50, 56, 68, 93, 94, 101, 105
churning 107
citizen politics 14, 55, 56
citizenship 51, 118, 123–125, 135
CityWorks 122
civic activism 41
civic engagement 19, 35, 41, 53, 104, 125
civic intelligence 51
civic mindedness 123
civic responsibility 32, 34, 36, 130
civil commons 118
class 6, 8, 9, 13–16, 22–26, 28, 29, 32, 33, 38, 40, 41, 48, 49, 53, 62, 66–70, 72, 73, 78–80, 83, 84, 86, 90–92, 100, 103–105, 109, 111, 112, 114–117
classed spaces, 9
classical experimentalism, 136
client 14, 27, 52, 57, 61, 62, 66, 69, 72, 97, 122, 132
Coalition for Community Schooling 26
Coalition of Essential Schools 26

159

SUBJECT INDEX

coalitions 42, 57
coercive and prescriptive solutions 129
coercive policies 25
cognitive ability 114
collaborative teaching arrangements 33
collateral damage, 113
collective action 42, 58
commodification and marginalization 98
common good 13, 18, 27, 108, 134
commonsense 90, 103–105, 115
communities of disadvantage 6, 15, 47, 50, 131
community activist 41, 43, 52, 54, 62, 127, 130, 131, 134
community and school renewal 10
community assets and resources 12, 124
community-based learning 24, 26, 30, 32, 34, 37, 41, 59, 116, 124
community capacity building 19, 31, 130, 131
community engagement 24, 27, 33, 37, 38, 132–133, 139
community house 28, 30, 65
community of learners 27, 31
community organizing 14, 43, 47, 57–60, 62, 69, 73, 131
community partnership 27, 41, 61, 124
community renewal 5–7, 12, 14, 19, 26, 27, 43, 47–74, 127–140
community resource 31, 35
community service model 37
Community services program 123, 124
community strengths 14, 28, 31, 42, 47, 61, 69, 131, 132
community voiced approach 14, 57–64
competition 20, 95, 99, 109, 113
competitive advantage 99
competitive assessment practices 133
compliant technicians 2
comprehensive state high schools 112
computer club 68
confluence of history and biography 3
connect 30
connectionist pedagogy 36
connection to place 32
conservative assault 26, 128
conservative backlash 106
constellation of orienting concepts 16, 62
consumerism 2, 51
context matters 128, 130
contextual portraits 11
contrived images 63
controllability 15
corporate ideology 108
corporate managerialist approach 24
corrosive effects 26
cost-center of business 14
counterfeit versions 64

counter-hegemonic 16, 127
counter-narrative 134
courtyard project 34, 116
craft labor system 107
craftsmanship 4, 8, 128, 135
crime 63, 65, 79, 81
crisis in institutional arrangements 5
critical and engaged citizenry 134
critical approach 9, 27, 36, 118, 128, 134–137
critical capacities of students 38, 144
critical citizenship 118, 123–125, 135
critical consciousness 119
critical constructivism 119
critical-democratic 46, 73, 119, 125
critical democratic approach 119
critical dialectic 8
critical educational scholarship 98
critical education researchers 77
critical educators 38, 40–41
critical ethnography 8, 9, 138
critical inquiry 104, 125, 128
critical literacy 105
critically engaged 19, 37, 41–43, 133, 135
critically engaged citizens 42
critically engaged classroom 133
critically engaged communities 135
critically informed citizens and workers 104
critical pedagogy 14, 26–27, 32–38, 132–134
critical pedagogy of place 14, 27, 32–37
critical pedagogy of school/community engagement 132–133
critical perspective 3, 134
critical reasoning 32
critical reflection 26, 93
critical researchers 78, 92, 94, 137
critical social science 90
critical social theorists 86, 87
critical sociology 8
critical spectators 73
critical thinking 22
critical/transformative 134
critical vocational education 125
critique of positivism and managerialism 90
cross-curricula themes 33
culpability of individual students 79, 103
cultural and political problem 50
cultural and political processes 50
cultural capital 25, 115
cultural deficits 115, 129
cultural narratives 50
cultural politics 10, 137
cultural politics of schools and communities 137
culture of poverty, 66, 70

# SUBJECT INDEX

## D

damaged community 65
damaged relationships 46
dangerous places 63
data-driven approaches 48
data surveillance 80
daunting challenges 13
deconstructing job hierarchies 110–116
decontextualized 103
deep respect for ordinary citizens 51
deficiencies in parenting 25
deficit 4, 8, 14, 15, 24, 41, 42, 50, 51, 66, 67, 70, 115, 121, 125, 127, 129, 134, 137
deficit/dependency 70
deficit narratives 127
deficit views 8, 24, 41
de-industrialization 1, 57
de-industrializing national economies 107
de-insitutionalizing relationships 14, 62, 65–66
deliberative democracy 37
delivery of service 52
democracy 20, 26, 36–38, 46–49, 52, 55, 95, 103, 104, 109, 118, 123–125, 135
democratic aspirations 118
democratic communal life 58
democratic pedagogy 42
democratic possibilities 98
democratic practices 26
democratic sensibilities 38, 134
democratic solidarity 48, 49
democratization of education 98
demonization of the poor 66
Department of Housing 66–68
dependence 57, 71
depoliticized citizenry 124
deregulation 40
devalued and marginalized 95
devolved educational responsibilities 12
dialectical theory-building 10, 94, 138
dialogic learning 26, 133
dialogue with outsiders 61
different kind of politics 14, 51–57, 62, 73, 128, 131
different kind of poverty knowledge 7, 67
diminished opportunities 20, 32
diminished self 24, 134
direct instruction 29, 78
disadvantage 1, 3, 4, 6–8, 10, 12, 13, 15, 19–21, 25, 33, 39, 40, 43, 45, 46,
disadvantaged communities 4, 6, 8–10, 15, 18, 27–28, 38–40, 45–47, 49, 50, 57, 69, 75, 103, 113, 127, 131, 139
disadvantaged schools 3, 6, 8, 10, 13, 15, 24, 25, 27, 40, 50, 103, 111, 127, 129, 130, 139
Disadvantaged Schools Program (DSP) 27
disadvantaging 78, 102, 111, 116
disaffected students 30
disciplinary work 88
disciplined lack of clarity 7
disciplining effects 3
discomforting 16, 104, 127
discourse of deceit 13, 14, 18–20, 43, 46
discourses of demonization 63
discourses of student engagement 46
discursive assault 45
discursive democracy 48
disengagement 42
dismantling social hierarchies 121
disparaging portrayals 12, 28
disruptive 104, 127
distancing 4, 64
distant and unengaged 54
distributive questions 52
diversity and pluralism 90
doing education 74, 93, 96–101
domesticate 9, 115
dominance of economic goals 129
dominant educational policy discourse 15
dominant policy paradigm 139
dumping ground 115

## E

early school leaving 13, 30, 34, 83, 108, 116
economically depressed areas 40
economically disadvantaged communities 18
economically equitable society 40
economic imperatives 18
economic instrumentality 14, 49
editing researchers in 10
educated hope 104, 125
educational activists 95, 102
educational credentialism 109
educational disadvantage 6–8, 13, 15, 19, 21, 28, 33, 39, 40, 43, 47, 75, 80, 130, 133, 136
educational inequality 103, 112, 139
educational leadership 95, 96, 98
educational market 21, 100, 102, 132
educational policy orthodoxy 14
education policies 18, 26, 43, 75, 88–91, 95–96, 98–99, 101, 103, 112, 127, 139–140
education standards 128
effective pedagogy 82
effective schools 76, 81, 83, 102
Effective Schools Model 83
egalitarian 26, 118
emancipatory ideals 130
embedded interviews 10
embedded networks 48
emotional work 85

161

SUBJECT INDEX

empowering education 117, 124
enclaves of resistance 43
engaged community 37, 61
enterprise 33, 75, 109, 120
enterprise education 33
entrenched inequalities 42
entrepreneurialism 19
environment 6, 12, 13, 18, 22, 23, 26, 28,
    33–35, 37–38, 41, 43, 51, 53, 75, 76, 81,
    88–90, 94, 100, 124, 129, 134–135
environmental threats 135
equitable communities 43
equity and social justice 96, 134
essential conversation 7, 8
ethic of care 34, 135
ethnicity 100, 137
ethnographic and theoretical sensibility 138
ethnographic insertion 11
ethnographic slices 11, 14
ethnography 8–10, 138
everybody's business 31
everyday citizens 56
everyday life 63, 82, 139
everyday politics 55, 57
evidence based 2, 9, 82–86, 88, 136, 138, 139
evolving criticality 137, 139
exclusion 2, 15, 27, 28, 50, 112, 127, 128, 137
existing social structure 95
expert 43, 48, 51, 52, 61, 70, 80, 85, 101, 118,
    131
exploitation 113, 135, 139
extended rational dialogue 48
externally prescribed solutions 31
externally produced curriculum 23

F

face-to-face 60, 66, 136
failing schools 89
falling educational standards 79
family background 15, 76, 77, 86
family effect 77
feisty critic 67
feminism 8
fragmentation 26, 107
freedom 19, 23, 26, 41, 43, 56, 104, 120, 125,
    132, 138
full service extended schools 39
functionalist 18, 85, 87, 89, 90
functional literacy 23
funds of knowledge 24, 25, 30–32, 34, 130

G

gay and lesbian students 38
gender 25, 105, 109, 116, 121, 134, 136, 137

generalizations or laws 87
generic learning outcomes 32
genocide 45
get a job 104, 105, 110
getting by 114
global capitalism 106, 125, 130
global competitiveness 19
global warming 37
good or bad schools 76
good or bad teaching 76
good social science 4
good work 4, 105, 109, 119, 120, 128, 135
governmentality 90
government speak 64
grassroots community organizing 58
grassroots reclamation 14
great place to live 13
grossly unequal 69
grounded theory 90

H

hands-on approach to learning 116
hard data 114
hermetically sealed 8
heroic formulations of school leadership 58,
    90
hero organizers 58
heuristic 16, 46, 96, 125, 138
hierarchical labor market 113
hierarchy of natural ability 112
hierarchy of school knowledge 111
hierarchy of school performance 84
Highlander Center 26, 41
highly skilled work force 39, 108
high school graduation rates 1
high stakes testing 21, 22, 25, 37, 43, 125, 129
historically neutral 94
homelessness 38, 41
homework centers 33
homophobic attitudes 36
hope 1, 8, 9, 14, 15, 19, 26, 29, 31, 39–43, 67,
    73, 75–102, 104, 125, 128–132, 136, 138,
    140
horizontal political relationships 72
horticulture 33–35, 103, 116, 117
hospitable spaces 129
How Young People Are Fairing 108
human capital 104–106, 108, 110, 115, 125
human entitlement 140
human interaction 70

I

idealized forms 49
identity formation 32, 48

# SUBJECT INDEX

ideological preference 49
ideological preparation 112
ideology 15, 48, 50, 84–90, 106, 108, 109, 111, 114
ideology of technicism 50
imagination 1, 5, 7, 9, 14, 16, 52, 127, 128, 135
impoverished technical views 51
improved attendance 30
improving life chances 25, 28, 59, 93
inclusive and educative possibilities 98
inclusive education 83
inclusive solutions 2
Indigenous Australians 17, 18, 20, 38, 43, 45, 139
indigenous culture 34, 133
indigenous leadership 42, 47, 58, 60, 132
individualism 3, 14, 27, 108
individual pathways 30
Industrial Areas Foundation 57, 59
inequalities 8–10, 17–22, 39, 40, 42, 43, 47, 50, 64, 79, 83, 89, 103, 112, 127, 130, 133, 134, 139
inequitable policies and practices 41
inequitable structures 32
informal knowledge 68
ingrained assumptions 93
inherent logic of school and economy 106
injustice 2, 17, 18, 38, 41, 67, 79, 103, 128, 135, 139, 140
innovative practices 23
inquiry of discomfort 127, 137
institutional contradictions 4
institutionalized relationships 65, 66
institution of schooling 48, 49, 66, 68
instructional experts 101
instrumentally thinking 102
instrument of economic and political ends 105
integrated studies 23, 29
intellectual and civic life 117
intellectual and methodological flaws 103
intellectual craftsmanship 3, 4, 8
intellectual exorcism 71
intelligence testing 112
intensification of teachers' work 22
interdependency 53, 61–62
inter-generational disadvantage 12
interloper 45
internal logic 88
international competitiveness 106
interpretive trail 34
investing ordinary people with power 61
Iraq War 22
Iron Rule 60
islands of democracy 38

## J

job market 110, 111, 116
Howard, John 17
just society 32, 41, 95, 96

## K

Rudd, Kevin 17
knowledge relations 9

## L

labor market 4, 78, 104–109, 112, 113, 125
landscape of exclusion 28
larger social struggles 50
leadership 6, 12, 28, 42, 47, 50, 58, 60–61, 70, 71, 78, 81, 83, 90, 95, 96, 98, 100, 115, 132, 133, 140
learning community 6, 26, 28–31
learning environment 81, 124
learning identity 9
learning opportunities 2, 41
learning potential 15
liberating education 130
liberation 92
license to experiment 35
life chances 25, 28, 59
lifelong learning 31
ligatures 93–95
linear, rationalist logic 89
listening for silences 10
literacy for stupidification 124
literacy practices 25
local and global 32, 40, 128, 135
local context 32, 97, 132
local decision-making 27
local empowerment 13, 24–25, 42
local history 32, 35
local knowledge 80, 99
local leadership 12, 81, 140
locally embodied 55
local school management 24
locational disadvantage 1
logic of deficits 50
logic of merit 50
logic of scarcity 50
logic of school effectiveness 79, 88–90, 103
logic of schooling 50, 51
logics of merit and deficit 50
Lone Pine Tree Project 35
low-paying service sector 104
low socio-economic communities 21, 38, 129, 130

# SUBJECT INDEX

## M

macro-forces 95
making a mess with method 7
managerialist practices 19, 129
manual skills 111
marginalized 3, 41, 42, 47, 57, 68, 74, 95, 99, 102, 105, 124, 127, 131
markers of disadvantage 20
market competition 20, 95, 99, 110
market economy 113
market fundamentalism 118
marketization 3, 19, 27, 89, 129
marketization of schools 19
market model of education 19
markets 3, 4, 18–21, 26, 27, 37, 40, 46, 51, 78, 89, 95, 97, 99, 100, 102, 104, 108–113, 115–118, 125, 127–129, 132, 139
market value system 118
mass consumption 135
McJobs 108
meaning making 10
mean streets 67
measurability 15
mechanistic reforms 49
meritocracy 49, 112, 114
method 4, 7–9, 76, 78, 80, 84, 86, 103, 123, 133, 136, 138
methodological luddites 7
middle class 12, 22, 25, 29, 38, 40, 48, 49, 66, 70, 78, 104, 112, 125, 129
middle class institution of schooling 48, 49, 66
middle class values 29, 66
mission statements 19
moral and ethical activist 138
multiculturalism 26
multi-locale ethnography 10
multiple and severe disabilities 40
mutually interrogate theory and data 102
Horton, Myles 41, 42

## N

narrow emphasis in schools 99
narrow focus 91
narrowing of the purposes of teaching 79
narrow performance indicators 101
narrow vocationalism 115
national goals of schooling 11
National Schools Network (NSN) 27
native leadership 60
naturally occurring phenomena 94
natural order 83, 88
needs-oriented deficit approach 42
negotiated cultural political choices 101

neighborhood advisory board 28
neighborhood identity 28
neighborhood renewal 12, 26, 28–30, 41, 57–61
neoconservative agenda 136
neo-conservative restoration 8
neoconservative values 102, 103
neo-Darwinism 113
neo-liberal 3, 9, 12–14, 18–21, 40, 41, 43, 46, 74, 75, 88, 95, 96, 99, 102, 106, 108, 116, 119, 124, 125, 127–130, 132, 137, 139
neoliberal discourse of deceit 13, 14, 19–20, 46
neo-liberal framework 96
neo-liberalism 13, 19–20, 106, 124, 137
neo-liberal policies 3, 9, 75
neo-liberal project 74
neo-liberal promise 116
neo-liberal reform 13, 19, 21, 40, 41, 95, 132
neo-liberal solutions 128
neo-marxist 8
neutral 4, 78, 84, 87–89, 91, 94, 99, 100, 102, 108
neutral institutions 91
neutral managerial devices 99
new authoritarianism 26, 128
new economic realities 106
new language of analysis 134
new managerialism 74, 79
new money 13
new paradigm 131
New Right 19, 20
new social imagination 127, 128, 135
new standards 21–22
No Child Left Behind 21
normalized 68, 89

## O

objects to be managed 89
Occidental college 59
OECD 109
Office for Standards in Education 81
official curriculum 35
official deficit views 8
official knowledge 38
officially sanctioned curriculum 133
official policy discourses 73
one size fits all approach 133
openly ideological 136
oppressive relationships 32
ordinary citizens 51, 124
organizing for power 47
othering 64, 134
over-romanticizing 69
ownership 12, 27, 29, 31, 39, 60, 70, 140
Oxfam 38

# SUBJECT INDEX

## P

paradigm of school improvement 129
parental choice 19, 113, 129
parent engagement 27
participative 76, 95, 96, 98
participative/professional 15, 96, 97, 100–102, 132
part-time, casualized, low paying, repetitive jobs 106
passive recipients 37
pastoral care 33
paternalistic 1, 69, 70, 90, 131
pathologizing 24, 47, 64, 113, 121, 128, 134, 137
pathologizing discourses 24, 113
pathologizing practices 128, 134
pathologizing process 64
pathologizing views 121
pattern language 56, 57
patterns and interconnections 4
pedagogical power 19
pedagogical question 104
pedagogy 14–16, 20, 22, 26, 27, 29, 30, 32–38, 42, 75–102, 119, 125, 128, 132–134, 138
pedagogy of entrapment 20
pedagogy of freedom 132
pedagogy of hope 15, 75–102, 128–142
pedagogy of indignation 138
pedagogy of poverty 13, 22
people-centered capacity building 6, 47, 128, 131
performance appraisals 19
performance-driven policy 6
performance management 23, 31
performance-related pay 50
performativity 13, 18, 82, 88, 89, 96–98
personalized learning 30
personal troubles 5
person-centered learning 18, 26
perspective of the other 71
Phillips community 52, 53
philosophic compass 18
physicality 53
place-based learning 32, 33, 36, 135–136
placed at disadvantage 47, 49, 131
playing dumb 114
pockets of hope 19, 26, 41, 43
pockets of influence 13
policy, pedagogy and research 16, 125, 128
policy reclamation 17–43
policy sociology 8, 9, 97, 98
political economy 26, 40, 67, 139, 140
politically and socially engaged research 137
politically neutral 84

political representation 16, 139, 140
politicized pedagogies 36
politics of blame 79, 129
politics of place 1
popular culture 36, 134
portraits 11–13
positive identity 70
positive narratives 63
positivist 2, 82, 85–88, 136, 138
positivistic 76, 84–86, 136
positivist knowledge 2
positivist research 86, 87
positivist science 76, 136
post structuralism 8
post-welfarist education reforms 97
potential strengths 61, 132
poverty 1, 7, 13, 18, 20–22, 25, 28, 29, 38, 41, 57, 66, 67, 70, 91, 135, 138, 139
poverty knowledge 7, 67
povo (poor) 36
power 6, 9, 10, 14, 19, 20, 35, 42, 43, 47, 48, 52, 53, 55, 58–62, 65, 68, 69, 72, 73, 78, 80, 90–93, 102, 105, 112, 115, 120, 121, 124, 127, 130, 131, 133, 135–137, 139
powerful resident 69
power games 68
power relations 60, 61, 78, 91, 93, 102, 115, 124, 130, 136
pragmatism 48, 52, 78, 80, 82, 85, 103
praxis 134
pre-conceived theoretical template 9
predatory culture 113
pre-existent knowledge 117
preferred methodology 8, 136
prescriptive meaning 61, 132
prescriptive policies 97
prevailing myths 25
prevailing policy rationality 89, 102
private schooling 21, 33, 40, 111, 113
private solutions to public problems 5
private *versus* public good 95
privatization 13, 40, 45, 46
privatized consumption 64
privilege 6, 21, 50, 99, 112, 115, 127, 137
problem-fixing 47
problem-posing 133, 134
problem-solving 84, 115, 133
process of becoming 117, 130
professional 6, 15, 22, 23, 26, 27, 41, 51, 81, 85, 89, 96–102, 107, 116, 122, 132
professional communities 27
professional judgment 89, 99, 101, 132
professional responsibility 102
Program for Students with Disabilities 83
progressive educational approaches 99
project based learning 29

165

## SUBJECT INDEX

proud community 12, 72
proximal factors 39
psychologistic explanations 136
public actors 61
public and social spaces 124
public good 95, 136
public intellectuals 2, 3
public issues 5
puncturing the mythologies 3, 8, 66, 73
punitive measures 36
purposeful conversations 10
pushed to the margins 13, 17, 88

## Q

quality 4, 21, 22, 40, 50, 52, 78, 80, 83, 90, 91, 98, 103, 114, 124, 129, 133, 135
quality assurance 133
quality instruction 80
quality of mind 4
quality outcomes 50
quasi-positivist 87

## R

race 53, 78, 91, 105, 109, 116, 121, 134, 137
racism 27, 41, 138
racist policies 3, 18, 42
radical listeners 71, 131
randomized controlled experiments 136
rational-technical approach 81
re-building relationships 65
recentralizing control 40
recipients of services 61
reclamation of educational policy 26–27, 43, 128–132
recognition 25, 35, 40, 46, 133, 139, 140
redistribution 16, 40, 139, 140
redistributive policies 80
reductionism 84, 86
reductionist teaching 79
re-emergent scientism 136, 138
re-enchantment with management 90
re-engaging young people 38
reflexivity, 9, 139
Registered Training Organizations (RTO) 103
reification 87
re-institutionalization 99
relational cultures 49
relational immediacy 59, 60
relationally-led backlash 49–51
relational politics 46, 51–52, 66, 74, 129
relational power 14, 43, 47, 60–62, 69, 131
relational touch 49
relationship 10, 14, 19, 20, 27, 29, 31, 32, 36, 42, 46–49, 52–55, 57, 58, 60, 62–66,

72–77, 80, 81, 83, 87, 91–94, 98, 99, 101, 106, 110, 111, 122, 123, 125, 130, 136, 138, 140
relay devices 90
re-making schools 131
renovating educational identities 10
renovating relationships 62–64
research method 7, 78, 84
residualization of public education 21, 129
residual place of last resort 113
residual school 113
resistance 9, 43, 93, 114, 137, 138
respect 1, 6, 20, 22, 31, 37, 41, 45, 47, 48, 51, 64, 65, 68, 117, 125, 129, 131, 140
reverse engineer 122
revitalization 14
rhetoric of knowledge economy 110
right-wing policy 89
rigorous and relevant curriculum 111
rust belt kids 20

## S

safety 13, 21, 28, 29, 37, 60, 63, 124
savage inequalities 18
school and community activism 51–52, 129
school attainment 78
school-based curriculum 23
school choice 20, 50, 125
school-community engagement 24, 27, 33, 38
school-community partnerships 41
school-community relationships 27, 31
school-community renewal 27
school/community renewal 127–140
school culture 6, 79, 114
school effect 77, 78
school effectiveness 9, 15, 26, 74–103, 129, 136, 139
school effectiveness logic 79, 88, 92
school effectiveness movement 15, 26, 74–77, 90, 92, 101, 129, 136
school effectiveness rationality 85, 89, 90, 94, 98
school efficiency and effectiveness 99
school failure 83, 115, 129, 136
school guidance officers 112
school improvement paradigm 75, 129, 131
schooling for critical democracy 26
school-level educational partnership 98
school level effects 130
school participation 30, 136
school pathology 128
school policies 79, 133
school reform 5, 6, 37, 40, 43, 50, 57, 62, 80, 82, 84–90, 127, 128, 130, 137
school retention 21, 33, 41, 43, 128

# SUBJECT INDEX

schools as annexes of economy 13
schools as communities 27
schools as democratic public spheres 125
schools as social cultural sites 92
schools compensating for society 77
schools in challenging circumstances 6
schools in disadvantaged contexts 50
schools make a difference 76
scientific evidence-based 136
scientific management 99
scientific research 5, 108
self-managing school 12
self-reflection 89
self-reliance 115
self-respect 20
semi-skilled and manual workers 107
sensuous practices 10
service 12–14, 24, 28–31, 33–35, 37, 39–41, 47, 52, 57, 61, 66, 69, 72, 91, 102–104, 106–108, 111, 123–125, 130, 139, 140
shared leadership 42
simply context 86
single parent families 13, 33
skill shortages 106, 113
skills training 109, 119, 135
slices of life 11, 62
small learning communities 29
social action 32, 119, 131, 140
social activism 38, 130, 137
social actors 10, 100, 101
social and cultural aspects 101
social and economic mobility 1
social and educational activism 1
social and institutional structures 5
social and political context 101
social capital 39, 51, 60
social construction of reality 90
social dialectic 49
social equity 76
social exclusion 15, 28, 137
social fabric of schools 49
social identity 128, 137
social imagination 127, 128, 135
social injustice 41, 128
socializing students 109
social justice activism 140
social justice and inclusion 95
social knowledge 52
socially constructed 4, 99, 119
socially critical 2, 4, 9, 16, 18, 19, 26–27, 36, 46, 118, 127, 128, 130, 134–137, 140
socially critical alternatives 18
socially critical approach 9, 27, 36, 118, 128, 134–137
socially critical intellectual work 4
socially critical response 140

socially critical scholars 4
socially critical school and community 19
socially-engaged learning 130
socially-engaged schools 14
socially engaged teachers 41
socially-just forms of schooling 128, 140
socially just relationships 19
socially just schooling 132
socially just society 95, 96
socially relevant ethnographic accounts 10
socially worthwhile 117
social order 80, 87
social or political critique 51
social power 20, 47
social production of research 9, 139
social services mentality 47
social solidarity 64
social theory 9, 94, 139
socio-cultural reality 138
socio-economic disadvantage 39, 138
sociological imagination 5, 7
sociological perspective 48, 78, 86, 129
sociology of education 76, 77
socio-political reality 104
solidarity 27, 28, 43, 45–74, 118, 127, 131
sorry 17, 23
space for challenge 47, 102
speaking data into existence 10
speaking identities 128
spectator citizenry 73
standardization 82, 118, 125
standardization of school procedures 82
standardized curriculum 21, 22
standardized testing 23, 24, 32, 133
standards 13, 17, 21–22, 25, 29, 34, 37, 39, 50, 79–83, 85, 91, 99, 109, 113, 121, 122, 128, 135
standards-based reform 21
statistical correlations 78
statistically controlled 86
stereotype 12, 36, 63, 64, 66, 67, 70, 71, 81, 87, 94, 102, 128, 134
storylines 16, 125, 127–140
story telling 48
stratified education system 21, 113
streaming (or tracking) 104, 118, 122, 133
street level bureaucrats 70
strong leadership 78
structural 4, 40, 59, 62, 94, 95, 102, 124, 134
structural and social reforms 40
structural inequalities 20, 47
structural relations 87, 102
structure 5, 23, 32, 43, 50, 56, 65, 66, 87, 92–94, 100, 102, 107, 118, 124, 137, 138
structure of opportunities 5
student alienation 42

167

## SUBJECT INDEX

student campaign for social justice 38
student centered 122
student engagement 13, 21, 30, 31, 33, 41, 43, 46, 133
student resistance 114
students as active initiators 37
students as agents of social change 38
students at risk 8, 33, 134
sub-ordinate cultures 92
sub-schools 33
success-oriented approach 36
sullen hostility 114
Summerhill school 49
super principals 50
supplanting societies 45
surveillance mechanisms 24
symbolic spaces 104, 116–118
symbolic violence 114
synoptic view 11

### T

tacit professional knowledge 85
TAFE [Technical and Further Education] 103, 108, 110, 111, 123
taken-for-granted assumptions 124, 133
target setting 19, 23, 24
teacher autonomy 79
teacher professionalism 76, 80, 89, 98, 101
teacher quality 22, 40
teacher technicians 85
teaching as transmission 79, 132
teaching to the test 13, 22–24, 132
teaching to transgress 26
technical 15, 19, 50, 51, 68, 81, 85, 88, 89, 96, 97, 99–103, 105, 110, 111, 118, 122, 129, 132
technical/managerial approaches 99, 102
technical/managerial elite 132
technical/managerial organization 96, 97, 99
technical/managerial policy 101–102
technical/managerial view 15
technical problem 50
technocratic view of schooling 86
TEE [Tertiary Entrance Examination] 110, 111
territorial stigma 63
texts of despair 128
textual dissenters 98
theoretically-informed ethnographic work 9
theory 9, 10, 52, 57, 82–84, 89, 90, 94, 102, 105, 106, 138, 139
thickend concept of engagement 73
thinking critically 128, 139
thinking space 559
thin or diminished view of accountability 61

thin view of engagement 73
top-down decision making 23
top-down managerial policy 90
toxic 113
tracking performance 114
training 15, 28, 30, 70, 103–105, 108–110, 115, 117–119, 121, 122, 125, 129, 131, 132, 135
transformation 14, 41, 47, 65, 69, 93, 116, 117, 130, 134
transformative education 19, 26, 37
transformative possibilities 137, 140
transformative schooling 43
transient population 63
transmission model of teaching 132
treated with respect 41, 65, 140
tree planting project 34, 35
trickle-up revolution 131
trouble-makers 15
troubling 66, 104, 125
troubling perspective 125
true partnership 72
truisms 89
trust 31, 39, 40, 43, 47, 72, 108, 129, 131, 138

### U

underemployment 20, 107
unemployment 5, 13, 20, 33, 38, 91, 106, 107, 115, 116, 124
unequal power relationships 62, 130, 132
unfinished business 74
unfounded perceptions 63
uninspiring instruction 22
union stock yards 57
university 8, 21, 30, 33, 53–55, 104, 110, 111, 123
unjust economy 40, 128, 140
unmasking ideological content 87
unreflexive mantra 9
user-pay principles 19
utilitarian purposes 19

### V

value-free 138
value-free objectivist science 136
value systems 66, 118
vertical relationships 52, 73
victim-blaming 1
visual things 64
vocational and academic dualism 122
vocational curriculum 111
vocational education 12, 19, 21, 102–105, 109, 110, 115–119, 121, 125, 129, 135

# SUBJECT INDEX

Vocational Education and Training (VET) in schools 103–105, 109, 115, 117–119, 121, 125, 129, 135
vocational guidance 112, 114
vocationalism 103, 106, 115, 118
vocational orientation 15, 124
voice 3, 9, 10, 14, 18, 24, 40, 49, 62, 64, 66, 71, 95, 114, 127
voiced and narrative lives 62
voiced research 10
voices of educationalists 95
voices of participants 9
voices of students and teachers 18, 24
voluntarism 12, 28, 36
vulnerability 2, 7, 26, 60
vulnerable policy landscape 41

## W

wages 40, 72, 105, 107–109, 119, 124
Wal-Mart factor 107
welfare 12, 13, 19–21, 25, 28, 32–34, 36–39, 57, 106, 120, 125, 130
welfare dependency 12, 13, 21, 33, 38, 41
welfare mentality 57
what counts 85, 88, 99
wider social arrangements 95
winners and losers 113, 116
work 1–9, 13–15, 19–22, 24–37, 39, 41, 42, 45–50, 53–59, 61, 62, 65, 67–70
WorkChoices act 107, 109
workforce participation 13, 33
working class 13, 14, 25, 28, 41, 48, 49, 67–69, 72, 73, 91, 103, 112, 114–116, 129, 130, 133, 134
working class culture 68, 112
working class identity 14, 67, 69, 72, 73, 130
working class solidarity 28
working class students 41, 104, 115, 116, 133
work-related studies 33

## Y

youth labor market 104, 105, 108, 125
youth unemployment 13, 106

## Z

zero work 108